The Best of the Midwest

Linda and Fred Griffith

The Best of the Midwest

Recipes from Thirty-two of America's Finest Restaurants

Illustrations by Stanka Kordic

VIKING
STUDIO
BOOKS

VIKING STUDIO BOOKS
Published by the Penguin Group
Viking Penguin, a division of Penguin Books USA Inc.,
375 Hudson Street, New York, New York 10014, U.S.A.
Penguin Books Ltd, 27 Wrights Lane, London W8 5TZ, England
Penguin Books Australia Ltd, Ringwood, Victoria, Australia
Penguin Books Canada Ltd, 2801 John Street,
Markham, Ontario, Canada L3R 1B4
Penguin Books (N.Z.) Ltd, 182–190 Wairau Road,
Auckland 10, New Zealand

Penguin Books Ltd, Registered Offices:
Harmondsworth, Middlesex, England

First published in 1990 by Viking Penguin,
a division of Penguin Books USA Inc.

3   5   7   9   10   8   6   4   2

Recipes and sketches of the restaurants represented in this book
appear by arrangement with the respective proprietors.
Grateful acknowledgment is made for
their assistance and cooperation.

LIBRARY OF CONGRESS CATALOGING IN PUBLICATION DATA
Griffith, Linda.
The best of the Midwest: recipes from thirty-two of America's
finest restaurants / Linda and Fred Griffith; illustrations by
Stanka Kordic.
p.   cm.
ISBN 0-670-82565-4
1. Cookery—Middle West.   2. Restaurants, lunch rooms, etc.—
Middle West.   I. Griffith, Fred.   II. Title.
TX715.G8442   1990
641.5977—dc20   89-40381

Printed in the United States of America
Set in Garamond No. 3
Designed by Francesca Belanger

To our children
Barbara Griffith,
Gwen Griffith and her new husband, Barry Drucker,
Rob Myers and his new wife, Tracy,
Wally Griffith,
and Andy Myers

May they all take pleasure in preparing a fine dish of food,
opening a bottle of good wine, and celebrating life's
ups and downs with loved ones and friends

Acknowledgments

Without our wonderful food-loving friends it would not have been possible for us to do a book like this. So many helped guide us to splendid surprises. First we thank Donald Patz, national sales manager of Flora Springs Wine Co. He has an impeccable palate and a remarkable taste memory. He sent us to many of the restaurants in this book. To Tim Anderson of Goodfellow's, an enthusiastic Midwestern transplant, to Pete Peterson of Tapawingo, to Richard Perry of Richard Perry, and to The Phoenix's Carl Bruggemeier, more thanks for making certain we did not overlook other fine talents. Thanks also to Steve Michaelides, editor of *Restaurant Hospitality* magazine, for all the resource books and magazines; Bill Rice of the *Chicago Tribune* for sending us to River Wildlife; to writers Lynne Rossetto Kasper and Marcia Adams, for guiding us in Minnesota and Indiana; and to the wonderful Larry "Fats" Goldberg, who taught us all about the real food life of Kansas City. We shall be ever grateful to Brenda and Evan Turner and Sandy and Peter Earl, who applauded every recipe they tasted; to Debbie and David Klausner, for traveling with us so that we could taste more; and to our dear friends Lydie and Wayne Marshall, who understood why all our travels have been west instead of east. (Additional thanks to Lydie for being a teacher's teacher.) And a toast to Hiroshi Tsuji, owner of Shujiro, one of the best Japanese restaurants in the country, whose wonderful sushi nourished us while we were writing this book.

More appreciation to Susan Cavitch, Linda's cousin and her grandmother's first great-grandchild, who is a throwback to Grandma; to Susan's sister Betsy Cohen; and to their mother, Mackie Miller (who isn't a throwback), for recipe testing. And also to Matt Cavitch, who has helped us all. Without Janus Small's encouragement and support, the project might not have been on schedule; it is she who taught us the mastery of deadlines. Sanford Hershkovitz, the fabled Mr. Brisket, maven of meats and poultry, made certain that all cuts of meat are referred to by their correct titles, and also that we were properly sustained during our toil.

We also thank George Orchin, purveyor of the best fish in Cleveland; fabled actor and splendid caterer Bob Snook, for volunteering his help in the testing process, and to Bob Fishman of the Grapevine for answering our wine questions. We bless Sue Conant, a patient recipe proofreader. Thanks must also go to Susan Sack, Linda's wonderful cooking-class helper; to Kevin McLemore, who helped Linda get back her old body; and to Laura Stephens, who cared so well for our creatures great and small while we were in parts unknown. And to our creatures—Dali, Bacchus, Pun'kin, Omar, Ginger, Mary Francis, Rosebud, and Pooh Bear—thanks for loving us even when we were gone so much, or so busy at home that the best they could expect was a perfunctory pat.

Special applause to The Cincinnatian Hotel in Cincinnati; the Fairmount Hotel in Chicago; The Whitney Hotel, Minneapolis; Schumacher's New Prague Hotel in New Prague, Minnesota; Old Rittenhouse Inn, Bayfield, Wisconsin; Strawtown Inn, Pella, Iowa; Lacorsette, Newton, Iowa; and The House on the Hill, Ellsworth, Michigan. Their gracious rooms, fine service, and wonderful breakfasts more than compensated for some of the lumpy beds and grumpy service we encountered in other hotels along the many miles we traveled.

About our wine selectors: every good plate of food tastes even better with a properly selected bottle of wine. To that end, we asked some of our friends to share their knowledge with all our readers who enjoy this book. In addition to Donald Patz (mentioned above), we thank: Sandra Jordan Earl, president of Winetrends; George Hammer, president of The Hammer Company; Gene Parrino, vice-president of Vintage Wine; Russ Vernon, proprietor of West Point Market; Nick Ambeliotis, proprietor of Woodland Markets; Chuck Masterpaul, owner of Napa Valley Bar and Grill and Noggins; Sandra MacIver, owner of Matanzas Creek Winery; John Giguiere, owner of R. H. Phillips Vineyard; and Dr. Leonard Calabrese and Dr. Ronald Bell, wine collectors with whom we shared many a delicious plate and bottle. We hope that you find their selections to be as interesting as we have.

Finally, we thank Michael Fragnito and our superb editor, Barbara Williams, at Viking Penguin for giving us this marvelous opportunity to discover the wonders of our own country and to share them in a book. Thank you also to Stanka Kordic for her gorgeous illustrations; to our fine copy editor, Lynn Warshow; to Francesca Belanger for our book's beautiful design; to Pa Griffith for teaching Fred the pleasure of a meat loaf well made; and to Gertrude LeVine, Linda's mother, for teaching her the joys of making yeast pastry as a young bride. And, above all, to Rob and Andy Myers, who convinced their mother, Linda, that no one could cook anything better—a million thanks and all our love.

Acknowledgments

Contents

Acknowledgments
vii

Introduction
xv

Ristorante Giovanni
BEACHWOOD, OHIO
3

The first restaurant to bring contemporary
fine dining to the Cleveland area.

Z Contemporary Cuisine
SHAKER HEIGHTS, OHIO
11

Owner/chef Zachary Bruell
brought the California style to Cleveland
and has adapted it to Midwestern palates.

The Baricelli Inn
CLEVELAND, OHIO
19

A beautiful renovated mansion
on the Case Western Reserve campus that
also has a small number of
elegant guest rooms.

Johnny's Bar
CLEVELAND, OHIO
27

A wonderful neighborhood tavern
that trots out the white linen and crystal
at night and turns into one of the
trendiest places in town.

The Palace
CINCINNATI, OHIO
35

In The Cincinnatian Hotel,
itself an outstanding facility,
The Palace is a superb showcase for its
young Cleveland-born chef,
Anita Cunningham.

The Restaurant at The Phoenix
CINCINNATI, OHIO
43

*A restaurant within a large
catering complex that manages to maintain
a separate identity. It is the elegant
domain of Carl Bruggemeier,
one of this country's genius restaurateurs.*

Peter's Restaurant
INDIANAPOLIS, INDIANA
53

*Peter's has a sophisticated contemporary
decor and a menu that emphasizes
regional products in heartland dishes.
Chef Tony Hanslits has been invited to do
a James Beard Memorial dinner . . . so
the word is beginning to spread
about Peter's.*

The Carriage House
SOUTH BEND, INDIANA
61

*In an old church that was built about 1850,
this restaurant is furnished with elegant wood
and antiques, tapestries and brocades.*

Tapawingo
ELLSWORTH, MICHIGAN
69

*On the edge of Lake Michigan, north of
Traverse City, this is Mecca in the middle of
rural Michigan, even in winter.*

Chez Raphael
NOVI, MICHIGAN
79

*One of the costliest restaurants of all our
travels, but also the most like a French three-
star restaurant in ambiance;
it is well worth every penny.*

Cousins Heritage Inn
DEXTER, MICHIGAN
91

*Chef Greg Upshur, a former rock-and-roll
singer, is a natural talent who developed his
skills mostly in Detroit. He is passionate
about the surrounding farm region and takes
advantage of local products.*

Yoshi's Café
CHICAGO, ILLINOIS
101

*A tiny, always packed restaurant that serves
simple but elegant food reflecting Yoshi's
Japanese heritage and his French training.*

Charlie Trotter's
CHICAGO, ILLINOIS
109

*Charlie Trotter gives you hearty food,
creative in its combinations and elegantly
presented. He may have the best
desserts outside of France.*

Frontera Grill
CHICAGO, ILLINOIS
117

Emphasizing Mexican regional cuisine, this successful restaurant demonstrates how sophisticated palates in the Midwest have become, since the Frontera's cuisine is definitely not the usual Tex-Mex variety.

The Everest Room
CHICAGO, ILLINOIS
125

The view is spectacular, since The Everest Room, living up to its name, perches forty floors high. The ingredients are regional, the style is simple, and the straightforward food is prepared by someone who is clearly a master.

Jackie's
CHICAGO, ILLINOIS
133

Here we have the finest regional ingredients, prepared with subtle Chinese touches. Owner/chef Jackie Shen is, more than anyone else, responsible for the current interest in edible flowers in this country.

Printer's Row
CHICAGO, ILLINOIS
141

The first restaurant opened by Michael Foley, who has been a pioneer in the use of regional products.

Café Provençal
EVANSTON, ILLINOIS
147

This restaurant used to be more French than not. Today it reflects a chef who understands what country food is all about.

Old Rittenhouse Inn
BAYFIELD, WISCONSIN
155

A fabulous Victorian mansion on the edge of Lake Superior that serves splendid food using mostly local products. Seasonal cuisine is the norm here, with wild mushrooms and berries from the forests, fish from the lakes, fruits and vegetables from the yard.

L'Étoile
MADISON, WISCONSIN
165

A twelve-year-old restaurant overlooking the state capitol that is not as French as it sounds. The owner has devoted years to working with Wisconsin farmers. The menu tempts sophisticated palates without intimidating any of its clientele.

River Wildlife
KOHLER, WISCONSIN
173

A rustic log cabin that is the site of superlative country cooking, which features Wisconsin game and indigenous products prepared by a staff that describes its style as "Kamikaze cookin'."

D'Amico Cucina
MINNEAPOLIS, MINNESOTA
181

*Gorgeous contemporary restaurant
in a renovated old warehouse. Italian-
inspired food done with a light hand,
using lots of local ingredients.*

Tejas
MINNEAPOLIS, MINNESOTA
189

*An inexpensive café that
serves outstanding Southwestern food in a
beautiful new downtown retail and office
complex called The Conservatory
on Nicollet.*

Goodfellow's
MINNEAPOLIS, MINNESOTA
197

*Owned by John Dayton and Stephan Pyles,
this restaurant is a stunner, and the
executive chef, Tim Anderson, deserves
all the raves he gets.*

Schumacher's New Prague Hotel
NEW PRAGUE, MINNESOTA
207

*Schumacher's serves German/Czech
heartland food in the middle of Minnesota
farm country. Its historic landmark building
was restored by John Schumacher, who was
raised on a nearby farm and trained at
the Culinary Institute of America.*

Strawtown Inn
PELLA, IOWA
215

*Lots of Dutch influence here,
both in the decor and in the food.
A pretty place that serves hearty Iowa/Dutch
stick-to-your-ribs meat and potatoes.*

Lacorsette
NEWTON, IOWA
223

*This gorgeous mission-style house,
built in the 1920s by a senator, is now
a bed-and-breakfast and restaurant.*

Stroud's
KANSAS CITY, MISSOURI
233

The best fried-chicken place we know.

Jack Fiorella's
Smokestack Bar-B-Que of
Martin City
MARTIN CITY, MISSOURI
239

*Wood smoking at its finest here.
From ribs to roasts, it's delicious.*

Tony's
ST. LOUIS, MISSOURI
247

*Tony's set the standard
for fine dining in St. Louis more than
twenty-five years ago. It still serves food
in elegant surroundings.*

Broadway Oyster Bar
ST. LOUIS, MISSOURI
255

*A wonderful neighborhood bar
serving some of the best seafood in town
on plastic-coated paper plates.
A restaurant that draws heavily on
St. Louis's Mississippi River roots.*

Richard Perry
ST. LOUIS, MISSOURI
265

*An elegant restaurant in
a newly restored small downtown hotel.
Owner Richard Perry draws his cuisine
from the traditional dishes of the old
riverboats, and even from some of
the boardinghouses of the region.*

Appendix
274

Addresses and Phone Numbers
279

Index
281

Introduction

Food is more than just fuel for the machine. It is central to virtually every ceremony of life. Interesting food attends the celebration of a wedding, a birthday, or a promotion on the job. Food is frequently part of a romantic interlude, a precursor to the attainment of higher levels of intimacy. People propose over food. Other people announce that it's time for a divorce. Some foods are reputed to have curative powers or the ability to restore sexual vigor. (One man we know ate a pint of raw oysters with a spoon every night before bedtime. He had a very happy marriage.) There is no major religion in which food does not play a significant role. Food is served at a wake, brought to the home by friends and relatives who perceive it as an offering of love and caring. In many cultures food has traditionally been stashed in the tombs of the departed, just in case. Even the convict, on his way to the execution chamber, is asked if there is something special he would like to eat before he is dispatched. Having dinner is a social transaction.

And in addition to all these familiar structured ceremonial uses of food, we routinely eat it two, three, or four times a day, seven days a week, for a lifetime, in the interest of keeping our bodies ticking. Food is celebrated because it is essential, because it is so good, because it is a metaphor for life. That, of course, is why people read and write about food, study food, and work to make better food. To cook well is one of the most wonderful and satisfying of skills. To work at learning to cook is to sharpen the senses, to improve the palate, and to better appreciate life.

We have both always been interested in food. Together we learned how much fun you can have in the kitchen. How food is grown, gathered, preserved, cooked, and eaten has been a passionate concern of ours. Together we have gone to every corner of the globe to understand and appreciate the cultural and anthropological significance of food. We have eaten street food in Kashgar, bannock fried in blubber in the northernmost settlement on the continent (Grise Fiord, Northwest Territories, Canada), saga cakes on Papua New Guinea's Sepik River, and yams and pork in that country's highlands. We have enjoyed picnics among giraffes, zebras, and wildebeests. There have been wonderful meals down home. And we have eaten in the greatest restaurants in the world—in Italy, France, New York, California, Beijing, and Hong Kong. We found that at their best those meals become art and drama, transcending the ordinary. Some of our most wonderful times have been spent at the table with friends, and often with strangers; and at home we are always happiest when we are at the stove cooking for our families, our friends, and ourselves.

Fred grew up with a lard-based cuisine. In southern West Virginia, before anyone ever heard of cholesterol, life was eggs, ham, bacon, sausage, biscuits made with lard and slathered with butter, pot roasts, chicken soup with lots of yellow chicken fat, chicken fried in lard, potatoes fried in lard (surely the best potatoes in the world), beans cooked with hambones or bacon ends, vegetables cooked to mush in rich, salty, ham-flavored pot liquor, juicy meat loaf accompanied by rich gravy made from the pan drippings, lumpy mashed potatoes loaded with butter and ground pepper, inch-thick hamburgers, plump frankfurters with sauerkraut and Uncle J. Emzy Malcolm's famous horseradish—so fresh and hot that it came close to ripping off the top of your head when you et it—chili that would stand up to a spoon and that tasted great even though there was no cumin in it (we didn't miss it because we had never heard of it), and pies with fresh cherries or apples or peaches, or mile-high cream, and meringue pies with crusts flaky and delicious because of the lard, which is where this paragraph began. For a decade, anytime he was not in school, he helped make and serve this food in his father's restaurant, the McFarland Lunch, in Charleston.

For Linda, the fat at mealtime came from chicken. This was also before people worried about cholesterol. She remembers that there were some good cooks among her relatives, especially her Grandma Weller, who made bread every Friday—bread that Linda's taste memory tells her was the best she ever had—and whose tsimmes was not only edible, which is usually the most you can expect of tsimmes, but delicious. Linda knew the meaning of schmaltz and ate it on her toast instead of butter. Grandpa Weller, the undertaker who dispatched so many of New Haven's great and near-great, showed her the delights of restaurants, establishments quite different from the McFarland Lunch of Fred's youth. These were the restaurants of New Haven, where Yale professors went and the stars from the Shubert Theater, who were trying out plays for Broadway. The restaurants served caviar on toast points and oysters Rockefeller, beef Wellington, duck à l'orange, Napoleons, and profiteroles. Grandpa Weller taught her to open an oyster, dismantle a lobster, and crack a crab. And on one day, which she will never forget, her grandfather's friend Oscar Hammerstein II taught her how to eat raw clams. Life was never the same for her after that. She survived college food, but as soon as she could have a kitchen of her own, she went to the stove and never left it.

So here were two non-natives about to embark on a culinary journey through the Midwest. But what was this book going to be? We really didn't know. We saw the Midwest as an area neglected by food writers, who suffer from a subtle perception that from a culinary standpoint there isn't much to take note of there. But we thought of the Midwest as a place rich with grain, produce, meat, and poultry. It was a place that abounded with wild game and wild mushrooms, wild fruits and berries, the kind of vegetables that were being used in the "American-style" dishes presented by fabled East Coast chefs. As we set out on this quest for the best of the Midwest, we didn't know what kind of experiences would move us the most. Would it be a homey hash house, a celebrated steak place, or a humble barbecue stand? Or would we discover the kind of sophistication and food-

as-art that we had found in the great chef-driven restaurants of the *Michelin Guide?* Would we look for the 1990s versions of great farm dinners, the feasts that were spread for threshers, who follow the ripening of the grain in their huge combines? Would we seek out some of the few remaining places that so wonderfully celebrated ethnic food traditions in the big cities of the Midwest? Would we look for a contemporary version of the covered-dish dinner at the church or the ice-cream social? Or would we go to those few city restaurants that were the bastions of old-fashioned French cooking and which had as their clientele the wealthy and the traveled?

The answer is "all of the above." Some of the restaurants in this book are working with food ideas that flow from regional history, developing recipes from produce grown in the immediate vicinity. These are surely heartland restaurants, offering dishes not all that different from old-time prairie food. But the criterion for inclusion in this book became not whether a restaurant used Door County

root vegetables or Lake Superior whitefish or wild mushrooms or Michigan wild cherries, although most of them did. Rather, the criterion had to do with a chef's creativity and skill in synthesizing these ingredients into a successful whole. Just as a chef in Quercy uses duck fat and truffles because they are available, so do Midwestern chefs celebrate the good things of their region. But when a cook can have snapper or swordfish jetted in and under his knife twenty-four hours after it is caught, why not? The world is a global village, after all, and sea fish on his grill does not make a chef any less of a Midwesterner.

We found an astonishing variety among the places we chose for this book. We found that, above all, each had a personality, a style that set it apart, that made us want to go back. We included a great Mexican restaurant in Chicago, a Dutch inn in Iowa that is still preparing and serving food as they did a generation ago, a quixotic place in St. Louis that flies in oysters every morning and serves them in grinders on paper plates, and a Kansas City fried-chicken restaurant. Most of the chefs are Midwesterners, but one is a classically trained Frenchman who has worked in this country for only a few years. Another is Japanese. One was born in Hong Kong. Some have spent their lives in the kitchen. Others are relative newcomers, having abandoned other careers for the hard work of running a restaurant. Some are elaborately trained, others are self-taught. All of them are in these pages because they have earned the right to be recognized nationwide for their superlative achievements.

For nearly a year we traveled and ate in as many places as we could, guided by what we had read, what our food friends told us, and in some cases by sheer serendipity. In our search for the best, we found many restaurants of great sophistication and style, generally chef-driven, offering a standard of quality and creativity on a level with the very best in New York and San Francisco. We also found some restaurants that came close to that level but that were either too big for the chef to maintain quality, or that had a chef who got irretrievably caught up in celebrity status, or that were overwhelmingly pretentious. Among those places where everything worked, the common denominators were generous portions, artfully conceived and prepared, and served by caring people with a lack of pretension that has come for us to typify the Midwest. We met some of the friendliest people in the world in these places. We found some geniuses among the cooks. Most of them are young and sophisticated, well trained and well traveled. They have the energy and drive to work eighteen-hour days and the leadership qualities to train and inspire their staffs. They are people who spend the afternoon of their only day off perfecting the taste or texture of a sauce or a new dessert. And they

are all different, each from the other. Each is doing his or her own thing; there are no copycats among them.

Chefs are nothing if not individualistic. No two from whom we solicited recipes gave us any in the same format. So we had the problem of somehow forging a style that could accommodate everybody without compromising any one individual. That wasn't easy. We kept the phones busy, checking details, quantities, techniques, and cooking times. But when we had gone through the process and sent the recipes back to the chefs for a final reading, they approved. Still, there are inconsistencies. One chef proofs yeast one way, another doesn't proof it at all. One always puts eggs in his pasta, another never does. There are different approaches to breadmaking in the book, and to the preparation of stocks, the degree of doneness of vegetables, and the making of a roux. Some of the chefs work meticulously, measuring every ingredient with precision. Others throw things together. We tried to keep some of these stylistic and personal characteristics in the recipes.

After we had selected the restaurants we wanted to feature in the book, we asked each chef to provide us with a menu for a complete dinner. Each responded differently. Some felt that they did not want to be constrained and instead provided a sampling of their favorite recipes, without concern for how they might work together. One chef gave us two fish entrees, for example. Several did not offer an appetizer. A few did not include a dessert. But we felt that now the reader would have an opportunity to mix and match items from the various menus. We ourselves have done that frequently, often using one chef's sauce with another chef's fish, one chef's chop with another chef's vegetable. Nevertheless, there have been many times we have prepared a complete menu from a single restaurant.

Readers may note how often ravioli appears in these pages and in the menus. We aren't quite sure why it is so ubiquitous, except that it is a convenient way of packaging a morsel of something delicious. There is also lot of red pepper and veal in Cleveland and cheesecake in Cincinnati. We also found many chefs using buckwheat. Duck and game are very popular in this part of the country. But every recipe, regardless of how similar its ingredients are to any other recipe featured herein, is unique. We felt every recipe was worthy of inclusion because of its spectacular success as an individual dish and because each is truly typical of the best food to be found in this region.

The chefs featured in this book routinely deal with complexity and difficulty in the preparation of their foods; some of their recipes are quite challenging. In testing and rewriting them, we tried to simplify as much as possible, but we realized that some are going to require care and patience in the kitchen. The rewards, however, will be great. In the back of the book are a few basic recipes for items that come up frequently, and a few notes on techniques. We also offer suggestions on how to find some of the unusual ingredients.

We enjoyed involving our wine-loving friends in this project, asking them to suggest appropriate selections to go with these menus. While we did not require that the wines be from the Midwest, we did ask them to confine their selections to wines from the United States and wines that are consistent from year to year, since we were not going to suggest vintages. We must confess to trying many of these food-and-wine combinations ourselves—just to verify the pairings, of course! It was hard work, but somebody had to do it.

Our work on *The Best of the Midwest* has shown us that this region is a sophisticated place, with people looking for culinary change and challenge. If this book does anything, it should demonstrate the richness of the food experiences that are available to anyone traveling in this wonderful and varied part of our lovely land.

The Best of the Midwest

Ristorante Giovanni

BEACHWOOD, OHIO

A few years ago Victor and Marcella Hazan, specialists in all things Italian, told a reporter for a California newspaper that they had finally found good Italian food in the United States and that it was at Ristorante Giovanni in Cleveland, Ohio. That answer surprised the reporter, but it did not surprise Clevelanders. For years Giovanni's, located on the ground floor of an office building in the Cleveland suburb of Beachwood, was Cleveland's only fine restaurant. Fiddlehead ferns, white truffles, fresh porcini mushrooms, and balsamic vinegar made their debuts in Cleveland at Giovanni's long before they turned up in the national food magazines. Today Ristorante Giovanni retains its luster and continues to be a place for culinary adventures. Owner Carl Quagliata is still the architect of every aspect of the restaurant. His mark is on the decor, the service, the menu, and the wine list. However, in recent years Carl has placed most of the responsibility for daily operations in the creative hands of Sergio Abramof, the executive chef, who also interprets many of the new menu ideas that Carl brings back from Italy.

We'll never forget the ethereal panzotti that Carl himself made for the Hazans. Panzotti are feather-light pillows of stuffed pasta. That day they were gently filled with goat cheese and crabmeat and sauced with a splendid fish fumet combined with cream, wonderfully reduced, then blessed with a bit of wine and some extra crab. But panzotti are prepared here in many ways; just recently they were lightly filled with a mousseline of ground veal and basil and served with a creamy Bolognese sauce. The kitchen at Giovanni also does marvelous things with fish. But perhaps the greatest dish we ever had there was a plump yellow pike, fresh from Lake Erie, poached to perfection and served with a sauce of fresh tomatoes and fresh peas. This is a humble Sicilian sauce that comes from Carl's grandmother's kitchen, but there is real elegance in that simplicity.

The printed menu offers a variety of pastas and many creative veal and fish dishes. We always ask for the daily specials, for it is in these that Sergio brings his taste and talents most evidently into play. Duck breast might be grilled and served with a truffle sauce; coho salmon might be sauced with lobster and scallops. Linda first discovered the joys of sweetbreads at Giovanni when Sergio served them as part of a mixed grill, along with a perfectly done lamb chop and a sublime veal chop, all with a sauce of caramelized onion and another of red wine, accompanied by grilled polenta and wild mushrooms. Sergio's mighty version of the veal chop, by the way, has achieved cult status among serious Cleveland cooks. They buy the same cut from Sergio's fabled meat purveyor, Mr. Brisket, who supplies the region's best restaurants. Known as the "Sergio Chop," it comes from a veal rack split in half and cut into seven chops, then trimmed of all but the wonderful eye itself. It is always on Giovanni's menu, grilled or sautéed and sauced in endless different ways. Other Sergio creations reflect his Brazilian/Jewish heritage, as he occasionally offers superb dishes with black beans or chilies or a perfectly poached chicken with its luscious broth.

The Old World decor is soft and lush. Carl prides himself on making changes that even the regulars rarely notice. They just sense that the room is always fresh. Dinner at Giovanni is always ceremonial. Tuxedoed servers move quietly and efficiently; this is the most professional serving staff in the entire region, making Giovanni popular with the power brokers in town. Final plating of most dishes is done tableside from long serving carts with warmers. There is elegant theater to all of this, especially to the dessert production of lighter-than-air zabaglione, a very special Giovanni version that is spooned into huge crystal goblets over fresh raspberries. Then, to complete the performance, a grand dessert cart is wheeled by with a flourish, presenting eight or so of Carl's phenomenal pastries rich with mocha ganache, silky custard, or berries and cream. Afterward you have room for only a cup of espresso from the enormous copper and brass machine that decorates a side wall.

As the years pass, this restaurant gets better and better. Carl Quagliata has recruited, trained, and kept a fine kitchen staff, but his passion for cooking has him in the kitchen all morning, around the flour bin, working with the pastries and pastas. No one does them quite as well as he, and at least once each week he works the line. Evening finds him in the front or moving about the dining room. No patron goes unwelcomed; no serving error goes unnoticed. He knows which of his patrons enjoys a discussion about the extensive wine list. He also knows who might prefer to remain unnoticed that evening! Many years have passed since Carl Quagliata set the standard for fine dining in Cleveland. While the competition has become keen in recent times, the fact is that he and his fine staff have kept Ristorante Giovanni about as good as a restaurant can be.

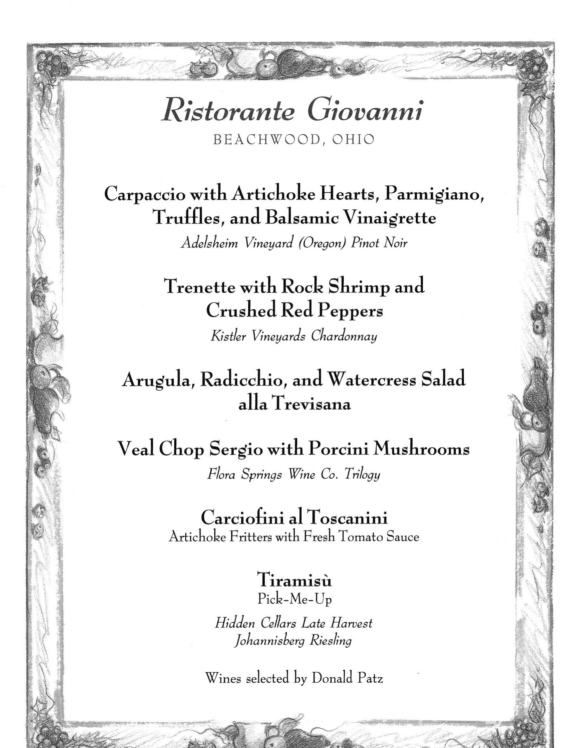

Ristorante Giovanni

BEACHWOOD, OHIO

**Carpaccio with Artichoke Hearts, Parmigiano,
Truffles, and Balsamic Vinaigrette**

Adelsheim Vineyard (Oregon) Pinot Noir

**Trenette with Rock Shrimp and
Crushed Red Peppers**

Kistler Vineyards Chardonnay

**Arugula, Radicchio, and Watercress Salad
alla Trevisana**

Veal Chop Sergio with Porcini Mushrooms

Flora Springs Wine Co. Trilogy

Carciofini al Toscanini
Artichoke Fritters with Fresh Tomato Sauce

Tiramisù
Pick-Me-Up

*Hidden Cellars Late Harvest
Johannisberg Riesling*

Wines selected by Donald Patz

Carpaccio with Artichoke Hearts, Parmigiano, Truffles, and Balsamic Vinaigrette

Be sure to use a really wonderful olive oil for this.

Serves 4

> 1 large tomato, peeled, seeded, and diced in ¼-inch cubes
> 1 teaspoon plus 3 tablespoons extra-virgin olive oil
> Balsamic vinegar
> Salt and freshly ground black pepper to taste
> 8 ounces center-cut beef tenderloin, silverskin removed, cut into 4 equal slices
> 1 fresh artichoke heart, cooked, cooled, and thinly sliced
> 3 ounces Parmigiano-Reggiano, sliced paper-thin
> 1 whole black truffle, sliced paper-thin
> 1 tablespoon balsamic vinegar
> 4 sprigs Italian leaf parsley

Marinate diced tomato with 1 teaspoon olive oil and a few drops of balsamic vinegar, salt, and pepper to taste.

Place each slice of beef tenderloin between two sheets of plastic wrap and gently pound with the flat edge of a meat cleaver until paper-thin. Remove top sheet of plastic wrap and place meat on serving plate meat side down. Remove other sheet of plastic. Sprinkle meat with salt and pepper. Repeat with 3 remaining slices on three more serving plates.

Garnish plates evenly with artichoke heart, Parmigiano, and black truffle. Drizzle 3 tablespoons olive oil and vinegar over beef. Divide tomato relish among the four plates, placing relish in the center of the plate. Place parsley over tomato. Add a few more grindings of pepper and salt if you wish.

Trenette with Rock Shrimp and Crushed Red Peppers

Serves 4

> ½ pound trenette, or fettuccine
> 1 pound rock shrimp, cleaned and peeled
> ¼ cup olive oil
> 2 tablespoons butter
> 1 tablespoon chopped fresh garlic
> 3 tablespoons chopped fresh parsley
> ½ teaspoon crushed red pepper (or to taste)
> Salt and freshly ground black pepper

Cook pasta al dente according to package directions; set aside.

Heat olive oil in a large sauté pan. Add shrimp and sauté about 1 minute. Add chopped garlic and continue cooking until garlic begins to brown.

Remove from heat. Add butter, parsley, red pepper, salt and pepper. Stir until butter has melted and the shrimp are well coated with the sauce. Toss with the pasta and serve at once.

Arugula, Radicchio, and Watercress Salad alla Trevisana

Serves 4

DRESSING

1¾ tablespoons raspberry vinegar
¾ teaspoon salt
½ teaspoon sugar
¼ teaspoon dry mustard
⅛ teaspoon freshly ground black pepper
5 tablespoons extra-virgin olive oil

4 bunches arugula
2 heads radicchio
4 bunches watercress
4 thin slices red onion
8 strawberries, sliced
¼ cup shelled unsalted pistachios

*P*our raspberry vinegar into a salad bowl; dissolve the salt, sugar, mustard, and pepper in the vinegar. Slowly whisk in the olive oil. Taste and adjust seasonings.

Carefully wash and dry all salad greens. Break them into bite-size pieces and put into a bowl. Add the onion, strawberries, and pistachios. Add the dressing, toss well, and distribute among four serving plates.

Veal Chop Sergio with Porcini Mushrooms

Serves 4

4 10-ounce veal chops (eye of rib, from a Frenched rack)
Flour
¾ cup clarified margarine
8 ounces fresh porcini mushrooms, or 2 ounces dried (soaked and sliced)
¼ cup Madeira wine
1½ cups Dark Brown Veal Stock (see page 277)
2 tablespoons butter, rolled in flour
¼ cup fresh tomatoes, peeled, seeded, and julienned
2 tablespoons minced Italian leaf parsley
Salt and freshly ground black pepper to taste

Sautéed or steamed seasonal vegetables and fresh herbs (such as parsley and thyme) for garnish

*P*reheat oven to 400°. Dust chops with flour. Heat margarine in a large sauté pan, add chops, and brown on both sides over high

heat. Transfer pan to the preheated oven and continue cooking 5 to 8 minutes, depending on thickness of chops.

Remove sauté pan from oven, place chops on a heated platter, and keep warm. Discard excess margarine from sauté pan.

Return sauté pan to stove and sauté porcini over medium heat about 1 minute. Add Madeira and scrape bottom of pan to loosen any particles. Then add stock and bring to a simmer.

Add floured butter to sauce and whisk until blended. Continue to simmer until sauce thickens slightly. Add julienned tomato and parsley and salt and pepper to taste.

Arrange chops on large, heated serving plates. Be sure to distribute mushrooms and tomatoes evenly as you sauce the chops. Garnish with some simple seasonal vegetables and herbs.

Carciofini al Toscanini
Artichoke Fritters with Fresh Tomato Sauce

Serves 4–6

    6 large artichokes
    ¼ cup cider vinegar
    2 lemons
    1 tablespoon flour

BATTER
    1 cup flour
    2 egg yolks
    3 tablespoons olive oil
    ¼ teaspoon salt
    ¼ teaspoon cayenne

    ¼ teaspoon cream of tartar
    ¾ cup milk

    3 large ripe tomatoes
  1½ tablespoons chopped garlic
    1 teaspoon sugar
    2 tablespoons chopped Italian leaf parsley
    Salt and freshly ground black pepper to taste
    ¼ cup extra-virgin olive oil
    1 dried hot red pepper, crumbled

  3–4 cups vegetable oil
    2 egg whites
    3 lemons, quartered, for garnish

*P*lace artichokes in a large bowl; cover them with cold water and the vinegar. Soak for at least half an hour. Remove artichokes from water and knock each one upside down on a hard surface to remove excess water and any remaining sand. Slice off any stem, then peel away outer leaves until you start to see the tender, more yellow leaves. Lay artichoke on its side and, using a sharp knife, cut off tight cone of leaves above the heart. Trim and shape heart carefully until no dark part remains. Repeat with remaining artichokes. Cut each heart into 8 wedges and spoon out any remaining choke. Soak in water with the juice and rinds of 1 lemon.

Fill a non-aluminum pan with water and the juice and rind of another lemon, 1 tablespoon flour, salt, and pepper. Bring to a boil, add artichokes, and simmer until al dente, about 8 minutes. Remove artichokes and chill in iced water; drain thoroughly and pat dry. (The recipe can be prepared a day ahead up to this point.)

Combine the first 6 ingredients for batter and blend well. Gradually whisk in milk and let batter rest in refrigerator for 1 hour.

        The Best of the Midwest

Wash the tomatoes, slice in half horizontally, and gently squeeze seeds from pulp. Preheat oven to 375°. Oil a small baking dish and place tomatoes in it cut-side-up. Sprinkle with garlic, sugar, parsley, salt, and pepper. Pour ⅛ cup of olive oil over tomatoes and bake for 1½ hours. Remove tomatoes from dish, drain, and purée through a food mill. Add remaining ⅛ cup of olive oil and hot pepper to taste.

Heat oil in a deep skillet to 365°. Beat egg whites until they are stiff but not dry. Fold into batter. Dip artichokes in batter; drain off excess. Fry in hot oil until golden brown (a few minutes). Drain on paper towels and keep warm. After all the artichokes are fried, sprinkle with salt and arrange on serving platter. Garnish with lemon slices and tomato salsa.

Tiramisù
Pick-Me-Up

There are as many versions of this wonderful dessert as there are of apple pie.

Serves 8 to 10

    3 large egg yolks
    7 tablespoons sugar
500 grams (1 pound, 2 ounces)
        mascarpone
    2 teaspoons Amaretto
    1 teaspoon vanilla extract
   30 Italian ladyfingers (*savoiardi*)
  1½ cups cooled espresso
    ½ cup (3 ounces) bittersweet chocolate,
        chopped
    ½ cup almonds, toasted and chopped
  1½ pints raspberries
    6 mint leaves, stems attached, for
        garnish

Whisk egg yolks and sugar in a mixing bowl until the yolks turn pale yellow. Add the mascarpone, Amaretto, and vanilla, and beat until well mixed and creamy.

Dip 10 ladyfingers lightly in espresso and arrange in two rows in a flat, deep-sided 8 by 12-inch baking dish that has been buttered and sugared. Spread ⅓ of the mascarpone mixture over the ladyfingers. Sprinkle with ⅓ of the chocolate, the almonds, and the raspberries. Repeat this layering 2 more times, garnishing top with remaining raspberries and the mint leaves. Chill several hours.

Z Contemporary Cuisine

SHAKER HEIGHTS, OHIO

Since it first opened in 1985, Z has been the trendiest, most talked about restaurant in Cleveland. Although the starkness of the restaurant mystifies some Clevelanders, we never fail to appreciate the perfect marriage between the award-winning architectural design and the elegantly straightforward cuisine. The 98-seat restaurant is exactly what owner/chef Zachary Bruell wanted it to be—a neutral canvas for the presentation of his artful food. The striking room, with its attractive servers in pastel shirts, sets a festive mood. It is a place for champagne and fine wines and beautiful people.

We have had periods when we've eaten four consecutive dinners here and not tired of the food because of its refined simplicity. We can count on Z for the best ingredients, simply handled, exquisitely sauced, and beautifully presented. The menu changes weekly, but the one dish that is always present is a side order of crisply fried shoestring potatoes liberally dusted with minced fresh herbs. First courses are especially delicious at Z. We look forward to summer, when the red bell peppers are small and richly flavored. We hope to see them on the menu, filled with American chèvre and fragrant herbs, roasted and served with a beurre blanc. Fascinated with Thai ingredients, Zach might offer smoked Thai sausage or crab fricassee or an impeccably fresh sautéed soft-shell crab, which rests in a bowl of rich chicken stock and is perfumed with cilantro and lemon grass with a zip of hot sauce. This is a dish that memories are made of. Fried calamari here are the best we have ever had; the tempura batter is so light it dissolves on your tongue. Salads at Z are more akin to a first course and are an opportunity for the chef to create imaginative combinations of heady herbs, farm-fresh vegetables, and briny shellfish. Soups are usually made with cream and are the texture of antique satin. A special favorite is the chilled red bell pepper soup, with its generous garnish of fresh tarragon.

Since nearly all main courses are grilled, they never overwhelm. From salmon to pork tenderloin, they are prepared rare and presented with a never-ending range of sauces. Perhaps we might enjoy the pork tenderloin accompanied by a horseradish sauce, or some sweetbreads with caramelized citrus. We love the veal tenderloin with a Hoisin-based Oriental sauce and its accompanying grilled Japanese eggplants. Another choice could be loin of lamb with potato and fennel purée, or tuna with port wine and ginger. A sure sign of spring is grilled salmon fillet presented with a light mustard sauce and a lattice of matchstick-thin haricots verts, sprinkled with finely diced tomato. This is a feast for the eyes as well as the palate. Another favorite is the superlative grilled pike with chanterelle mushrooms, grilled corn, and a cabernet butter sauce. We happen to love the caramelized smokiness of corn done on a grill, and in this dish it adds a satisfying contrast to the pike and the cabernet sauce. All entrees are accompanied by simply prepared vegetables, frequently presented as a decorative arc across the top of the plate.

However delicious our meal might be, we always plan to save room for one of the luscious desserts prepared by Amy Whitelaw, Zach's sister. Trained in classical French baking, she creates an endless variety of tarts, ice creams, and sorbets. Sometimes dessert can be a sampler platter with four or five small servings of the evening's best. This is a dessert lover's orgy, since there are at least four different chocolate confections each day. We love all her fruit tarts, as well as the crème brulée tart. And anything made with passion fruit is worth becoming passionate about.

Zach is among that extraordinary crew of brilliant young American chefs coming out of Michael's, a restaurant in Santa Monica owned by Michael McCarty. As a student at the Wharton School of Business in Philadelphia, Zach began his cooking career in self-defense: he needed to cook if he wanted to eat. When he then decided to attend Philadelphia's Restaurant School, he became a chef only to learn all facets of this complex business. But he is a genius in the kitchen! After a stint with McCarty, his former roommate, out in Santa Monica, Zach returned to Cleveland. While he was working and catering, he was always on the lookout for the right location for his own place. With the help of his dad he finally found it. The two planned to go into business together, but alas, it was not to be. When Z finally opened, the first week was dedicated to raising money for the Ernest Bruell Memorial Cancer Research Fund at the Cleveland Clinic. And Zach's partner was his young wife, Laurie.

The restaurant is on the ground floor of a Shaker Heights office tower designed by the late Walter Gropius, and every facet of its design had to be approved by Gropius's firm, Architects Collaborative. The Bauhaus lives on in this very white space with its dark gray carpet, chrome and black leather chairs, and large abstract paintings. While patrons from New York and California rush to Z when they visit Cleveland, it has taken some local diners a bit longer to appreciate, but Clevelanders have now grown accustomed to the white room and have finally accepted Zach Bruell's very personal vision.

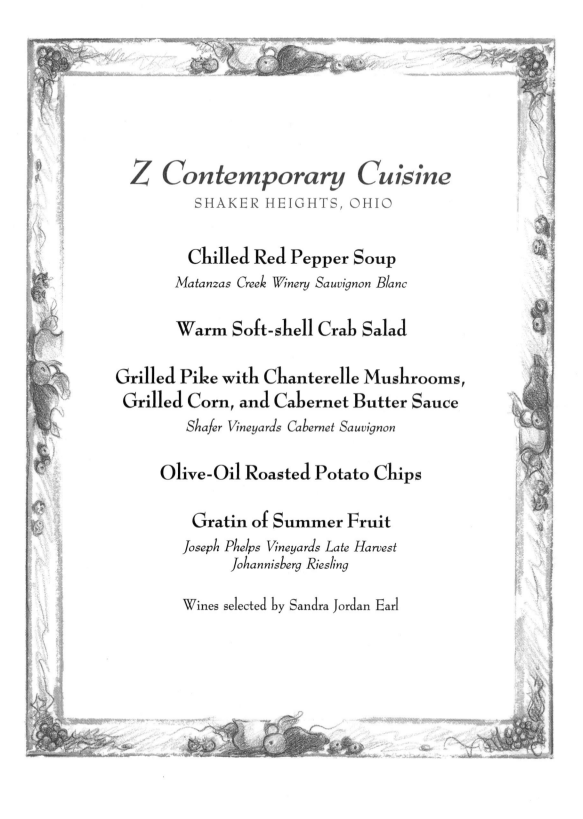

Z Contemporary Cuisine
SHAKER HEIGHTS, OHIO

Chilled Red Pepper Soup
Matanzas Creek Winery Sauvignon Blanc

Warm Soft-shell Crab Salad

Grilled Pike with Chanterelle Mushrooms, Grilled Corn, and Cabernet Butter Sauce
Shafer Vineyards Cabernet Sauvignon

Olive-Oil Roasted Potato Chips

Gratin of Summer Fruit
*Joseph Phelps Vineyards Late Harvest
Johannisberg Riesling*

Wines selected by Sandra Jordan Earl

Chilled Red Pepper Soup

Serves 4

½ pound unsalted butter
1 Spanish onion, thinly sliced
3 tablespoons fresh tarragon
1 head garlic, unpeeled, cut in half
    horizontally
6 large red bell peppers, deveined,
    seeded, and sliced
3 cups Chicken Stock (see page 276)
1 cup heavy cream
    Salt and freshly ground black pepper
    to taste

    Sour cream and chives for garnish

*I*n a heavy saucepan, melt the butter and sweat the onion, tarragon, and garlic by covering them with wax paper and cooking them over low heat until onions are transparent.

Remove wax paper, add sliced red peppers to onion mixture, and cook over low heat 5 minutes. Cover with stock and simmer until stock is reduced by half. Add heavy cream and cook slowly 5 minutes.

Purée mixture in food processor and pass through a sieve. Chill in refrigerator. Season with salt and pepper before serving.

Serve in chilled soup plates and garnish with a dollop of sour cream and chives.

Warm Soft-shell Crab Salad

Serves 4

4 fresh soft-shell crabs
2 cups milk
16 or more baby asparagus spears
16 leaves Belgian endive
1 head radicchio
1 bunch arugula
8 baby yellow pear tomatoes, or cherry
    tomatoes

FISH FUMET CREAM
3 cups Fish Fumet (see page 275)
2 cups heavy cream
    Salt and freshly ground black pepper
    to taste
1 tablespoon fresh thyme
1 tablespoon minced chives
    Juice of half a lemon

    Olive oil
    Flour
1 teaspoon cold unsalted butter

    Fresh thyme and chives for garnish

*C*lean crabs by removing lungs, eyes, and intestines (or ask your fish merchant to do this for you when you buy the crabs). First, lift up sides of upper shell and remove gills. Place crab on a wooden board and, using a sharp knife, cut off head immediately behind eyes. Use a butter knife to scrape out the lungs and intestines through this opening. Rinse well under running water. Then turn crab over and pull open the "apron," or turned-under tail, and cut it off with a sharp knife or scissors. Soak crabs in the milk for at least 1 hour.

Cut off the tips of the asparagus, discard the stems, and blanch tips in boiling water about 30 seconds, until barely cooked. Plunge into a bowl of ice water, drain, and set aside.

Carefully wash and dry all greens. Arrange alternately on four large plates, making a decorative bed for the crab. Place asparagus and tomatoes in a circle on top of the greens.

Then, make the fish fumet cream: In heavy saucepan, bring the Fish Fumet to a boil; then reduce heat and simmer briskly until liquid is reduced to just a glaze. Whisk in the heavy cream and cook 2 to 3 minutes, until thin enough to pour but not too runny. Season with salt, pepper, thyme, chives, and lemon juice. Set aside in a warm place.

Pour just enough olive oil into a large skillet to glaze the bottom. Heat to smoking. While oil is heating, remove crabs from milk, pat dry, and dredge lightly in flour. Season lightly with salt and pepper. When oil begins to smoke, quickly add the butter. Before the butter's milk solids begin to burn, add the crabs, shell side down. Sauté 1 minute, or

until bright red and slightly browned. Turn and do the same on the other side.

Drain crabs and gently blot with paper towel to remove excess oil. Place in center of the prepared salad plates. Drizzle crabs and greens with warm fish fumet cream. Garnish with fresh thyme and chives.

Grilled Pike with Chanterelle Mushrooms, Grilled Corn, and Cabernet Butter Sauce

If you cannot find chanterelles, substitute another flavorful mushroom, such as portobellos or shiitakes; chanterelles are especially good because of their buttery flavor. A very clean, Pam-sprayed, hot grill is essential for this dish.

Serves 4

2 cups Cabernet Sauvignon wine
1 cup red wine vinegar
2 tablespoons dried shallots
4 tablespoons heavy cream
¾ pound unsalted butter
3 ears of corn, shucked and rinsed
8 ounces chanterelle mushrooms
Salt and freshly ground black pepper to taste
3 tablespoons minced fresh basil
4 8-ounce pike fillets, skinned
Olive oil

Fresh basil and chives for garnish

*H*eat a gas or charcoal grill until very hot.

In a heavy 1-quart saucepan, combine the wine, vinegar, and shallots. Bring to a boil, reduce heat to a brisk simmer, and cook until mixture is reduced to 2 tablespoons of liquid. Whisk in heavy cream and then, over high heat, whisk in ½ pound of butter, a bit at a time. Hold sauce while you finish this recipe by setting the pan in a larger saucepan filled with hot water and keeping it in a warm place. Don't keep cooking or sauce will break down. (If that happens, whisk in a bit more heavy cream.)

Place the ears of corn on the grill and cook until lightly golden on all sides, 4 to 6 minutes. Remove from grill and slice kernels off the cob.

Melt ¼ pound of butter in a large skillet and sauté the mushrooms over medium heat 10 minutes. Add the corn kernels, salt, pepper, and basil. Keep warm.

Wipe pike fillets with oil and sprinkle with a bit of salt and pepper. Place on hottest portion of grill and cook approximately 1½ minutes on each side (depending on thickness of fillets and temperature of the grill).

Place fillets in center of warm plates. Arrange corn-mushroom mixture in a free-form fashion over the plates. Pour sauce around the fish. Garnish with chives and basil leaves.

Olive-Oil Roasted Potato Chips

It is somewhat amusing to think that with all of the extravagant food on the menu at Z, the simple fact is that Zach is most famous for his fabulous frites, lavishly sprinkled with herbs. From time to time, however, there are other potato dishes available as well. Mr. Brisket always calls ahead for the mashed potatoes with garlic. Zach's personal favorites are these terribly simple oven-roasted potato chips, which he prefers to serve in the summer. We love them at any time of year.

Serves 4

2 large baking potatoes
About ½ cup extra-virgin olive oil
Kosher salt to taste
Freshly cracked black pepper to taste
2 ounces fresh rosemary, finely minced

Fresh rosemary for garnish

*P*reheat oven to 425°. Using a mandolin or food processor, carefully slice the potatoes diagonally to a thickness of ⅛ inch.

Thoroughly oil a baking sheet with extra-virgin olive oil. Then, using a pastry brush, coat each slice of potato with olive oil on both sides. Sprinkle with salt, cracked black pepper, and the fresh rosemary.

Bake the potatoes until lightly brown; this will take between 15 and 30 minutes. When they are done, remove them from the oven and drain on paper towels. Serve warm or at room temperature. Garnish with rosemary.

Gratin of Summer Fruit

Serves 4

CRÈME ANGLAISE
½ vanilla bean, split in half lengthwise
2⅓ cups milk
¾ cup sugar
6 large egg yolks

½ cup shelled unsalted pistachios
½ pint fresh red raspberries
½ pint fresh golden raspberries
2 whole fresh peaches, peeled and sliced
3 whole fresh apricots, peeled and sliced
3 whole fresh plums, sliced

Spread the pistachios in a baking pan. Place in hot oven and brown, turning frequently. Don't let burn.

Make the crème anglaise: Combine split vanilla bean and milk in a heavy saucepan. Add sugar and bring to a boil.

Whisk egg yolks in a medium-sized mixing bowl. Temper the yolks by gradually whisking the hot milk mixture into them. Then turn the mixture back into the saucepan, return to the stove, and cook over low heat, whisking constantly, about 10 minutes, or until mixture is thick enough to coat the back of a spoon. Pass the mixture through a chinois (cone-shaped strainer) and cool. Stir from time to time to prevent skin from forming.

Divide the crème anglaise equally among four individual gratin dishes that can be put under the broiler. Arrange the fruit on the custard. Just before serving, put the gratin dishes under a hot broiler to lightly brown. Scatter the pistachios over the fruit and serve.

The Baricelli Inn

CLEVELAND, OHIO

Cleveland's University Circle has long been one of the most celebrated areas of the city. Nowhere else in the country is there such a confluence of cultural, medical, and educational institutions. Although the area had for years been without a fine restaurant or a quality place to stay, we are now able to enjoy an elegant restaurant and inn that has been transformed from a fortress-like mansion in Little Italy. Dr. and Madame Giovanni Baricelli had been well known in Cleveland. He was a physician and she taught Romance languages at nearby Western Reserve University. After their deaths, their large brownstone home, surrounded by university and hospital buildings, attracted the attention of many developers. But it was a well-known neighborhood restaurant family, the Minnillos, who undertook the costly renovation and construction. The project went on for more than a year and many of us thought they had lost their senses. But the Minnillo family knew what they were doing, and when they opened in the summer of 1985—having dropped an *r* from the name of the inn at the request of the Baricelli family—we saw a restaurant and inn of great charm and quality.

The seasonal menu is strongly influenced by the fine restaurants of Europe, but the ingredients and style are American. Chef Paul Minnillo has developed relationships with regional purveyors who keep him supplied with the finest ingredients available in the Midwest. We consider the delicate pink peppercorn ravioli filled with Maytag blue goat cheese to be one of Paul's finest accomplishments. Garnished with toasted hazelnuts, the ravioli are napped with a saffron butter sauce and dusted with orange zest. Another of our favorites is the buckwheat blini served with smoked Scottish salmon and eggplant caviar. A lover of freshwater grass shrimp, Paul might offer them sautéed with pasta, or poached and chilled in a summer salad. And, when available, a variety of Cape Cod oysters baked with fresh smoked buffalo milk mozzarella is outstanding. Another summer favorite is a calamari salad garnished with a julienne of peppers, piqued with red onion, lots of garlic, and Niçoise olives. Soups here are superb, but a Maryland crab bisque punctuated with a swirl of watercress purée and miniature crabmeat ravioli is sublime. And corn chowder garnished with tiny oysters poached in champagne is simply "the best."

We always share a pasta course when we go to Baricelli. Delicate lemon fettuccini make a marvelous foil for shellfish. Red bell pepper pasta is especially successful in combination with smoked duck. Our single favorite dish, however, is the roasted loin of lamb wrapped in veal and spinach mousseline and accompanied by a rosemary tarragon sauce. The boneless loin is rosy pink; the mousseline is pastel green. Redolent of fresh herbs, this dish makes a gorgeous presentation that is as delicious as it looks. Veal medallions are also generally on the menu. We have had them with Marsala cream sauce and accompanied by sautéed wild mushrooms, pancetta, capers, and tomatoes with an herbed cream sauce. A thick veal chop and smoked Michigan pheasant are also winners. The kitchen does fish superbly at Baricelli. We have enjoyed baby coho salmon and baby halibut, gently grilled and enhanced by a sauce of Chardonnay cream and caviar. And we must congratulate the chef on the sautéed red snapper in black currant butter, garnished with toasted macadamia nuts—a stimulating orchestration of tastes and textures. Great food cries for fine wine, and to our delight, there is an outstanding wine list at Baricelli to further enhance any meal.

Finally, there is dessert. Ice cream here is wonderful, and if the passion-fruit torte is on the menu, don't pass it up. In fact, all of Baricelli's pastries are delicate and delightful.

Everything about The Baricelli Inn is elegant. As part of the renovation, a gracious entrance and adjacent dining room were built across what had been the back of the house. The main dining room, with a soaring glass ceiling, seats about sixty people. Soft grays and greens are accented by pink and salmon. Large green trees and generous bouquets of flowers enhance the celebratory nature of the room. Other dining areas are smaller and more intimate. The original veranda is enclosed with glass and looks over a small private garden onto Cornell Road, one of the busiest in the circle. The open kitchen is in the center of the building, although there is an enormous prep kitchen down below. In keeping with the atmosphere, service is formal and efficient but never pretentious. Most servers are also quite knowledgeable about wine. Regulars appreciate having their personal preferences remembered; new patrons enjoy a warm welcome.

The Minnillo family is an institution in University Circle. Their first restaurant, Minnillo's, a hangout for university and hospital people, was opened by Paul's father, Paul Minnillo, Sr., and his wife, Amy. In the mid-seventies, their sons remodeled the place and changed the name to The Greenhouse. Now Tom Minnillo is in charge. Paul Minnillo runs the kitchen at Baricelli, and his brother, John, divides his time between it and the Ninth Street Bar and Grill in downtown Cleveland's Galleria. While they work in team fashion, it is Paul's hand that shapes the food at Baricelli. Trained in this country and in Europe, he brings a splendid palate to the kitchen. He is a dark and intense man of enormous talent and considerable modesty. In this age of chef as celebrity, Paul is the first to rave about others and to celebrate competition. Both Paul and John travel as often as they can in this country and in Europe. Their standards are high; they do not allow complacency in themselves or their staff. The patrons of The Baricelli Inn are now the beneficiaries, and the skeptics among us are now believers.

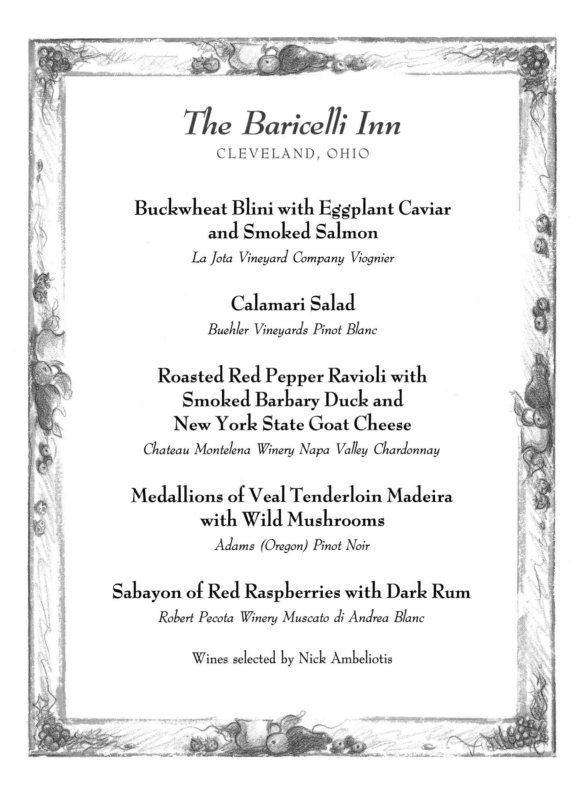

The Baricelli Inn
CLEVELAND, OHIO

Buckwheat Blini with Eggplant Caviar and Smoked Salmon

La Jota Vineyard Company Viognier

Calamari Salad

Buehler Vineyards Pinot Blanc

Roasted Red Pepper Ravioli with Smoked Barbary Duck and New York State Goat Cheese

Chateau Montelena Winery Napa Valley Chardonnay

Medallions of Veal Tenderloin Madeira with Wild Mushrooms

Adams (Oregon) Pinot Noir

Sabayon of Red Raspberries with Dark Rum

Robert Pecota Winery Muscato di Andrea Blanc

Wines selected by Nick Ambeliotis

Buckwheat Blini with Eggplant Caviar and Smoked Salmon

Sometimes this is served with dollops of real caviar, which may be gilding the lily, but we are not ones to applaud restraint! This recipe makes about 18 blini, 3 to 4 inches in diameter.

Serves 6

BATTER

    1 cup buckwheat flour
    1½ tablespoons all-purpose flour
    2 large eggs
    1 tablespoon dark brown sugar, firmly
        packed
    ¼ teaspoon salt
    1⅔ cups milk
    5 tablespoons corn oil

    2 medium red bell peppers
    2 medium eggplants, peeled and finely
        diced
    2 tablespoons olive oil
    1 garlic clove, minced
    1 large shallot, minced
    1 tablespoon minced chives
    3 ounces black olives, finely chopped
    Salt and freshly ground black pepper
        to taste
    Butter
    9 ounces smoked salmon, thinly sliced

    1 cup sour cream and minced chives
        for garnish

Mix flours, eggs, brown sugar, and salt in a large bowl; gradually whisk in milk until smooth. Blend in oil. Let batter rest at least 30 minutes.

Roast the peppers in the broiler on a rack placed 6 inches from the heating element. Turn when skins are blistered and blackened. Place the peppers in a plastic bag, seal, and allow them to steam 10 minutes. Peel away skin, slice in half, remove seeds, rinse and pat dry. Dice and set aside.

In a large skillet, sauté eggplant in hot olive oil 2 to 3 minutes, or until tender. Add garlic and shallot, and sauté another minute. Remove to a large bowl. Add diced peppers, chives, olives, salt and pepper. Blend and adjust seasoning.

To make blini, heat a small, well-seasoned, lightly buttered crêpe pan that is 3 to 4 inches in diameter over high temperature. When hot, add 1 tablespoon of batter to the hot skillet. Quickly tilt to distribute batter evenly over pan. Reduce heat to medium and cook about 1 minute. Turn blini gently with your fingers or a spatula and cook about ½ minute on the other side. Turn out on a tea towel; repeat until all the batter is used. Add more butter to pan only if necessary. Keep warm.

To serve, place blini on warm serving plates. Cut salmon into thin strips and place just inside the outer rim of the blini (i.e., in a circle). Place eggplant caviar inside the salmon, again forming a circle. Spoon a dollop of sour cream in the center and top with minced chives.

Calamari Salad

Paul Minnillo suggests combining this salad with chilled pasta for a nice summer supper.

Serves 6

2½ pounds fresh calamari, cleaned*
Flour
¼ cup cottonseed oil†
1 large red bell pepper, seeded,
    deveined, and finely julienned
1 large yellow bell pepper, seeded,
    deveined, and finely julienned
1 large poblano pepper, seeded,
    deveined, and finely julienned
½ small, sweet red onion, peeled and
    thinly sliced lengthwise
4 cloves garlic, minced
Salt and freshly ground black pepper
    to taste
4 tablespoons extra-virgin olive oil
4 ounces chopped fresh basil
¼ cup pitted Niçoise olives, quartered
Balsamic vinegar

Curly endive, radicchio, and/or
    arugula for garnish

Cut calamari into ⅛-inch rings, cut tentacles in small pieces, and lightly flour. In an oversized skillet (calamari cook much better if there's a small number of them in a large pan), heat the cottonseed oil over high heat. Add calamari, cover pan loosely, and sauté until brown on one side. Add peppers, onion, and garlic. Flip calamari, sprinkle with salt and

pepper, and cook about 2 minutes, until brown and done.

Remove ingredients from pan with tongs, trying to drain the cottonseed oil. Put in a bowl and add olive oil, basil, and olives. Add more salt and pepper if needed. Toss. This salad should be served warm, not hot.

Arrange on large serving plates, surrounded by pretty greens sprinkled with olive oil and balsamic vinegar. If you have nasturtium blossoms, use them for garnish, too.

*The best way to obtain clean calamari is to have a cooperative fish merchant! If you wish to clean them yourself, begin by soaking the calamari in salted water for 2 hours. Then hold head and tentacles in one hand and the body sac in the other and gently pull off fins and skin from the outer body, leaving only the white squid body. Remove and discard cellophane-type backbone from inside body. Clean inside of sac thoroughly. Cut tentacles above the eyes. Discard remaining part of the head.

†Cottonseed oil can take a very high heat without burning. Wesson Oil is cottonseed oil.

Roasted Red Pepper Ravioli with Smoked Barbary Duck and New York State Goat Cheese

This recipe makes a marvelous pasta. If there is more than you need for ravioli, cut the rolled strips for fettuccine, dust the strips with cornmeal, and freeze for another delicious meal. If you have difficulty obtaining smoked duck, contact Mr. Brisket at 4118 Silsby Road, University Heights, Ohio 44118, (216) 923–8628. He is an excellent source for all the difficult-to-obtain fowl and meats in this book.

Serves 6 (20 to 30 ravioli)

4 to 6 red bell peppers, roasted, peeled,
    seeded, and drained
5 cups flour
1 large egg
3 to 4 pounds smoked Barbary duck, meat
    coarsely chopped
1 cup fresh New York State goat
    cheese

¼ cup unsalted pistachios, toasted and
coarsely chopped
Salt and freshly ground black pepper
to taste
Egg wash made by mixing 1 egg yolk
with 1 tablespoon water
Cornmeal
3 cups heavy cream
2 cloves garlic, peeled

Fresh herbs, such as chives, thyme,
and flat-leaf parsley, for garnish

Purée the peppers in the bowl of a food processor to make ¾ to 1 cup purée. Pour into
a tea towel and wring to press out excess
water.

Combine 4 cups of flour, purée, and egg in
the bowl of an electric mixer. Using the paddle, mix on slow speed until dough forms into
a ball. Add more flour if too sticky. Cover
with a towel and let rest a half hour in the
bowl.

Meanwhile, mix duck meat, goat cheese,
and pistachios together in a bowl. Add salt
and pepper to taste.

Follow instructions on page 274 to knead
and roll dough in the pasta machine. Then,
using a 2–4-inch round cookie cutter, cut
rolled pasta dough into circles. Brush circles
with egg wash. Place 1 tablespoon duck mixture in the middle of half the circles. Cover
each with another circle and pinch the edges
to seal together. Place 1 inch apart on a baking
sheet that has been dusted lightly with cornmeal. Cover and chill until time to cook.

Combine cream and garlic cloves in a large,
heavy saucepan. Simmer briskly until cream
has thickened. Remove garlic and season with
salt and pepper to taste.

Cook ravioli in slowly boiling water until
tender, about 3 minutes, stirring with a

wooden spoon as necessary to prevent stick-
ing. Drain very carefully.

Spoon the sauce into the center of six warm
serving plates and place 3 or 4 ravioli on top.
Garnish with fresh herbs.

Medallions of Veal Tenderloin Madeira with Wild Mushrooms

This recipe is quite versatile. The tenderloins
can be grilled and then sliced, or they can be
sliced into medallions and quickly grilled over
charcoal or pan-broiled in a skillet. At Baricelli the plate might be garnished with
blanched small carrots that still have their
stems, blanched sugar-snap peas, and some
nasturtium blossoms.

Serves 6

2 quarts Dark Brown Veal Stock (see
page 277)
1 cup Madeira wine
1 tablespoon finely minced shallots
2 teaspoons minced fresh tarragon
½ pound wild mushrooms (preferably a
combination of golden chanterelles
and shiitakes)
2 tablespoons butter, plus more if
necessary
2½ pounds veal tenderloin
Salt and freshly ground black pepper
to taste

Steamed or sautéed seasonal
vegetables and fresh tarragon for
garnish

Preheat oven to 500°. Pour Veal Stock into heavy saucepan and cook briskly until reduced to 2 cups. Combine Madeira and shallots in a small saucepan and cook over medium heat until reduced by half. Combine with Veal Stock. Add tarragon. If sauce is not thick enough, whisk in some cold butter, bit by bit, until thickened . . . but do this just before serving.

Gently brush the dirt from the chanterelles and thinly slice them and the other wild mushrooms. Melt 2 tablespoons butter in heavy skillet and sauté mushrooms 2 to 3 minutes on high heat. Add more butter if necessary. Season with freshly ground black pepper.

Lightly season tenderloins with salt and pepper. Roast in preheated oven 15 minutes. Remove and let rest 10 minutes in a warm place.

To assemble, slice veal tenderloins into 18 equal pieces. Spoon some of the sauce in the middle of six warm serving plates and arrange 3 slices of meat on each plate. Divide mush-rooms among plates, along with cooked vegetables, making a decorative arrangement. Carefully spoon a small amount of sauce over meat, but do not completely cover meat with sauce. Sprinkle with a few grindings of pepper. Decorate with sprigs of tarragon.

Sabayon of Red Raspberries with Dark Rum

Serves 6

6 large egg yolks
3 tablespoons orange juice
1 tablespoon plus 2 teaspoons dark rum, preferably Myers's
1 tablespoon plus 2 teaspoons granulated sugar
3 pints red raspberries

Place egg yolks, orange juice, rum, and sugar in a medium-sized glass or copper bowl. (A zabaglione pot is perfect.) Place bowl over a larger saucepan filled with simmering water and whisk over low heat. Make certain that the bottom of the bowl is never too hot to the touch. Keep whisking until sabayon emulsifies and becomes thick and creamy. This will take about 8 minutes.

Cool sabayon over ice water, whisking constantly.

Distribute raspberries among six oven-proof gratin dishes. Spoon just enough sabayon over berries to coat them. Just before serving, place under a hot broiler, turning the dishes to glaze evenly. Serve immediately.

Johnny's Bar

CLEVELAND, OHIO

Hidden among some of Cleveland's toughest streets, in a once thriving Italian neighborhood on the city's west side, is Johnny's Bar. It is a neighborhood watering hole that eases out the bar clientele at 6:00 p.m., covers the tables with white linen and sparkling fine china, and turns itself into the hottest, trendiest restaurant in town by 7:00! This is a place that thrives on Saturday night, crowds, and chaos.

The menu is created by Joe Santosuosso, one of three owner-brothers. It is Joe who shapes the look of the restaurant as well as the taste of the cuisine. He draws upon his childhood food memories, as well as from his frequent trips around this country and Europe. It is a highly personal menu, one that will often offer dishes that Joe has a particular hunger for that day. The only certainties are the ever-present gnocchi and pasta.

The light-as-air gnocchi are made right on the premises according to a recipe created by Joe's mother, Frances Santosuosso. One of our favorite dishes is pasta puttanesca, a huge plate of red-bell-pepper pasta generously covered with a creamy cayenne sauce, freshly cooked shrimp, and scallops. ("Puttanesca," by the way, seems to be the preferred spelling for a word which means "whore's pasta"; it is a dish that is prepared about as many different ways as it is spelled.) Another splendid pasta dish is the perfectly cooked angel hair tossed with escargots sautéed in a handful of garlic, fresh Italian parsley, and sweet butter.

Joe's preparations of fish are always tempting. For example, we always manage to sample the mussels marinara—Joe's is an updated version of the traditional dish, one that requries the confidence not to overcook the tomatoes. Another of our favorites is stuffed baked calamari, gently bathed in a special variation on the house marinara sauce. Fillets are generally grilled at Johnny's. And while we love them rubbed with some olive oil and herbs, Joe makes an outstanding champagne sauce that always tempts us, and we think that the lime beurre blanc is perfect with Pacific salmon. As for meat, sweetbreads in a sauce of wild mushrooms, reduced veal stock, and madeira are outstanding. Veal tenderloin, grilled rare and served on sautéed romaine with thyme beurre blanc, is luscious. The rack of lamb is satisfying any way Joe prepares it. Sometimes it is boned and wrapped in puff pastry; at other times it is grilled and covered with a handful of fresh herbs picked from the yard in summer or the greenhouse in winter. Portions are enormous and all dishes are served with a vegetable, usually a timbale. We are rather partial to their winter timbales of squash or carrots. Finally, Joe serves the best version of Bananas Foster we have ever tasted. There is also a well-chosen wine list that always offers some interesting gems from California and France as well as from Italy.

Johnny's developed under Eugene and Frances Santosuosso. When they retired in the late 1970s, their sons Johnny, Joe, and Bo took over. While the decor has changed considerably in recent times, it never strays too far from the building's roots as a tavern in the days when Art Nouveau was on the wane and Art Deco was just beginning. The back dining room has striated dark paneling and extraordinary murals of bare-breasted nymphs and muscular gods surrounded by tropical exotica, both animal and vegetable. A huge Art Nouveau chandelier throws soft light on the rose-tinted room. The front dining room has mahogany walls with silver bands between the panels; black leather banquettes line two walls. Here the feeling is of Radio City Music Hall, with marble wall sconces and two enormous hyperrealistic paintings of balustrades and staircases by George Kozman which seem to jut at peculiar angles into the room. A faux-leopardskin carpet covers the floors in both dining rooms, while the floor around the mahogany-and-granite bar is covered in a geometric pattern with small Italian tiles in the colors of the leopard carpet. There are twelve whimsical chrome-and-leather barstools. Both dining rooms suggest the slightly bizarre humor of the brothers, who have for years loved to confound patrons with contrasts of elegance and kitsch.

Those dining in front have a nice view of the tiny bar, which absorbs the seemingly unlimited number of patrons who are forced to wait for a table on weekend evenings. Despite the noise and occasional chaos, people crowd into Johnny's because it is so enjoyable. It is a place where quality food is entertainingly served in a fascinating atmosphere. Some people come for a romantic dinner for two; others come with a group for a convivial evening, some business people work while eating, and many people come to see and be seen. Some people are dressed to the nines, others wear jeans and a sweater. Johnny's embraces them all. About a hundred souls can dine at one time, and there is hardly a night when they don't try. Clevelanders know a great restaurant when they find one.

Johnny's Bar

CLEVELAND, OHIO

Pasta Puttanesca

Joseph Phelps Vineyards Gewurztraminer

Stuffed Calamari

Marinara Sauce

Qupé Zinfandel

Veal Medallions over Braised Romaine
with Thyme Beurre Blanc

Clos Pegase Homage

Bananas Foster

Wines selected by Sandra Jordan Earl

Pasta Puttanesca

We have had many versions of this dish, but never has it been as wonderful as at Johnny's. The pasta, by the way, is Grandma Landi's egg-rich variety, the only kind the Santosuosso brothers have ever known. It is interesting to compare this sweet-red-pepper pasta recipe with the one from Baricelli to see how different they are.

Serves 6

SWEET-RED-PEPPER PASTA

    3 cups flour
    1 teaspoon salt
    3 large eggs
    3 large egg yolks
    1 4-ounce jar pimientos, drained and puréed
    3 tablespoons extra-virgin olive oil

PUTTANESCA SAUCE

    2 tablespoons butter
    1 teaspoon minced garlic
    Salt and freshly ground black pepper to taste
    Cayenne to taste
    ½ teaspoon crushed red pepper seeds
    1 pound shrimp, peeled and deveined, plus extra for garnish
    ¼ cup Parmesan cheese
    ½ cup or more heavy cream
    1 tablespoon olive oil

*T*o make the pasta, combine flour and salt in food processor. In a separate bowl, mix remaining ingredients. While food processor motor is running, add the wet ingredients to the flour and salt. Remove dough from processor bowl and knead on a well-floured board. Add just enough flour to make a smooth, pliable dough.

Follow instructions on page 274 to knead and roll dough in a pasta machine. Cut into fettuccine and dry.

In a heavy sauté pan, melt butter and slowly cook garlic, salt, pepper, cayenne, and red pepper seeds. Do not brown the garlic. Add shrimp and sauté until opaque. Add cheese and heavy cream. Remove from heat.

Cook pasta in boiling water until al dente, about 3 minutes. Drain well and toss with the olive oil. Add to the sauté pan and toss over very low heat. Add more cream if needed. Serve on warm plates immediately. Garnish with a few shrimp.

Stuffed Calamari

Serves 6, or 10 as an appetizer

SAUCE

    1 tablespoon flour
    Salt and freshly ground black pepper to taste
    2 cloves garlic, minced
    12 leaves fresh basil, chopped
    6 leaves fresh sage, chopped
    2 sprigs fresh thyme, leaves only
    ¼ cup dry sherry
    1¼ cups Marinara Sauce (see page 31)

    5 pounds fresh calamari, cleaned*
    1½ pounds bacon, chopped
    1 large red onion, finely chopped
    1 medium green bell pepper, seeded, deveined, and finely chopped

*To clean calamari, see instructions accompanying Baricelli Calamari Salad recipe, page 22.

1 medium red bell pepper, seeded,
    deveined, and finely chopped
7 cloves garlic, minced
¾ teaspoon cayenne pepper
½ teaspoon freshly ground black
    pepper
1 teaspoon salt
½ cup white wine
½ cup dry sherry
½ cup Chicken Stock (see page 276)
¼ cup lemon juice
3 large eggs
½ cup grated Parmesan cheese
    Bread crumbs
    Flour
¼ cup extra-virgin olive oil

    Fresh herbs, such as thyme, sage, and
      basil, and lemon slices for garnish

*I*n a small saucepan over high heat, combine flour, salt, pepper, garlic, and herbs. Add the sherry and simmer briskly for several minutes until liquid is reduced by three-fourths. Add Marinara Sauce and heat through. Keep warm while preparing the rest of the dish. Cut calamari tentacles into pieces and set aside. Place calamari bodies in pot of water and bring to a boil. Simmer 5 minutes to reduce liquid. Drain in colander and cool to room temperature.

    In a large sauté pan, cook bacon, onion, and peppers until onion is translucent. Add garlic and seasonings, and cook for several minutes. Add liquids and cook over medium heat until reduced to just a bit of moisture. Let cool and add eggs, cheese, and enough bread crumbs to hold mixture together.

    Place stuffing in a pastry bag with a large tip and stuff calamari (don't overstuff). Dredge in flour.

    Heat olive oil in a large skillet until smoking. Carefully, and without crowding, arrange stuffed calamari in the hot oil, cover, and cook 2 to 3 minutes on each side until brown. (Be sure to cover skillet, because calamari pop in hot oil.) Remove calamari from the oil and keep warm. To cook tentacles, dredge in flour and either sauté in the same pan or deep-fry for several minutes until brown. (Joe prefers deep-frying.)

    Serve calamari by arranging on a very large warm platter and spooning sauce over the top. Garnish with herbs and lemon slices.

Marinara Sauce

This makes an excellent sauce for any kind of pasta.

Makes 8 cups

    ½ cup extra-virgin olive oil
    1 stick butter
    6 cloves garlic, minced
    1 medium onion, minced
    1 large carrot, scraped and shredded

2 28-ounce cans crushed Italian plum
   tomatoes
2 teaspoons dried basil
½ teaspoon dried oregano
1 teaspoon crushed red pepper seeds
⅛ teaspoon cayenne pepper
   Salt and freshly ground black pepper
   to taste
½ teaspoon baking soda

*I*n a large, heavy saucepan, heat the olive oil and butter. Add the garlic, onion, and carrot, and sauté until the carrots are soft. Next, add remaining ingredients through cayenne and stir. Bring to a boil, reduce heat, and simmer 20 minutes. Add salt and pepper to taste, then add baking soda and stir well. This sauce is delicious over fettuccine with Parmesan cheese or steamed mussels sprinkled with fresh chopped parsley.

Veal Medallions over Braised Romaine with Thyme Beurre Blanc

Serves 6

4 tablespoons olive oil
2 bunches romaine lettuce
   Garlic salt
   Freshly ground black pepper to taste
12 2-ounce veal medallions, cut from
   the tenderloin
   Flour
7 tablespoons unsalted butter
4 cloves garlic, minced
   Salt to taste
6 sprigs fresh thyme, leaves only

1 tablespoon sugar
3 ounces tarragon vinegar
⅓ cup heavy cream

   Fresh herbs (thyme sprigs, parsley,
   and chives) and sautéed or
   steamed seasonal vegetables for
   garnish

*H*eat olive oil in a large skillet. Add romaine, garlic salt, and pepper. Cook until lettuce is wilted. Remove from skillet and arrange on warm dinner plates.

   Dredge veal in flour. Heat 4 tablespoons butter in skillet and sauté medallions about 2 minutes per side (longer if very thick). Remove from skillet and distribute on top of the romaine. Keep warm.

   Add garlic, salt, pepper, thyme, sugar, and vinegar to sauté pan. Cook over high heat until liquid is reduced by one-quarter. Add cream, cook until hot, then lower heat and simmer briskly until thickened. Swirl in 3 remaining tablespoons butter, a bit at a time. Adjust seasonings. Spoon sauce around the medallions. Garnish with herbs and lightly cooked fresh vegetables.

Bananas Foster

Serves 6

½ pound unsalted butter

⅛ teaspoon ground cinnamon

⅓ cup extra-light brown sugar, firmly
    packed

6 firm ripe bananas, peeled and cut in
    half lengthwise

¼ cup crème de banane liqueur

3 tablespoons Myers's dark rum

1 quart Vanilla Ice Cream (see page
    204)

*I*n a large sauté pan or chafing dish, over medium heat, whisk together butter, cinnamon, and brown sugar until ingredients are thoroughly mixed and contents begin to boil. Do not caramelize.

Add bananas and sauté on each side 45 seconds. Add both liqueurs to the pan, ignite, and let flame burn off.

Scoop ice cream into six serving bowls. Distribute bananas and sauce among the dishes.

The Palace

CINCINNATI, OHIO

The Cincinnatian Hotel is one of the most stunning, best run hotels we have had the pleasure to visit. From the elegantly upholstered chairs to the exciting contemporary art on the walls, the Cincinnatian ownership has paid attention to every detail. The building, over one hundred years old, is on the National Register of Historic Places. It was renovated at a cost of $23 million and reopened in February 1987. The architects have preserved the original staircase, with its well-worn marble treads, in the lobby, and added the extraordinary old safe that was in the hotel's office at the turn of the century. The hotel's intimate size allows the staff to recognize the guests by name and make them feel very welcome.

For decades the best known restaurant in Cincinnati has been The Maisonette, regarded as one of the finest French restaurants in the Midwest. Because of The Maisonette's popularity, it has been especially difficult for more contemporary food trends to take hold in this community. The Palace cuisine is miles away from the very rich, elaborate classic cuisine of France, but its menu offers just enough of the familiar to make diners feel comfortable. Pan-seared oysters in a delicate vermouth saffron cream sauce make a heavenly appetizer. Barely floured, and cooked just enough to brown, each oyster is placed on a fresh basil leaf and lightly surrounded with fragrant sauce. Blue cornmeal pancakes with Texas-barbecued quail are accompanied by a crispy jicama salad. Silky-sweet onion fettuccine is delicious with grilled tiger prawns and spicy salsa butter. Wild-mushroom broth with shrimp dumplings is heavenly, and happens to be among the menu items designated as "heart-healthy."

Salads are not to be overlooked at The Palace. Spinach salad with California chèvre is dressed with a splendid oregano mustard-seed vinaigrette. Smoked trout and salmon served with potato pancake and a Bibb lettuce and cucumber salad can also be a superlative appetizer. And we must tell the world that the Palace Caesar salad with lobster-and-boursin croutons is the best version of an old favorite that we have had outside our own kitchen. There are nice chunks of lobster meat as a garnish, and the croutons just melt in your mouth. This is one of the few restaurants we have visited that have a wide variety of really delicious salads and dressings in their repertoires.

We almost fought over the swordfish and tiger prawns marinated in tequila and lime and served with a sun-dried-tomato butter sauce, punctuated with opal basil. Grilled over hickory, applewood, and mesquite, the fish and prawns are barely cooked, the varied fragrances of the woods adding another dimension of flavor to the plate. We also enjoyed halibut and Pacific salmon, grilled to perfection and accompanied by a truffle sauce generously garnished with that delicious black French "diamond." Other winners from the grill are king salmon and lobster tail accompanied by braised radicchio and merlot butter, a veal chop with a Port Salut cream sauce, and sirloin steak in a red chile-pepper crust. The kitchen also offers several dishes from the wok. We found it hard to resist the mahi-mahi with ginger pecan sauce and glazed shrimp. While each dish has its own accompaniments, side orders of potatoes and vegetables are also available. We were especially tempted by the mashed potatoes zipped with horseradish.

The biggest problem here is saving room for dessert. The pastries, from tarts to tortes, are light as air and delicious. The crème brûlée, however, gets our vote as number one. This is not the baked variety but a cream that gets its body from lots of egg yolks and heavy cream, slowly cooked and stirred. It is then poured into a tissue-thin pastry crust, allowed to set up, then lightly coated with sugar and quickly caramelized. Served with a raspberry and strawberry sauce, it is sublime.

Chilled mineral water is poured for each guest, and a fine wine list is knowledgeably presented. The dinner is consummated by a silver "tree" of twice-dipped strawberries, generously showing their coats of white and dark chocolate.

The Palace is definitely the jewel in the hotel's diadem. With its two small side rooms, the restaurant holds only about eighty-six people. Decorated in shades of peach, pink, violet, and lavender, The Palace reinforces the post-modern architectural feel of the hotel lobby. Mirrors are used judiciously to create an illusion of space. Two windows to the street are covered in translucent white drapery and accented by exquisite tiebacks of watered silk. Some of the woodwork appears to be mahogany, some painted ivory. Upholstery in peach and lavender echoes the colors of the architectural details in the hotel's atrium and bar. Table linens are ivory damask, the napkins are pink; the silverware is large and heavy, and the china is a pale-gray-and-white pattern by Schonwald that features hexagonal dinner plates. Each table is ornamented with a splendid small lamp with a silver filigreed shade and silk fringe. Although the ceiling is low in the dining room, one can easily look off to the soaring space of the distant atrium. Adding to the quality of this dining experience is a staff that is faultless in its attention to the guests.

Every detail is in the hands of a tiny dynamo, Anita Cunningham. Under thirty and a graduate of Philadelphia's Restaurant School, this Cleveland native possesses limitless energy and impeccable taste. From before sunrise to about midnight she is busy overseeing the total food operation of the hotel. Not even breakfast orders escape her notice. And no tea cake slips out if it is not perfectly finished. She says that she thrives on the pace. When we talk about the hotel and restaurant, her face glows and her eyes dance as she tells us how much she loves what she does. And how well we can tell!

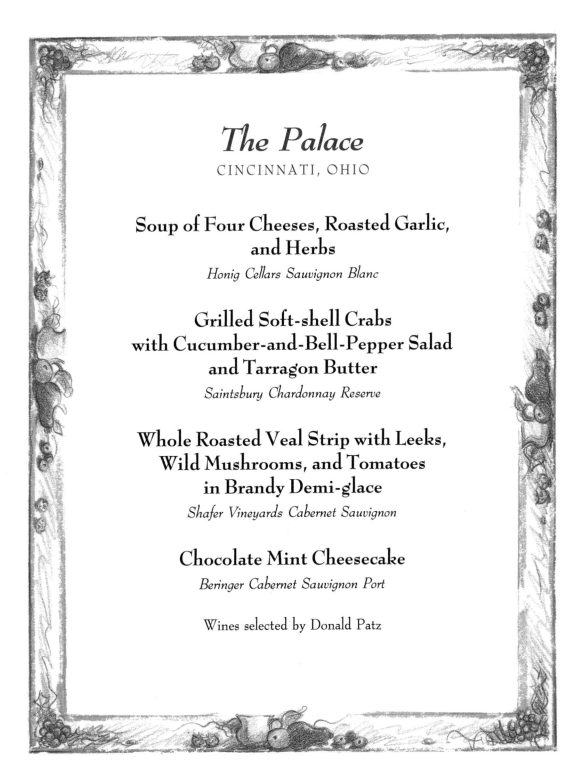

The Palace

CINCINNATI, OHIO

Soup of Four Cheeses, Roasted Garlic, and Herbs

Honig Cellars Sauvignon Blanc

Grilled Soft-shell Crabs with Cucumber-and-Bell-Pepper Salad and Tarragon Butter

Saintsbury Chardonnay Reserve

Whole Roasted Veal Strip with Leeks, Wild Mushrooms, and Tomatoes in Brandy Demi-glace

Shafer Vineyards Cabernet Sauvignon

Chocolate Mint Cheesecake

Beringer Cabernet Sauvignon Port

Wines selected by Donald Patz

Soup of Four Cheeses, Roasted Garlic, and Herbs

You can really be creative with this and use any four of your favorite cheeses. Experiment and keep track of favorite combinations.

Serves 8 to 10

3 tablespoons vegetable oil
½ cup whole garlic cloves, peeled
6 tablespoons clarified butter
2 medium yellow onions, chopped
6 tablespoons flour
5 cups Chicken Stock (see page 276)
5 cups heavy cream
½ pound each grated Cheddar, Swiss, smoked mozzarella, and jalapeño jack cheese
Salt and white pepper to taste
Worcestershire sauce to taste
Tabasco sauce to taste
1 cup mixed fresh herbs, such as oregano, basil, tarragon, dill, or rosemary

Fresh herbs for garnish

Preheat oven to 400°. Heat oil in medium-sized skillet and sauté garlic cloves over medium heat 5 minutes. Pour contents of skillet into a baking dish and place in hot oven. Roast 10 minutes, or until cloves are dark brown.

Meanwhile, heat clarified butter in a 3–4-quart saucepan. Add onions and sauté 5 minutes. Add entire contents of garlic dish and sauté about 2 more minutes. Stir in flour and keep stirring to make a well-blended roux; cook roux for total of 5 minutes, stirring constantly.

Slowly add the stock and cream to the saucepan, whisking over medium heat until it is brought to a boil. Reduce heat and simmer 20 minutes. Slowly add cheese, stirring constantly. When cheese is completely melted, turn off heat. Add herbs and immediately put a small amount into a blender or food processor. Purée until very smooth. Repeat in small batches until all the soup is puréed. Return to saucepan and season to taste. Serve garnished with sprigs of fresh herbs.

Grilled Soft-shell Crabs with Cucumber-and-Bell-Pepper Salad and Tarragon Butter

A very clean, Pam-sprayed, hot grill is essential for this dish.

Serves 8 to 10

8 to 10 fresh soft-shell crabs

VINAIGRETTE
2 teaspoons Dijon mustard
⅛ teaspoon minced garlic
2 tablespoons chopped fresh tarragon
⅓ cup red wine vinegar
1 cup extra-virgin olive oil
Salt and coarsely ground black pepper to taste

2 cucumbers
1 each red, yellow, and green bell pepper, seeded, deveined, and finely julienned
1 red onion, finely julienned
4 heads Bibb or red-oak-leaf lettuce
Olive oil

TARRAGON BUTTER

    1 teaspoon cracked peppercorns
    1 bay leaf
    1 cup heavy cream
    ½ teaspoon minced shallot
    ⅛ teaspoon minced garlic
    1 pound unsalted butter, cut into small
        pieces, at room temperature
    Juice of 1 lemon
    Salt and freshly ground black pepper
        to taste
    Tabasco to taste
    Worcestershire sauce to taste
    3 tablespoons chopped fresh tarragon

    Fresh tarragon sprigs for garnish

Clean crabs by removing lungs, eyes, and intestines (or ask your fish merchant to do this
for you when you buy the crabs). First, lift up
sides of upper shell and remove gills. Place
crab on a wooden board and, using a sharp
knife, cut off head immediately behind eyes.
Use a butter knife to scrape out the lungs and
intestines through this opening. Rinse well
under running water. Then turn crab over and
pull open the "apron," or turned-under tail,
and cut it off with a sharp knife or scissors.
Rinse crabs again and set aside on a large dish,
cover well, and chill until needed.

Combine next 6 ingredients in a large mixing bowl, whisking well to emulsify. Prepare
the cucumbers by partially peeling (in alter-
nate strips lengthwise), cutting in half lengthwise, removing seeds, and slicing into thin
half-moons. Marinate cucumbers, peppers,
and onion in the vinaigrette at least 1 hour.
Clean and dry lettuce.

To make Tarragon Butter: In a heavy saucepan combine the first 5 ingredients and reduce by two-thirds over medium heat.
Quickly whisk in butter a piece at a time.

Remove from heat and add everything but
the tarragon. Pass the sauce through a strainer
into a medium-sized mixing bowl. Keep warm
by placing bowl in a larger saucepan filled
with hot water. Whisk in tarragon just before
serving.

When ready to serve, spray grill with Pam
and heat to very hot. Rub crabs with olive oil
and place on the hottest portion of the grill
3 minutes on each side. Keep warm. Quickly
toss marinated vegetables with lettuce. Distribute among the serving plates. Place crabs
on top of salad in center of plate, spoon tarragon butter over crab, garnish with tarragon,
and serve.

Whole Roasted Veal Strip with Leeks, Wild Mushrooms, and Tomatoes in Brandy Demi-glace

This is definitely a luxury dish, since veal strip
is quite costly. We find that a cut that weighs
a tad over 2 pounds after trimming will serve
5 to 6 people when there are good accompaniments and starters.

Serves 8 to 10

    3 to 4 pounds strip portion of veal T-bone
        Salt and freshly ground black pepper
        to taste
    2 tablespoons vegetable oil
    2 leeks, cleaned very well, trimmed of
        their tops, and julienned into
        2-inch pieces
    ½ pound wild mushrooms, sliced
    1 teaspoon minced shallots
    1 teaspoon minced garlic
    ¼ cup brandy

½ cup Pommery mustard

2½ cups Veal or Beef Demi-glace (needs to be somewhat thick; see page 278)

4 tomatoes, peeled, seeded, and diced

Sautéed or steamed seasonal vegetables and chives for garnish

*P*reheat oven to 425°. Rub meat with salt and pepper. If there is a thinner end to the strip, fold this end in half and under itself. In a very large skillet (cast iron is best), heat oil on high heat. Quickly sear veal on all sides. Transfer veal to a roasting pan and roast in preheated oven about 20 minutes, or until a meat thermometer reads 115–120°.

While meat is roasting, add leeks, mushrooms, shallots, and garlic to the skillet that was used for browning the loin. Sauté on medium heat about 1 minute, stirring well. Then pour brandy over contents (be careful of flaming), stirring constantly. Simmer until liquid is reduced by half, then set aside.

When meat is done, remove from oven, coat with mustard, and return to oven for 6 minutes.

While meat is finishing, return skillet to heat and stir in demi-glace. Add tomatoes, salt, and pepper to taste. Heat thoroughly.

Let meat rest 5 minutes, then slice so that each person gets 3 pieces. Sauce with demi-glace. Garnish with potatoes and vegetables.

Chocolate Mint Cheesecake

CRUST

¼ pound lightly salted butter

2 cups finely ground chocolate wafer crumbs

¼ cup sugar

FILLING

2 pounds cream cheese

1¼ cups sugar

1 tablespoon Vandermint liqueur

1 teaspoon mint extract

Pinch salt

3½ ounces Maillard's Eagle sweet chocolate, or Baker's German sweet chocolate, melted in double boiler or in microwave

4 large eggs

2 ounces chocolate mint soufflé or mint-flavored dark chocolates (Droste Mint Pastilles, for example), chopped in food processor to size of small chocolate chips

TOPPING

2 cups sour cream

¼ cup sugar

1 teaspoon white crème de menthe

*P*reheat oven to 350°.

Melt butter over very low heat. Combine with chocolate wafer crumbs and sugar, and blend very well. Press mixture over bottom and up sides of a 10-inch springform pan. There should be enough to coat the entire pan.

In bowl of an electric mixer, combine cream cheese and sugar and beat 2 minutes, or until soft (cream cheese need not be at room temperature). Add liqueur, mint extract, salt, and melted chocolate. Blend thoroughly. Keeping the mixer speed on low (not to beat too much air into mixture), add the eggs one at a time. Mix just until each egg has been incorporated into the batter. Fold in mint bits. Pour batter into prepared crust and bake in preheated oven 40 minutes. If ingredients were not at room temperature, add 5 minutes to baking time.

Remove from oven and *let stand on a countertop 10 minutes* while you prepare the topping. This is an essential step.

Combine sour cream, sugar, and crème de menthe, and blend well. Spread evenly over top of cooled cake and return to 350° oven for 10 minutes. Remove from oven and cool in refrigerator at once (this will prevent cracks from forming in cheesecake). Cool completely before serving.

The Restaurant at The Phoenix

CINCINNATI, OHIO

Like the bird of mythology, The Phoenix was given a second chance at life. The building opened in 1893 as a private club for Cincinnati's Jewish businessmen. Abandoned and neglected, it was bought in spring 1987 by Carl Bruggemeier, the restaurant world's great gift to Cincinnati. Today it shines in pristine glory, from its top-floor ballroom with glorious stained-glass windows to its grand staircase sweeping down to the street, lovingly restored and refurbished. The Phoenix provides the city with phenomenal facilities for private parties and a 100-seat restaurant that has few equals.

The chef's taste treat changes nightly. Sometimes it might be a silky smooth chicken or liver pâté. Other times it might be a delicate and frilly rosette of smoked shellfish purée served with toast points. Whatever it is, your taste buds immediately tell you that it is going to be a splendid evening. While the menu changes seasonally at The Phoenix, the phyllo purse filled with smoked scallops and langoustine is constant throughout the year. Along with the shellfish, the little package gets added texture and flavor from a fine julienne of zucchini and red onion. Served in a pool of lobster sauce, and with generous dollops of golden and sturgeon caviars, this dish is simply sublime. Crispy-skinned Ohio white quail, stuffed with smoked duck and crunchy walnuts, is accompanied by a Cabernet-elderberry sauce. Delicate sweet potato and ginger pancakes are spiked by sour cream and chives; and polenta, crisply fried yet creamy on the inside, is presented with tangy Gorgonzola, a blessing of fresh tomato sauce, and a sprinkling of toasted pine nuts. And in the chill of winter, what could be better than a plate of three sausages—one of venison, another of boar, and the third an andouille—its spice showing Carl's passion for Louisiana—served on light and creamy mashed potatoes with a demi-glace?

Whether fresh tomato and vegetable or smoked chicken and wild rice, soups are elegant and filled with flavor. Salads are creative and highly satisfying. A fine dice of crisp apple mixed with tender watercress is lightly dressed in a honey-and-herb mayonnaise and studded with toasted pecans. Chunks of marinated mushrooms fill a radicchio cup garnished with fresh Bibb lettuce and diced red peppers and enlivened by a finely made Dijon vinaigrette. Pencil-thin green beans are mixed with slices of the sausages and red Bliss potatoes, making a scrumptious, albeit substantial, appetizer. And for citrus lovers, slices of navel oranges are mixed with crunchy romaine and zipped by warm cashews and balsamic vinaigrette. It is all so good that one almost forgets to leave room for the main course.

Cincinnatians like their meat and potatoes, so young chefs can get mighty discouraged if they try to be too inventive. We've been told that sweetbreads will never make it in this city. The test of a fine chef here, therefore, is to serve fairly straightforward dishes that are light, flavorful, and beautifully presented. Paul Sturkey, The Phoenix's executive chef, does this well indeed. The Colorado lamb chops are outstanding. Served on slices of Roma tomatoes and accompanied by rosemary-garlic beurre blanc and fried shoestring sweet potatoes, the dish takes on another dimension as the lamb, tomatoes, and sauce all mingle with each bite. Perfectly grilled salmon is served with champagne sauce and accompanied by leeks and caviar. A thick pork chop is delicious with its accompaniment

of sautéed pears and apples. Breast of chicken reaches new heights when served with corn, black beans, and choron sauce (a Béarnaise sauce to which fresh tomato purée has been added). Deep-fried cornmeal-battered catfish and smoked tenderloin of beef are also winners.

As everywhere in the Midwest, people here love their bread and their desserts. A cracked-wheat black bread is served at each table. Studded with raisins and flavored with molasses, it can become addictive. Pastries are also superb. Crème brûlée is exquisite served with a luscious almond cookie. Bananas Foster cheesecake is creamy and moist, and served with a perfectly made caramel cream sauce. A white-and-dark-chocolate checkerboard terrine answers the prayers of every chocolate lover. And the tray of tiny tarts and cakes would bring tears of delight to the eyes of any French three-star chef.

The Phoenix looks just the way we want it to when we are in the mood for an evening of elegant dining. There is an intimate bar with gorgeous window shades and comfortable chairs. The charming Chef's Dining Room has a glass wall looking into the kitchen. And the Library Dining Room still retains the magnificent wall of paneling and the bookcases and shelves that were there in the nineteenth century. All three rooms are exquisitely decorated with fine wallpapers and draperies. Confronted with twenty-foot ceilings, huge windows, and enormous fireplaces, only a skilled hand could have created the feeling of warmth and intimacy that has been achieved. Servers are among the best we have ever encountered. Captains, in blazers and flannel pants, are knowledgeable about wine, enthusiastic about the food, and attentive even to the tables not assigned to

The Best of the Midwest

them. No one seems to hover, but no need is overlooked, either. People are greeted warmly upon entering; goodbyes are by name whenever possible.

Raised in Cleveland, Carl Bruggemeier returned to Ohio after years of experience at Commander's Palace in New Orleans and The Potomac in Washington. He knows what it takes to build customer loyalty—the secret is in his staff. General Manager of The Phoenix is Dan Zwillweger, a charming young man who has worked many years with Carl. Ex-ecutive chef and a native of Akron, Ohio, Paul Sturkey is newer to the Bruggemeier philosophy, but is thriving under it. While the restaurant serves about one hundred on a given night, the entire operation, combined with the Cincinnati Club next door (which they also manage), can serve as many as two thousand guests a day. Cincinnati is a city on the move these days. We have every confidence that The Restaurant at The Phoenix will become part of its fame. Carl Bruggemeier has already become a part of its leadership.

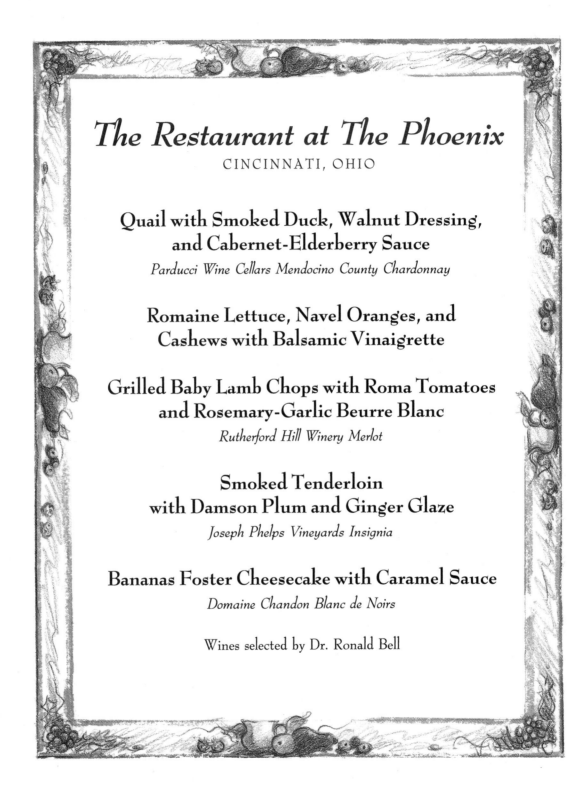

The Restaurant at The Phoenix
CINCINNATI, OHIO

Quail with Smoked Duck, Walnut Dressing, and Cabernet-Elderberry Sauce
Parducci Wine Cellars Mendocino County Chardonnay

Romaine Lettuce, Navel Oranges, and Cashews with Balsamic Vinaigrette

Grilled Baby Lamb Chops with Roma Tomatoes and Rosemary-Garlic Beurre Blanc
Rutherford Hill Winery Merlot

Smoked Tenderloin with Damson Plum and Ginger Glaze
Joseph Phelps Vineyards Insignia

Bananas Foster Cheesecake with Caramel Sauce
Domaine Chandon Blanc de Noirs

Wines selected by Dr. Ronald Bell

Quail with Smoked Duck, Walnut Dressing, and Cabernet-Elderberry Sauce

Another source for game fowl and smoked fowl besides Mr. Brisket (see The Baricelli Inn ravioli recipe, page 23) is D'Artagnan, Inc., at 399 St. Paul Avenue, Jersey City, New Jersey 07306, (201) 792–0748. You can also purchase fresh foie gras from them.

Serves 8

8 quail, boned except for legs and
    wings
Salt and freshly ground black pepper
    to taste
6 tablespoons butter
½ cup chopped celery
2 teaspoons finely minced shallots
¼ teaspoon minced fresh sage
1 teaspoon minced fresh rosemary
18 ounces smoked duck breast
4 large eggs

1¼ cup walnuts, roasted and coarsely
    chopped
1 cup fresh elderberries (or red
    currants; if necessary use canned
    berries from specialty stores)
½ cup heavy cream
Melted butter

CABERNET-ELDERBERRY SAUCE
7 tablespoons unsalted butter
2 tablespoons finely diced shallots
1 cup Cabernet Sauvignon wine
⅔ cup Duck Stock (see page 278)
1 cup Demi-glace (see page 278)
6 tablespoons elderberry jam
Salt and freshly ground black pepper
    to taste
½ cup heavy cream
½ cup port wine

Fresh rosemary and sage for garnish

*P*reheat oven to 375°. Season quail inside and out with salt and pepper. Melt butter in small skillet; add celery, shallots, sage, and rosemary; cover directly with wax paper and sweat over low heat until celery is translucent. Remove from heat and transfer celery mixture into large mixing bowl.

Remove and discard duck skin and coarsely grind duck meat in a meat grinder or food processor. Add to celery mixture. Add eggs, walnuts, ½ cup elderberries, and ½ cup cream. Mix well. Moisten with some duck stock if necessary. Stuff quails; form to resemble unboned quail. Brush with melted butter. Place quails on rack in roasting pan. Roast in preheated oven 15 to 20 minutes, or until golden.

Meanwhile, in a heavy 1-quart saucepan, sauté shallots in 4 tablespoons butter. Add wine and stock; reduce by two-thirds. Add demi-glace, then elderberry jam. Season to taste with salt and pepper. Add remaining cream and boil 1 minute. Strain well.

Return strained sauce to heat and whisk in remaining 3 tablespoons butter. Finish with port wine.

Spoon sauce into middle of eight heated serving plates. Put quail on sauce. Garnish with remaining elderberries and sprigs of herbs.

Romaine Lettuce, Navel Oranges, and Cashews with Balsamic Vinaigrette

Serves 8

¼ cup balsamic vinegar
2 tablespoons Dijon mustard
2 teaspoons minced garlic
1 tablespoon minced fresh thyme
½ teaspoon chopped fresh rosemary
    Salt and freshly ground black pepper
      to taste
½ cup extra-virgin olive oil
3 heads romaine lettuce
1 small Bermuda onion, thinly sliced
¼ cup cashews, lightly roasted in oven
6 navel oranges, each peeled and sliced
      into 6 equal slices

    Romano cheese (optional)

Combine first 6 ingredients in a medium-sized mixing bowl. Let stand at least 10 minutes. Slowly whisk olive oil into mixture; whip well to emulsify. Chill thoroughly.

Wash and core romaine and tear into bite-size pieces. Chill well. Just before serving, combine with onion and nuts. Toss with half the vinaigrette. Divide among eight chilled

salad plates. Arrange 4 slices of orange at the base of each plate. Grind a bit of pepper over each plate. Serve remaining vinaigrette on the side.

For a nice touch, heat the cashews just before tossing the salad. Also, we like to offer freshly grated Romano cheese at the table for sprinkling.

Grilled Baby Lamb Chops with Roma Tomatoes and Rosemary-Garlic Beurre Blanc

This dish is delicious when garnished with roasted cloves of garlic. Just slice off the very top of a few heads of garlic, loosen some of the skin, and place heads in a baking dish just large enough to hold them. Pour ⅓ cup Chicken Stock (page 276) in the bottom of the pan, coat the garlic with olive oil, sprinkle with freshly ground black pepper, cover with foil, and roast in 325° oven 1 hour. Remove foil, drizzle with more olive oil, and bake 20 minutes more.

Serves 8

2 cups extra-virgin olive oil
1 tablespoon fresh rosemary, chopped
1 tablespoon minced garlic
1 cup Cabernet Sauvignon wine
5 bay leaves
24 center-cut lamb chops
1 tablespoon minced shallots
2 tablespoons dried rosemary
1 tablespoon minced garlic
2 cups fumé blanc or comparable dry
      white wine
2 pounds unsalted butter, softened to
      room temperature

1 tablespoon chopped fresh rosemary
Tabasco sauce to taste
Salt
8 Roma tomatoes (or substitute very
    good quality pear tomatoes)

Crisply roasted potatoes and sautéed
    or steamed seasonal vegetables for
    garnish
Sprigs of fresh rosemary and bunches
    of watercress for garnish

Combine first 5 ingredients in a medium-sized mixing bowl. Whisk well. Arrange chops in a glass baking dish, pour oil mixture over them, and marinate overnight.

Combine shallots, dried rosemary, garlic, and white wine in a small saucepan and simmer briskly until liquid is reduced by two-thirds. Remove from heat and whisk in butter in 5 equal parts, whipping until sauce emulsifies. Strain sauce and season with the fresh rosemary, Tabasco, and salt to taste. Return to saucepan and keep warm by placing saucepan in a larger saucepan filled with hot water.

Slice tomatoes into 4 equal slices each and arrange along the outer edge of eight large heated dinner plates, overlapping slightly in a fan along the outer edge of one side of the plate.

Clean grill thoroughly, spray with Pam, and heat until very hot. Remove chops from marinade and grill until medium rare, about 5 minutes a side. Place meat part of 3 chops on the overlapping tomato slices, with the bone ends toward the center of the plate. Sauce the chops with the beurre blanc. Garnish plates with some crispy potatoes and a mélange of vegetables. Finish with some fresh rosemary, watercress, and a few cloves of roasted garlic, if desired.

Smoked Tenderloin with Damson Plum and Ginger Glaze

Serves 4

2½ to 3 pounds tenderloin of beef,
    silverskin removed

MARINADE
  2 cups vegetable oil
  3 tablespoons minced garlic
  3 tablespoons minced shallots
  4 tablespoons cracked black
    peppercorns
  2 tablespoons kosher salt
  2 cups Cabernet Sauvignon wine
  3 sprigs fresh rosemary

GLAZE
  1 cup port wine
  2 cups Cabernet Sauvignon wine
  2 tablespoons minced garlic
  ½ teaspoon dried chile peppers
  1 tablespoon minced fresh ginger
  2 tablespoons minced shallots
  1 cup Damson plum pulp (made from
    peeled, pitted, and puréed plums)
  1 cup sugar
  ¼ cup rice vinegar
  1 quart Beef or Veal Demi-glace (see
    page 278)
  Salt and freshly ground black pepper
    to taste
  ¼ pound unsalted butter, softened
  2 pounds hickory chips soaked in
    water 1 to 2 hours before grilling

Watercress for garnish

Combine all ingredients for marinade in a large mixing bowl and whip together. Add beef and marinate in a deep bowl 12 to 24 hours.

Combine the first 6 ingredients for the glaze in a heavy medium-sized saucepan and simmer briskly over moderate heat until reduced by half.

Combine plum pulp, sugar, and vinegar, and purée in blender or food processor. Add to the wine reduction and reduce by another one-third.

Add Demi-glace to the reduction, bring to a boil, and then lower heat to a simmer. Skim off any scum that might form on top and let simmer approximately 30 to 40 minutes.

Strain glaze, adjust seasonings to taste with salt and pepper, return to saucepan, and whip in butter, a bit at a time. Keep warm by placing saucepan in a larger saucepan filled with hot water.

Light coals in an outdoor barbecue grill and let burn down until embers glow red. Cover coals with wet chips to create a moderate smoke. Place marinated tenderloin on grill and close lid. Smoke approximately 30 to 40 minutes. It is important that the internal temperature of the grill does not exceed 125°, to avoid overcooked tenderloin and too heavy a smoke. Test with an oven thermometer.

Remove tenderloin from grill and let rest 10 to 15 minutes.

Slice tenderloin into 12 equal slices. Spoon glaze to cover bottoms of four heated dinner plates. Place 3 slices overlapping down the center of each plate. Garnish with watercress.

Bananas Foster Cheesecake with Caramel Sauce

They must love cheesecake in Cincinnati, because we saw several versions on menus of the restaurants we visited. The one from The Palace and this one from The Phoenix are, in fact, quite different from one another, and both are superb. This one has the same creamy texture that makes Bananas Foster so satisfying. And speaking of Bananas Foster, we only saw it in one restaurant of the many we visited during our year of travel—Johnny's Bar in Cleveland—and we have that recipe for you, too (page 33).

Serves 12

CRUST
 1½ cups graham-cracker crumbs
 ½ cup sugar
 4 tablespoons unsalted butter, melted

FILLING
 2 tablespoons unsalted butter
 3 tablespoons brown sugar
 1 pinch cinnamon
 2 large ripe bananas, sliced into
  quarters
 1½ tablespoons banana liqueur
 3 tablespoons light rum

 12 ounces cream cheese, at room
  temperature
 6 tablespoons sugar
 ¾ teaspoon vanilla extract
 1 pinch cinnamon
 1 large egg
 2 large egg yolks

   1¼ cups sour cream
   2 tablespoons sugar
   ½ teaspoon vanilla extract
   1 tablespoon dark rum

SAUCE

   1¼ cups superfine sugar
   1¾ cups Crème Fraîche (see page 275)
   ½ cup milk

*P*reheat oven to 350°. Combine all ingredients for crust and mix until evenly distributed. Pat evenly into the bottom and sides of an 8-inch springform pan.

Heat butter, brown sugar, and cinnamon in a sauté pan until bubbly. Add bananas and sauté until golden. Add liqueur and rum, then ignite. When flame goes out, remove bananas with a slotted spoon and reserve. Simmer liquid briskly until reduced to a bubbling syrup and pour over bananas. Set aside.

Combine cream cheese, sugar, vanilla, and cinnamon in the bowl of an electric mixer and beat with the paddle until very creamy and smooth. Scrape down mixing bowl and beat again. Add whole egg, then yolks, one at a time, beating slowly until blended. Scrape bowl and pour in banana mixture. Mix only long enough for bananas to break apart into large chunks. Do not overmix. Pour into prepared crust.

Bake in the preheated oven 20 to 25 minutes, until golden brown and slightly springy to the touch. *Remove from oven and let stand on countertop for 10 minutes while you prepare the topping.* This is an essential step.

Combine all ingredients for topping in a mixing bowl and blend well. Gently spoon topping onto the cheesecake and spread evenly. Bake cheesecake at 350° 8 to 10 minutes longer and remove from oven. *Refrigerate immediately* (this will prevent cracks from forming in cheesecake) and cool completely before serving.

To make the sauce, heat Crème Fraîche to just below boiling. Remove from heat and set aside. Put sugar in a caramel pot or a small saucepan. Slowly heat and stir over medium heat until sugar has dissolved and turned a beautiful golden brown. Remove from heat and pour in half the warm Crème Fraîche. Return to low heat and stir until caramel is well blended with the Crème Fraîche. Once blended, remove from heat and whisk in remaining Crème Fraîche. Let cool.

Just before serving, heat milk in a small saucepan. Pour caramel into top of double boiler. Over simmering water, carefully heat caramel and gradually add warm milk, whisking thoroughly, until proper sauce density is achieved. Spoon a small amount of sauce on each dessert plate and place a slice of the cooled cheesecake on top.

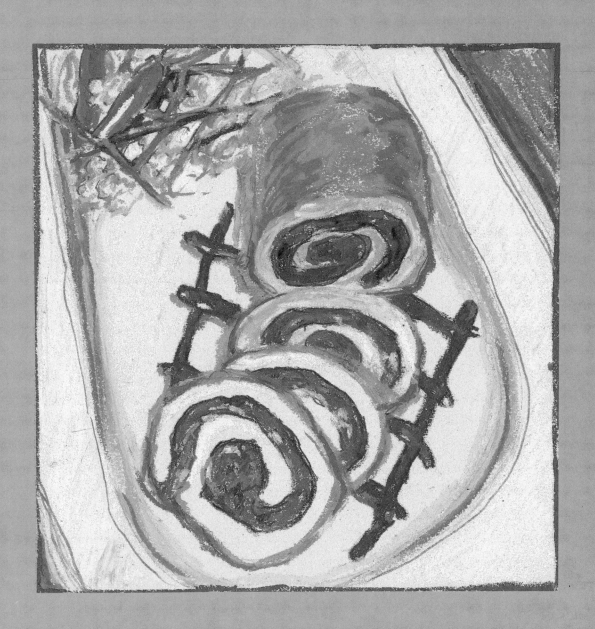

Peter's Restaurant

INDIANAPOLIS, INDIANA

Indianapolis is definitely a city on the move. We were astonished at the renaissance evident in its downtown area. Like so many of the industrial cities in the heartland, Indianapolis has enjoyed good times and bad. Fortunately, the city is now fighting back from bad times and winning. Major efforts are under way to bring visitors to Indianapolis for trade shows and conventions. We know that many of them will grab a cab and visit Peter's, a mile or so from the center of town in a wonderful old area now undergoing a lot of renovation. Although in a part of the country that expects fine dining to be served in a French Provincial setting, Peter's makes a contemporary statement in decor and really, as the saying goes, sticks its neck out. Peter George and executive chef Tony Hanslits have been offering Midwestern regional cuisine since they opened in 1985. Peter's was among the first restaurants to promote the heartland, but unfortunately the national press has been slow to recognize them. Peter's has cuisine that sincerely celebrates the wonderful culinary traditions of the Hoosier state, and it is a cuisine that splendidly showcases the bounty of the region.

Menus at Peter's change frequently. On a chilly autumn night we thoroughly enjoyed venison chili with sage biscuits. Moist cubes of venison, punctuated by tomato and white beans, are served on a sage biscuit in a copper ramekin—all presented on a larger plate that is garnished with a superlative mushroom salad and ringed by some of the crumbled biscuit. Roast quail with persimmon-bread stuffing is simply heavenly. A delicate Kentucky bourbon sauce, sautéed apples, and a small green salad garnished with nuts completed the presentation. We were intrigued by the three-cheese terrine, which consists of layers of Maytag Farms Edam, white Cheddar, and blue cheeses. And we were tempted by a salad of grilled whitefish and Bibb lettuce dressed with balsamic vinaigrette. Chef Hanslits is proficient at smoking, so there are often offerings of hickory-smoked meats and game. The kitchen is also skilled in the preparation of soups. From a smoked-duck consommé to a tomato bisque, they are rich and flavorful.

Entrees at Peter's best showcase the chef's creativity. Pan-fried fillets of catfish and gingered onions together make one of the best versions we have ever had of that delicious fish. Accompanied by peanut-butter sauce, hair-fine julienne of white radish and snow pea pods, melt-in-your-mouth hush puppies, and corn and red pepper relish, this is a dish to remember. Roasted Indiana duck with pear chutney is moist on the inside and crispy on the outside. Accompanied by perfectly prepared Brussels sprouts and wild-rice cakes, the duck is, thankfully, allowed to shine on its own without floating in sauce. Equally skillfully prepared is a small whole Indiana chicken served with delicate rye pancakes and accompanied by a pan sauce with morels. Oven-roasted pheasant pot pie, filled with parsnips, turnips, carrots, and pearl onions, and lamb turnovers with feta cheese, grilled eggplant, and green tomatoes are outstanding contemporary interpretations of old farm classics.

From appetizers to desserts, Peter's is a breath of culinary fresh air, and it never forgets where it is. While he is creative and innovative, the chef also remembers that folks in the heartland enjoy their sweets, especially their pies and ice creams. A separate dessert menu is offered that defies resistance. There are talented hands involved in pastry here. Cakes and pies are delicate and light; fillings and sauces are delicious, often ingenious. But while fruit cobblers and bread puddings are luscious, and homemade ice creams with white chocolate sauce are tempting, the white-and-dark-chocolate pâte with cappuccino is, quite honestly, one of the best desserts we have ever tasted.

This 50-seat restaurant is in a wonderfully designed contemporary environment that is a perfect setting for the style of food offered. In a way that retains the vintage look of the exterior, the interior has been gutted and redesigned in Bauhaus simplicity. Colors are creamy off-white, light grays, and dark grays; black lacquer-and-cane chairs are complemented by the light-gray-wool-upholstered banquettes. Skillful use of mirrors and halogen torchères adds decorative shadows that further enhance the sophisticated atmosphere. Highly professional servers further complement the entire dining experience by quiet attention to detail. Wine is taken seriously at Peter's; in fact, visitors are invited to tour the wine cellar and even to enjoy a sip or two down there, and it takes little effort to engage the staff in a stimulating conversation about their fine collection.

It is clear that Peter's is managed by highly experienced hands. Peter George quite literally learned the business at his mother's knee. Growing up in South Bend, he was "schooled" at The Carriage House (see page 61), where he watched his mom, Evelyn George, do it the way it ought to be done. After graduating from Purdue's School of Restaurant, Hotel, and Institutional Management, he worked with his mother for many years before moving to Indianapolis. Also an Indiana native, Tony Hanslits graduated from Johnson and Wales in Providence before returning to South Bend and joining the staff of The Carriage House. After four years, he moved to Vermilion, Ohio; but it was not difficult for Peter George to persuade him to join the Indianapolis project. His enthusiasm is infectious; thoroughly dedicated to Peter's, Chef Hanslits sometimes carries the work ethic too far. We learned that his child's birth was carefully arranged to coincide with his day off! While we sympathize with his beleaguered wife, we must salute Tony Hanslits's creativity and dedication. He and Peter George have dared to challenge the culinary traditions of Indianapolis—and they are doing it wonderfully well.

Peter's Restaurant
INDIANAPOLIS, INDIANA

Salad of Arugula, Radicchio, and Duck
with Raspberry Vinaigrette
Pheasant Ridge Winery (Texas) Sauvignon Blanc

Roasted Pork Loin
with Persimmon-Bread Stuffing and
Applejack and Port Wine Sauce
Kalin Cellars Sémillon

Veal Sweetbread Pancakes with Hazelnut Yogurt
Clos du Bois Flintwood Chardonnay

Sweet Potato and Coconut Pie
Quady Essensia

Wines selected by Nick Ambeliotis

Salad of Arugula, Radicchio, and Duck with Raspberry Vinaigrette

Serves 4

RASPBERRY VINAIGRETTE
- 1½ cups salad oil
- 1 large egg
- ¼ cup rice wine vinegar
- ¼ cup raspberry vinegar
- Salt and freshly ground black pepper to taste

- 2 boneless duck breasts
- Salt and freshly ground black pepper
- 1 large head radicchio, leaves separated, washed, and dried
- Hearts from 2 heads of romaine lettuce, washed and dried
- ¼ pound arugula, well washed and dried
- 2 ounces goat cheese, cut into tiny pieces
- ½ pint raspberries

*I*n a small mixing bowl, whip salad oil and egg together slowly until thick and pearl-white in color. Add the vinegars and whisk well. Season with salt and pepper. Set aside.

Clean grill thoroughly and spray with Pam. Heat to hot. Meanwhile, using a sharp knife, score duck breasts at half-inch intervals, partially through the fat. Rub with some salt and pepper. Cook on a hot grill, skin side down, for 4 minutes. Turn and grill 3 minutes on the other side. Or place under a hot broiler with rack about 3 inches below element. Broil skin side up 4 minutes, turn breasts and broil 3 minutes. Let breasts rest in a warm place.

Arrange radicchio leaves on each of four serving plates. Tear romaine hearts into a mixing bowl, then divide among the plates. Slice the duck breasts into ¼-inch strips and divide among the four plates. Scatter arugula over the strips, then pieces of goat cheese, and, finally, the raspberries.

Dress salad with vinaigrette and a few grindings of pepper.

Roasted Pork Loin with Persimmon-Bread Stuffing and Applejack and Port Wine Sauce

At Peter's, this roast would be accompanied by Veal Sweetbread Pancakes with Hazelnut Yogurt (see page 58). By the way, the persimmon bread freezes beautifully; just wrap it very well. It makes a fine addition to the Thanksgiving table. This stuffing would also be wonderful for quail or squab, or even a wild turkey. It is light and delicious. Persimmon pulp can be purchased from Dillmon Farms, 4955 West Street, Route 45, Bloomington, Indiana, 47401; (812) 825–5525.

Serves 4

PERSIMMON BREAD
- 3½ cups flour
- 1½ teaspoons salt
- 2 teaspoons baking soda
- 1 teaspoon ground mace
- 2 cups sugar
- 2 sticks unsalted butter, melted and cooled
- 4 large eggs
- ⅔ cup brandy
- 2 cups persimmon pulp
- 2 cups coarsely chopped pecans
- 1 cup sultanas (golden raisins)

STUFFING

½ pound pork loin, diced
½ loaf Persimmon Bread, diced
1 cup sultanas (golden raisins)
½ cup dried cranberries, or chopped
  fresh cranberries
2 ounces pork fat, finely diced
¼ cup walnut oil
1 cup finely shredded fresh red
  cabbage
3 scallions, cleaned and thinly sliced
2 large egg whites, beaten to soft peaks

SAUCE

2 cups port wine
¼ cup applejack brandy
2 tablespoons maple syrup
2 tablespoons molasses
2 teaspoons arrowroot

PORK ROAST

3 pounds boneless pork loin
Flour
Egg wash, made by mixing 1 egg
  with 1 tablespoon water

1 cup cornbread crumbs
1 stick butter

Fresh watercress and chives for
  garnish

To make bread: Preheat oven to 350°. Sift flour, salt, baking soda, mace, and sugar into a large mixing bowl. Make a well in the center and add the cooled melted butter, eggs, brandy, persimmon pulp, nuts, and raisins. Lightly mix until blended. Grease and flour two 9 × 4-inch loaf pans. Fill pans three-quarters full with batter and bake in preheated oven 1 hour, or until a cake tester inserted in center comes out clean. Let cool 15 minutes before removing from pans. Finish cooling on wire racks.

To make stuffing: Place the diced pork loin in food processor fitted with a steel blade and process until pork is a smooth paste. Dice half a loaf of persimmon bread and store the rest. Combine pork paste, diced persimmon bread, raisins, cranberries, and pork fat in a mixing bowl. Heat walnut oil in a non-stick skillet until hot. Add cabbage and scallions and sauté 1 to 2 minutes, being careful not to let burn. Cool and add to mixture in bowl, blending well. Fold in egg whites. Set aside.

Combine port, brandy, maple syrup, and molasses in a small saucepan and bring to a boil. Lower heat and simmer until liquid is reduced by one-third. Dissolve arrowroot in a bit of water and stir into sauce. Bring heat back up just near boiling and cook 2 minutes. Remove from heat and strain. Reheat just before serving.

Preheat oven to 375°. Cut pork loin lengthwise about halfway through the meat. Fold out and place between two double sheets of plastic wrap. With the flat edge of a meat cleaver, gently pound pork loin to ¼-inch thickness.

Spread sautéed persimmon stuffing on pork and roll it up as you would a jelly roll. Tie with kitchen cord. Dust pork with flour and roll in egg wash, then in cornbread crumbs.

Warm an ovenproof skillet over medium heat and add the butter. Brown the roast evenly on all sides. Then roast in the pre-heated oven 25 minutes. Remove from oven and let rest 10 to 15 minutes in a warm place.

Spoon some sauce on each of four heated serving plates. Slice roast and arrange over the sauce. Serve with more sauce on the side. Garnish with watercress and chives.

Veal Sweetbread Pancakes with Hazelnut Yogurt

Serves 4

BATTER
    1 lemon
    ¾ pound veal sweetbreads
    ¾ cup flour
    ½ teaspoon salt
    2 teaspoons sugar
    1 teaspoon baking powder
    1 large egg, beaten
    1 cup half-and-half
    2 tablespoons butter, melted
    1 teaspoon minced fresh thyme
    Vegetable oil

HAZELNUT YOGURT
    1 cup plain low-fat yogurt
    ½ cup hazelnuts, roasted, skinned, and
        chopped
    1 tablespoon champagne vinegar

    1 teaspoon hazelnut oil
    Salt and freshly ground black pepper
        to taste

    Fresh herbs, such as thyme,
        watercress, and chives, for garnish

*S*lice lemon in half. Fill a medium-sized bowl with cold water and 1 lemon half. Add sweetbreads and 1 teaspoon lemon juice from other lemon half. Soak sweetbreads at least 2 hours, changing water and adding another teaspoon of lemon juice at least once. This removes any traces of blood. Drain sweetbreads well, place in a saucepan, and cover with cold water. Bring to a boil, lower heat, and cook 8 to 10 minutes. Drain and cool in cold water. When cooled, remove tough filaments from sweetbreads and break into 1-inch pieces, removing and discarding sinews. Place sweetbreads in food processor fitted with a steel blade and process until smooth.

Sift next 4 ingredients into a large mixing bowl. Combine egg, half-and-half, and melted butter. Add to the dry ingredients. Whisk in sweetbread purée and thyme. Set aside.

Combine all the ingredients for the yogurt in a stainless-steel mixing bowl and mix until smooth. Chill.

Just before serving, heat a large cast-iron skillet with enough vegetable oil to cover the bottom. Pour about 2 tablespoons of batter for each pancake into the skillet, making about 4 at a time. Fry over medium heat until bottom is brown and bubbles begin to appear on the top. Carefully turn and fry on other side until browned. Keep warm until all pancakes are made. Serve with Hazelnut Yogurt and garnish with herbs.

Sweet Potato and Coconut Pie

CRUST

    1¼ cups flour
    ½ teaspoon salt
    1 teaspoon sugar
    ½ cup (1 stick) unsalted butter, cut into
        small pieces
    ¼ to ½ cup ice water

FILLING

    3 eggs, lightly beaten
    ⅓ cup sugar
    ½ cup shredded unsweetened coconut
    1 cup light cream
    ¼ cup cream of coconut
    ¼ teaspoon ground cinnamon
    1 teaspoon vanilla extract
    Pinch each of ground nutmeg,
        ground allspice, and salt
    4 medium sweet potatoes, baked,
        peeled, and mashed
    ¼ cup (½ stick) unsalted butter, melted

1 quart Vanilla Ice Cream (see page
    204)

Chill all crust ingredients thoroughly before beginning. Combine flour, salt, and sugar in mixing bowl. Using your fingers or a pastry blender, cut in butter until mixture resembles a coarse meal. Add water 1 tablespoon at a time, blending lightly with a fork or your fingers, until the mixture holds together. Dough should not be too wet or sticky. Shape into a ball, wrap with plastic, and let rest in refrigerator 1 hour.

Roll dough between two sheets of wax paper to 1/16-inch thickness. Remove one sheet of wax paper and place the dough, exposed side down, in a 9-inch pie plate. Remove top sheet of paper, trim dough, and flute the edges. Chill until ready to fill and bake.

Preheat oven to 400°. Combine first 7 filling ingredients in a large mixing bowl, add the spices, and whisk until combined. Add the mashed sweet potatoes and stir until thoroughly mixed. Add melted butter and mix well.

Pour into the prepared crust and bake in the preheated oven 45 to 55 minutes, or until a knife inserted into the filling comes out clean.

Let cool half an hour and serve with Vanilla Ice Cream.

The Carriage House

SOUTH BEND, INDIANA

We had never been there before, but as we drove through South Bend, we felt as though we had. There is something nostalgic about Notre Dame and the mystique of that famous university. We felt at home; we sensed its history. Perhaps it is fitting, then, that the best restaurant around is situated in a building that has a long historical tradition of its own. Evelyn George, mother of Peter George (see page 54), bought the property in 1975, and although previous tenants had referred to it as a carriage house, the truth is that it was never used for that purpose. Built in 1851 and located somewhat northwest of the original settlement of South Bend, just a mile south of the Michigan state line, it began as a Brethren church. In 1910 the building was no longer used for worship and became a community center, a place for family gatherings and celebrations. Today, as a splendid restaurant, it continues to be a place for family gatherings and celebrations.

Appetizers at The Carriage House are outstanding. We are fans of steak tartare from way back, but rarely enjoy it prepared in a restaurant. Here the high-quality tenderloin is scraped, using a dangerously sharp knife, into paper-thin slivers and garnished with capers, sweet onion, freshly grated horseradish, and a raw egg. When fresh oysters are available, they are not to be missed, either *au naturel* or gently sautéed with a superb curry sauce and accompanied by puréed cucumbers and a dollop of caviar. Presented on a large black dinner plate, it is really a dish to celebrate. From Brie baked in puff pastry to grape leaves filled with lamb, rice, and pine nuts, the selection is wide and the results are delicious. Soups change daily and are very well made. We especially applaud a hearty, flavorful cream of carrot and potato.

Salads are dressed with delicious high-quality olive oil; greens are varied and perfectly selected. We normally prefer our salad to follow the entree; the only exception to that is Caesar salad. While there are at least four salads available on the menu, we knew that the Caesar here would be outstanding, and it is! With just the right zip from smashed garlic, the romaine leaves are perfectly dried, allowing the dressing to coat properly. The salad sets a perfect stage for a delicious rack of lamb glazed with honey and soy, sprinkled with sesame seeds, and roasted to pink perfection. Another outstanding dish is the beef fillet grilled with caramelized onions and roasted potatoes with garlic. If veal is your preference, you will have many choices here. There is even osso bucco, those tasty veal shanks that are slowly braised with lots of vegetables and wine.

For fish lovers, The Carriage House offers an excellent selection. Crispy fried Great Lakes whitefish is presented in a horseradish and watercress sauce. Norwegian salmon is baked and served with a tarragon cream sauce. Every dish has delicious accompaniments; presentation is thoughtful and attractive; portions are substantial.

But it is important to save room for something from the dessert cart, because the pastries are wonderful. Reminding Fred of his dad's restaurant, the McFarland Lunch, where Myrtle Long made phenomenal pies, The Carriage House has fabulous banana cream, Boston cream, and lemon meringue pies; they are miles high, with flaky crusts, and filled with flavor. There might be a chocolate torte or two, bowls of berries, and delicious whipped cream, but the pies alone are worth the drive to South Bend, especially when accompanied by a glass of dessert wine from Evelyn George's terrific wine list.

We are certain that Mrs. George has not overlooked a single detail relating to fine dining. The two dining rooms are gorgeously decorated. Exposed beams and brick walls are accented by richly colored fabrics, fine paintings, and antiques. Rose carpeting, dark-green wallpaper, and red balloon shades create an airy atmosphere of Old World elegance in the main dining room. Heavy linen and beautiful china and wineglasses complete the setting. Shortly after guests are seated, they are offered some delicious liver pâté and crackers. When wine is ordered with a meal, Mrs. George herself will pour it into one of her large collection of old crystal decanters.

The menu at The Carriage House is fairly traditional in style. The large clientele from Notre Dame as well as the area's corporate community finds the cuisine comfortable, not challenging. But comfortable does not mean uninteresting; lightness and freshness are evident in every dish. Greens are impeccably fresh; sauces are delicate and light. Evelyn George's years of food-service experience prior to opening The Carriage House are felt both in the kitchen and in the dining room. Her servers are highly skilled and gracious; her kitchen staff is outstanding. While Mrs. George has chosen a calling that is physically demanding, she has clearly chosen one for which she has great talent. Visitors to The Carriage House are fortunate, indeed, that she is there.

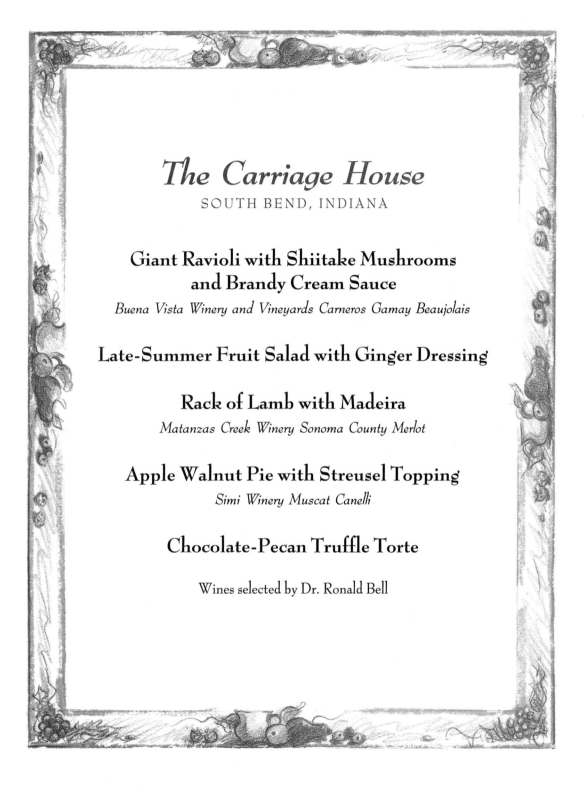

The Carriage House
SOUTH BEND, INDIANA

Giant Ravioli with Shiitake Mushrooms and Brandy Cream Sauce

Buena Vista Winery and Vineyards Carneros Gamay Beaujolais

Late-Summer Fruit Salad with Ginger Dressing

Rack of Lamb with Madeira

Matanzas Creek Winery Sonoma County Merlot

Apple Walnut Pie with Streusel Topping

Simi Winery Muscat Canelli

Chocolate-Pecan Truffle Torte

Wines selected by Dr. Ronald Bell

Giant Ravioli
with Shiitake Mushrooms and
Brandy Cream Sauce

Serves 6

    3 eggs, at room temperature
    2 cups flour
    ¼ pound butter
    2 finely minced shallots
    1 pound shiitake mushrooms, stems
        discarded, coarsely chopped
        Salt and freshly ground black pepper
        to taste
    2 teaspoons minced chives
        Egg wash, made by mixing 1 egg
        white with 1 tablespoon water
        Cornmeal
    ¼ cup brandy
    1½ cups heavy cream
    2 tablespoons unsalted butter
    2 tablespoons minced chives

    Chives for garnish

Mix eggs and flour in food processor just until a ball is formed. Wrap in plastic and let rest 1 hour on countertop.

Meanwhile, melt butter in a large skillet and sauté the shallots and mushrooms until tender. Season with salt, pepper, and chives. Set aside.

Follow instructions on page 274 to knead and roll dough in a pasta machine. Plan your ravioli to be about 5 × 4 inches and cut rolled dough sheets accordingly. Remove mushroom mixture from pan with a slotted spoon and place about 1 tablespoon on each of half of the pasta rectangles. Moisten pasta edges with a finger dipped into egg wash. Then cover with another pasta rectangle and pinch to seal. Carefully set ravioli an inch apart on a baking sheet that is dusted lightly with cornmeal. Cover and chill until time to cook. Reserve skillet and remaining juices from filling.

Return skillet to stove and heat over medium heat. When skillet is heated, deglaze by adding brandy and stirring well to loosen any particles from the pan. Be careful, because brandy will flame. Add the cream and simmer until liquid is reduced and thickened. Whisk in the butter. Add chives and keep warm.

To cook ravioli, bring lightly salted water to a boil in a large, deep skillet or shallow saucepan and lower ravioli carefully, a few at a time, into water. Do not crowd. Let simmer briskly for several minutes. The cooking time will depend on how long the uncooked ravioli have been in the refrigerator—about 4 minutes for drier pasta and 3 minutes for dough that is still fairly moist. Remove with a large Chinese strainer or slotted spoon. Then place 1 each in a heated soup plate. Spoon the brandy/cream mixture gently over the ravioli and garnish with some long chives.

Late-Summer Fruit Salad with Ginger Dressing

Serves 6

½ cup lime juice
2 tablespoons honey
1 teaspoon powdered ginger
½ pound mache, arugula, or watercress
6 romaine lettuce hearts, torn into
    bite-size pieces
6 plums, thinly sliced
3 peaches, thinly sliced
3 nectarines, thinly sliced
3 blood oranges, thinly sliced
    (optional)

Combine first 3 ingredients and whisk thoroughly. Set aside. Combine mache and torn romaine hearts, and distribute among six salad plates. Arrange fruits on top. Drizzle with dressing and serve.

Rack of Lamb with Madeira

Serves 6

1½ whole racks of lamb (about 3
    pounds, trimmed)
    Freshly ground black pepper to taste
3 teaspoons dry mustard
1 cup Madeira wine
⅓ cup unsalted butter
1 tablespoon fresh thyme
    Salt to taste

Fresh thyme and mint for ganish

Preheat oven to 450°. Make sure that lamb is well trimmed of extra fat along the lower part of the bones. Rub with dry mustard and pepper. Sear in a lightly buttered skillet over high heat. Place lamb fat side up on a rack that fits inside a large, shallow roasting pan and roast, uncovered, in the preheated oven 15 minutes. Let rest at least 10 minutes in a warm place.

While lamb is roasting, pour the Madeira into the skillet used for browning and cook over high heat, scraping well to loosen browned particles that have adhered to the pan. Then lower the heat and gradually whisk the butter into the skillet until mixture thickens well. Add salt, if desired. Stir in the thyme.

Slice lamb racks into chops. Spoon sauce among six heated dinner plates and lay chops attractively on sauce. Add herb garnish.

Apple Walnut Pie with Streusel Topping

This is a delicious dessert and is different from the standard apple pie. If your sweet tooth isn't very well developed, omit the final glaze.

Makes 1 10-inch pie

FILLING
6 cups tart Granny Smith apples,
    peeled, cored, and thinly sliced
6 tablespoons flour
1 cup sugar
    Juice of 1 whole lemon
1 teaspoon ground cinnamon
2 pinches nutmeg
½ cup raisins
½ cup walnut pieces
2 tablespoons unsalted butter, cut into
    small pieces

1 unbaked 10-inch pie shell, edges
fluted (see Sweet Potato and
Coconut Pie recipe, page 59)

TOPPING

1 cup brown sugar, firmly packed
½ cup flour
½ cup unsalted butter, melted
2 teaspoons ground cinnamon

GLAZE

¾ cup confectioner's sugar
1 teaspoon vanilla extract
3 tablespoons unsalted butter, melted

Preheat oven to 375°. Combine all filling ingredients except the butter in a large mixing
bowl. Pour into the prepared pie shell and
dot with butter. Bake in the preheated oven
40 minutes.

While pie is baking, combine all the topping ingredients in a mixing bowl and blend
well.

After pie has baked 40 minutes, distribute
streusel mixture evenly over top. Reduce heat
to 350° and bake 15 minutes more.

Meanwhile, combine ingredients for glaze
in a small mixing bowl. If not pourable
(should be the consistency of thick cream),
add a bit more melted butter. When pie is
just slightly warm, pour glaze over the top
and continue cooling until hard.

Chocolate-Pecan Truffle Torte

Makes 1 9-inch torte

CRUST

1½ cups sifted flour
¼ teaspoon salt
½ cup shortening
¼ cup unsalted butter
2–3 tablespoons ice water

GANACHE

8 ounces semi-sweet chocolate, melted
and cooled
2 tablespoons unsalted butter, room
temperature
1 cup heavy cream

FRENCH CREAM

1½ cups heavy cream
1 cup water
½ cup cornstarch
½ cup sugar
8 egg yolks
1 teaspoon white vanilla flavoring

TOPPING

4 tablespoons unsalted butter
6 tablespoons granulated sugar
6 tablespoons light brown sugar, firmly
packed
½ cup heavy cream

1 teaspoon vanilla extract
1½ cups coarsely chopped pecans

Whole pecans for garnish

*T*o prepare crust, place flour, salt, shortening, and butter in a large bowl. Using a pastry cutter, blend with short strokes until mixture is texture of cornmeal. Sprinkle with ice water and gather together into a ball with a large-tined fork. Wrap in plastic wrap and let rest in refrigerator 1 hour before rolling.

Thoroughly dust rolling surface with flour. Carefully roll pastry into an 11-inch circle, trim, and place in a tart pan with a removable bottom. Gently ease pastry into place. There should be enough pastry to go well above the sides of pan; fold that over to give more strength to the sides of the tart, but make sure you have an upstanding rim slightly above the top all around. Crimp the sides decoratively and refrigerate shell for 1 hour.

Preheat oven to 425°. Prick sides and bottom of pie shell. Place parchment paper in shell and fill with pie weights or dried beans. Bake in upper third of oven for 8 minutes. Remove weights and carefully prick bottom of shell in about 6 places. Return to oven and bake until brown, about 8 more minutes.

Remove shell from oven and cool on a rack.

To make ganache, blend chocolate and butter until smooth. Whisk in cream and mix until blended. Evenly spread ganache in bottom of cooled shell.

To make French cream, place cream in a small saucepan. Set it on the stove within easy reach. Mix water with cornstarch in the top of a double boiler and cook until warm to the touch. Whisk in sugar. Then add egg yolks and beat over medium heat until very thick. While whisking yolk mixture, heat cream, then add to yolk mixture. Continue cooking until mixture is very thick. Remove from heat and cool. Add white vanilla and blend. When it is thoroughly cool, spread mixture over ganache in tart shell. Chill.

To make pecan topping, melt butter in heavy saucepan over low heat. Add both sugars and cook about 5 minutes over medium heat, stirring occasionally. When sugars are melted, add cream and continue to cook for 2 minutes. Remove from heat and add vanilla and chopped pecans. Blend well. Spoon topping over French cream. Decorate with walnut halves. Serve at room temperature.

Tapawingo

ELLSWORTH, MICHIGAN

Almost heaven, northern Michigan! It's not hard to understand why Harlan "Pete" Peterson left a successful career as an automotive designer to cook fabulous food in the sparsely populated Michigan woods. We, too, now feel drawn to a part of our country that is truly heaven-blessed by a nearly pristine shore along Lake Michigan, woods dotted with aspen and birch and filled with morels and berries, rich farmlands, and natural lakes running with trout and salmon. It is an area that has been treated kindly by planners and developers as well as by travelers. And this is a part of the United States that has nurtured one of this country's most talented chefs, Pete Peterson.

Tapawingo may epitomize all that is good about Midwestern cuisine. The ingredients are mostly regional; the dishes often have roots in farm food from the past. The preparation is in the hands of someone well trained in traditional French techniques; the generous portions are presented with an eye for design—which is never too extreme—and the flavors are hearty. During the season Tapawingo is packed every day; in fact, about a thousand people may dine there each week. This makes for a frenetic pace, especially when the chef has constant problems obtaining most food products. After all, there is not a food market down the road. Fortunately, however, Pete is well supplied by area farmers and foragers whose daily visits keep the kitchen stocked with the land's bounty. Although winter brings new challenges, even then he can choose from delicious elk, venison, or pheasant to keep diners happy.

Meals always begin with a taste teaser from the chef. Our favorite is a Lake Michigan whitefish mousseline rosette in a tiny cup of tissue-thin pastry. Bigos, a Polish hunter's stew, is a lusty appetizer, with chunks of venison, lamb, veal, and sausage that have been slowly simmered in a rich red wine sauce, garnished with cabbage, paper-thin slices of apple, morels, and geranium petals, and served in a copper ramekin. Minnesota wild-rice soup is a creamy-rich chicken stock given a tender smokiness by local hickory-smoked bacon. Terrines and pâtés are silky and moist. A game terrine of duck, quail, and pheasant, with a hint of juniper, is studded with pistachios and wrapped in thin slices of bacon, then dusted with a fine mincing of red pepper, napped by a tart currant sauce, and garnished with pineapple mint flowers and sprigs of rosemary. In addition, Pete has become famous for his delicate savory cheesecakes. We are especially fond of one made with Montrachet goat cheese and rosemary garnished with a succulent sun-dried-tomato relish. And we can think of no better way to celebrate springtime than to enjoy the creamy northern Michigan cassoulet of asparagus, morels, and fiddleheads, with its hint of Madeira, basil, and thyme. A simple house salad consists of Boston lettuce, romaine, peppery nasturtium blossoms, a julienne of green apple sprinkled with pomegranate seeds, and a dressing of creamy vinaigrette. The special autumn salad is a colorful combination of purple cabbage and Belgian endive, bits of Illinois blue-veined goat cheese, and julienned fennel dressed with a creamy vinaigrette of the same chèvre.

One of the most exciting entrees we have ever enjoyed is to be found at Tapawingo. It is a symphony of morels and a signature dish for the restaurant. Dried morel powder is worked into a tender fettuccine, while other morels become the base of a richly fragrant cream sauce that clings to the pasta and flavors the delicately sautéed scallops of veal; whole morels are liberally strewn about the plate. Chunky vegetables, cooked lightly, complete the dish. Exquisite rack of local lamb, grilled just to pinkness and perfumed by a liberal sprinkling of herbs, is another of our favorites. Venison and wild game birds are often available, and fish are superlative. We are not sure which lake produces the best whitefish, Michigan or Superior, but we *are* sure that it's fun to compare. Ducks are outstanding at Ta-

pawingo; what could be better than grilled duck breast with a wild-rice burrito and onion confit—unless it is pork loin medallions marinated with mustard, grilled to perfect doneness, and garnished with Pete's own black-cherry chutney? This latter is spiked by whole peppercorns and then assembled with a gratin of potatoes, turnips, and Montrachet chèvre. Each plate is carefully orchestrated to present contrasts of color, texture, flavor, and fragrance. Edible flower petals and herbs are often used for punctuation.

We were once fortunate enough to spend an afternoon tasting as the chef tested new dessert recipes. They run the gamut from a highly sophisticated bittersweet truffle torte, baked with Michigan tart cherries, to warm gingerbread with pear sauce. A frozen white chocolate mousse made with chunks of white chocolate, Grand Marnier, pistachios, and raspberry sauce is the ultimate decadence. Chocolate bread pudding made with fresh brioche is ethereal; pecan lace with raspberry cream is one of those dishes that inspire the poet in us all. Not essential, but a welcome addition, is a glass of dessert wine selected from among many outstanding bottles available on the restaurant's excellent wine list.

With a magnificent vista opening onto a small lake, Tapawingo was built in the 1920s as a beautiful summer home. The house continues to have great charm, since the remodeling has been done with a very light hand. One sees the artistic training and impeccable taste of the owner-chef in every detail. Dinner plates have a wild trillium painted in the center; beautiful wine goblets and handsome silver complete the service. A paneled room off the entrance serves as a charming bar. The colors are soft and soothing; a stone fireplace dances with the reflections from the evening fire. In summer, the back wall of glass opens onto carefully planted gardens. Swans in the lake swim obligingly past.

In the early stages of our book research, it seemed that the name Pete Peterson came up whenever the discussion turned to talented young chefs. We were amazed by the respect given to this North Dakota native by his peers in such a competitive field. Once we met him, we understood. Pete had always enjoyed cooking, but when he spent a summer vacation in Paris studying at La Varenne, he knew he would change his career as an industrial designer for the Ford Motor Company. Ultimately risking it all, he left Ford, moved to the north, and began a seven-year association with the famous Rowe Inn in Ellsworth. Then, in 1984, he moved down the road and opened Tapawingo, retaining the Indian name that had been given to the house when it was first built. The seasonality of the business is both a blessing and a curse. Since the area is primarily a summer resort (although cross-country skiers are growing in numbers), he is certain of a huge crowd three or four months a year, but business is unreliable during the other months. Thus Pete has time to travel and develop new recipes, although he must be flexible and creative about sporadic availability of ingredients. Pete is the perfect person for this dynamic way of life. He thrives on the contrasts. The travel revitalizes him; the quiet time lets him concentrate on his work. He is a kind and patient man who has inspired exceptional loyalty both from his staff and from his patrons. We'll always return to northern Michigan so that we can be renewed by the beauty and peace of the region, and nourished by one of the country's most talented chefs.

Tapawingo
ELLSWORTH, MICHIGAN

Cream of Spring Greens Soup
Merlion Winery Coeur de Melon

Cassoulet of Morels, Fiddleheads, and Asparagus
Buena Vista Winery and Vineyards Pinot Noir Reserve

Tart Red-Cherry Granita

Grilled Ducklings with Wild-Rice Burrito and Onion Confit
Flora Springs Wine Co. Cabernet Sauvignon

Lingonberry Citrus Sauce

Pecan Lace with Raspberry Cream
Eberle Winery Muscat Canelli

Rhubarb Cobbler

Wines selected by Sandra Jordan Earl

Cream of Spring Greens Soup

This soup is also delicious served hot; just substitute chopped parsley for the chervil.

Serves 8 to 10

> 1 quart Chicken Stock (see page 276)
> 4 medium potatoes, peeled and coarsely cut
> 1 pound fresh asparagus, cut in 1-inch pieces, tips reserved
> 2 cups fresh spinach leaves, stems removed
> 2 cups fresh sorrel leaves, stems and tough ribs removed
> 2 cups watercress leaves
> 2 cups heavy cream
> Salt and freshly ground black pepper to taste
> Freshly grated nutmeg to taste
>
> Chervil sprigs for garnish

Combine Chicken Stock and potatoes in a heavy stainless-steel saucepan and bring to a boil. Reduce heat and cook about 5 minutes before adding the asparagus. Continue cooking until asparagus is just tender, about 4 minutes or longer, depending on thickness of asparagus. Then add spinach, sorrel, and watercress. Immediately remove from heat.

When completely cool, purée mixture in batches in a food processor or blender, then strain through a fine sieve. Chill.

Fill a small saucepan with water; add a pinch of salt and bring to a boil. Put the reserved tips in the boiling water 30 seconds, drain, and plunge into a bowl of ice water. When chilled, drain and reserve.

When puréed mixture is cold, add cream and seasonings. Thin further, if desired, with a bit more stock or cream.

Serve the soup in chilled bowls garnished with blanched asparagus tips and fresh chervil sprigs.

Cassoulet of Morels, Fiddleheads, and Asparagus

Serves 6

> 4 cups fresh or 2 ounces dried morels or other mushrooms
> 1 tablespoon unsalted butter
> 3 tablespoons chopped shallots
> 1 teaspoon minced garlic
> 1 cup heavy cream
> ⅓ cup Madeira wine
> Salt and freshly ground black pepper to taste
> 6 ounces (about 1½ cups) thin asparagus, cut in 1½-inch pieces
> 6 ounces (about 1½ cups) fresh fiddleheads, cleaned of brown leaves
> ½ cup fresh white bread crumbs
> ⅓ cup freshly grated Parmesan cheese
> ⅓ cup freshly grated Swiss cheese
> 1 teaspoon chopped fresh thyme leaves
> 1 tablespoon chopped fresh basil

Preheat oven to 375°. Remove the stems from the morels and reserve for another use. If using dried morels, soak in hot water 30 minutes. Melt the butter in a large skillet over medium heat. Add the morels and shallots; stir and sauté 8 minutes. Add the garlic and sauté 2 minutes more. Add cream, Madeira, salt, and pepper, and simmer over medium-low heat 5 minutes. Remove the mushrooms and continue to cook the liquid until it is thick enough to coat the back of a spoon. Then return mushrooms to the sauce. Set aside.

Blanch the asparagus and fiddleheads in boiling salted water 3 minutes. Drain and refresh with ice water; drain again. Divide among six well-buttered ovenproof 1-cup ramekins.

Combine bread crumbs, cheeses, and herbs; mix well and set aside.

Spoon equal amounts of the mushroom cream sauce over the asparagus and fiddleheads. Top with the crumb mixture. Bake in the preheated oven 10 minutes. Place under a hot broiler to brown the top. Serve immediately.

Tart Red-Cherry Granita

Pete makes this marvelous mid-meal palate cleanser when the northern Michigan cherries are in season in the summer. It's good even with the imported cherries that we see in Midwestern markets in the springtime. But don't use Bing cherries for this recipe; they are too sweet.

Makes 16 small sorbet servings or 8 dessert servings

>   1 cup dry white wine (Sauvignon
>   Blanc)
>   ½ cup sugar
>   4 cups tart cherries, pitted
>   3 tablespoons Kirsch
>   Juice of ½ lemon
>
>   Mint leaves for garnish

Combine wine and sugar in a medium-sized saucepan and cook over low heat just until the sugar is dissolved. Chill.

Finely chop the cherries by hand or in a food processor. Reserve the juice. Add cherries and juice to the chilled syrup. Then add Kirsch and lemon juice.

Freeze in an ice-cream machine according to manufacturer's directions, or place in a flat container in the freezer, stirring every half hour until firm. Serve a small scoop for each person in a pretty crystal goblet and garnish with mint leaves.

Grilled Ducklings with Wild-Rice Burrito and Onion Confit

Not only is this a delicious dish, it also happens to look terrific on the plate. We like to do as Pete does and accompany this with a stir-fry of carrot chunks cut on the diagonal, asparagus spears cut into 1-inch lengths, squares of red bell pepper, and snow-pea pods that are notched on the ends. Pete also uses some edible flowers for added color.

Serves 6

ONION CONFIT
>   3 tablespoons olive oil
>   1½ pounds (1½ large) onion, thinly
>   sliced
>   1½ teaspoons dried thyme
>   1 bay leaf
>   1½ cups Duck or Chicken Stock (see
>   pages 278 and 276)
>   Salt and freshly ground black pepper
>   to taste
>
>   3 4-to-5-pound ducklings
>   ¾ cup soy sauce, plus more for basting

The Best of the Midwest

¼ cup plus 2 tablespoons port wine

3 large garlic cloves, chopped

1 tablespoon plus 2 teaspoons grated
  orange zest

4 tablespoons sesame oil

BURRITOS

1 cup milk

1 large egg plus 1 large egg yolk

½ cup all-purpose flour

¼ cup whole-wheat flour

1 teaspoon salt

¼ teaspoon freshly ground black
  pepper

2 tablespoons unsalted butter, melted

1 cup cooked wild rice

½ teaspoon minced fresh winter thyme

¼ cup minced parsley

1 tablespoon unsalted clarified butter
  Lingonberry Citrus Sauce (see page
  76)

Fresh parsley, thyme, sage, or
  watercress for garnish

*F*irst, make the confit: In a large skillet, warm oil over moderate heat. Add the onions, thyme, and bay leaf, and cook, uncovered, stirring frequently, for 20 minutes, or until onions are golden and soft. Make certain that the heat is low enough to prevent burning or the onions will become bitter. Add the stock and continue to cook until the liquid is almost completely evaporated. Season to taste and reserve.

Next, prepare the ducks. Preheat oven to 325°. Bone the ducklings (see instructions on page 274), remove the breasts, and reserve wings and remaining carcasses.

Score breast halves by making parallel lengthwise slashes ½ inch apart through the skin and part of the fat. Combine the re-maining ingredients in a shallow dish, add the breasts, and marinate at least 2 hours.

Place the duck carcasses in a large roasting pan. Brush the leg portion of the ducks with a little soy sauce. Roast in a preheated oven 2½ hours, or until the leg bone turns and is tender. Remove from the oven and let cool; when cool enough to handle, remove the duck meat with skin attached and shred into bite-sized pieces. Set aside. Save the remainder of the carcasses for making stock.

Then make the burritos: In the bowl of a food processor or blender, combine the milk, egg, egg yolk, flours, salt, and pepper. Process until smooth. Pour into a mixing bowl and stir in the melted butter, ½ cup of the wild rice, thyme, and parsley. Let batter stand at least 30 minutes.

Brush a 4½–5½-inch crêpe pan with clarified butter and warm over medium heat. When sizzling, pour in about 3 tablespoons of the batter and immediately tilt the pan so that the entire bottom is covered, then quickly sprinkle with a scant tablespoon of the remaining rice. Cook the burrito for less than a minute; flip with a spatula and cook the other side till the batter is just set. Remove to a rack and repeat with remaining batter to make 5 more burritos. Save remaining batter (this will yield at least 12 burritos) and make more burritos for breakfast, along with some sausage or bacon. If you wish, the burritos can be made a few hours ahead, cooled on the rack, then placed on a cookie sheet and lightly covered with foil. Just before serving place the covered sheet in a warm oven about 5 minutes.

To assemble the dish, spray a clean grill with Pam and heat it to medium high (a large cast-iron skillet just brushed with vegetable oil may also be used). When hot, grill the breasts skin side down for 5 to 6 minutes, or until the skin is darkened and caramelized. Do not burn, as the fat will flame. Turn the breasts and cook on the other side about 2 minutes, or until just medium rare. Let rest 10 to 15 minutes in a warm place.

In a medium-sized sauté pan, combine the shredded duck meat, ¾ cup onion confit, and 1 cup Lingonberry Citrus Sauce. Bring the mixture just to a boil and season with salt and pepper if needed. Keep warm. While the duck breasts are resting, spoon ⅓ cup of the mixture just in from the edge of each burrito, distribute it evenly down the side, roll that side over the filling, and continue to roll the whole burrito. Carefully turn the burrito onto the outer seam and keep in a warm oven until time to serve, or place on well-heated dinner plates while you are slicing the breasts.

Slice each duck breast half against the grain, perpendicular to the scoring, at about ½-inch intervals. Each half will yield about 8 slices. Place a filled burrito on each of six warm serving plates and fan the slices of half a duck breast out along one side of each plate. Garnish with about 3 tablespoons onion confit and ¼ cup Lingonberry Citrus Sauce. If desired, garnish the plate with fresh thyme, sage, or watercress.

Lingonberry Citrus Sauce

Makes 1½ cups

> 4½ cups Duck, Chicken, or Veal Stock (see pages 278 and 276)
> ¾ cup fresh orange juice
> 3 tablespoons lemon juice, or more if desired
> ¾ cup port wine
> ¾ cup lingonberry preserves
> ¾ teaspoon grated orange zest

Salt and freshly ground black pepper to taste
2 teaspoons arrowroot dissolved in 2 tablespoons port (optional)

*I*n a heavy 1-quart saucepan, simmer the stock until liquid is reduced by half. Add the juices and port; reduce by another one-quarter. Add the lingonberry preserves and orange zest. Bring to a boil and season with salt and pepper. Add more lemon juice if desired. If sauce needs to be thickened, add the arrowroot mixture and simmer 5 minutes.

Pecan Lace with Raspberry Cream

Be sure to use very good quality non-stick pans for the cookies so that they will bake evenly.

Serves 8 to 10

> ½ cup light brown sugar, firmly packed
> ⅓ cup heavy cream
> 2 tablespoons butter
> ½ cup finely chopped pecans
> 1 tablespoon flour

FILLING

　　1 quart fresh red raspberries
　½ cup sugar
　　2 tablespoons lemon juice
　¾ cup heavy cream
　½ cup sour cream, or Crème Fraîche
　　　(see page 275)

Fresh mint for garnish

*P*reheat oven to 350°. Combine brown sugar, cream, and butter in a small saucepan. Heat slowly until mixture bubbles. Add pecans and flour. Stir mixture until it bubbles once more. Remove from heat. Drop 1 full tablespoon of the mixture toward the end of a lightly buttered non-stick baking sheet and another tablespoonful toward the other end.

Bake in the preheated oven 6 to 7 minutes, or until firm and golden brown. (It is possible to bake two sheets at a time.) Cookies will have spread out to about 6 inches in diameter and will have lacy holes. Remove from oven and let stand about 2 minutes. When they just begin to firm, quickly remove from cookie sheet with a spatula and lightly press into a dishlike shape within, or over, small bowls and allow to cool completely. Remove gently, as the lace "cups" are very fragile.

Purée 3 cups of the berries and the sugar in a food processor. Then strain to remove seeds. Add lemon juice and chill. Whip cream until firm, then fold in the sour cream, ¾ cup whole berries, and ¼ cup raspberry purée.

Distribute remaining raspberry purée among six dessert plates. Spoon the cream mixture into the six "cups" and position on the plates. Garnish with fresh berries and mint.

Rhubarb Cobbler

Both the baking time and the amount of sugar needed will vary, depending on whether the rhubarb is hothouse or garden, early season or late season. It is difficult to give a hard-and-fast rule, but usually the hothouse and early-season varieties will be more tender and less tart than the garden and later-season varieties.

Makes 8 servings

　　2 cups sugar
　　2 teaspoons grated lemon zest
　　2 cups flour
　　8 cups fresh red rhubarb, cut in ½-inch
　　　pieces
　　2 teaspoons baking powder
　½ teaspoon salt
　　8 tablespoons unsalted butter
　　1 large egg plus 1 large egg yolk,
　　　lightly beaten
　　2 tablespoons sugar

Vanilla Ice Cream (see page 204)

*P*reheat oven to 375°. Combine 1½ cups sugar, lemon zest, and ¼ cup flour. Add rhubarb and toss lightly. Distribute among eight well-buttered 1½-cup baking dishes.

Combine the remaining ½ cup sugar, 1¾ cups flour, baking powder, and salt. With your fingers or a fork, blend in the butter until the mixture looks like coarse cornmeal. Pour in the beaten eggs and mix just until mixture holds together. It will be coarse and lumpy. Distribute this dough over the rhubarb. Sprinkle each cobbler with additional sugar. Bake in the preheated oven about 35 minutes, or until top is nicely browned and crusty and rhubarb is bubbling. Serve warm with Vanilla Ice Cream.

Chez Raphael

NOVI, MICHIGAN

We think Chez Raphael can be counted among the best restaurants anywhere—not only in the Midwest. Beginning as a nouvelle French restaurant, Chez Raphael changed direction when Chef Edward Janos arrived in May 1988 to team with maître d' Achille Bianchi and business manager Kevin Aspinall. Chef Janos presents menus that are highly personal and daring. Trained in classic French technique, he has a brilliant understanding of how to handle food but does not try to recreate French food. It is a style of cuisine that defies a simple label. In his use of sauces from natural juices and stocks, and in his avoidance of many sauces rich in butter and cream, he is on the cutting edge of the changes in fine contemporary cuisine that are just beginning in France and the United States. The result is food that is lusty and sensual.

The range of appetizers immediately alerts diners to this chef's talents. A simple flan of warm potatoes and onions is lightly dressed with a black truffle vinaigrette. A memorable gratin is composed of the first morels of the season, stuffed with an airy filling of vegetables and herbs, dusted with grated cheese, and served with a port-wine sauce and three toast points on edge between them. Briny-fresh oysters wrapped in paper-thin beef carpaccio are served with a black pepper vinaigrette. A salad of chilled sweetbreads, lobster, fennel, and pea pods with a saffron dressing is luscious. A warm salad of monkfish liver, smoked sturgeon, eggs, salmon caviar, onions, and tomatoes with a balsamic vinaigrette is wonderfully intriguing. These are not safe, familiar dishes, but Janos's fans trust him and eagerly anticipate the challenge. Poached New York foie gras is enormously flavorful, satiny and tender. Served with caramelized plums, onion compote, and a sauce of reduced duck stock and finely minced ginger, the foie gras is topped with crisp slices of potato. Ravioli of smoked duck, mushrooms, and herbs are delicate and delicious in their game broth studded with vegetables and herbs. And we must applaud the sauté of Gulf white shrimp and scallops, accompanied by a delicate garlic custard, all served with a light white-wine sauce and garnished with a mince of tomatoes, basil, and pine nuts.

We would never pass on the soups at Chez

Raphael. A light purée of broccoli is garnished with chanterelles, red peppers, and leeks. A soup of tomato, basil, and lobster is given an extra dimension by fine Parmesan cheese. A purée of cauliflower is thinned with cream and garnished with tiny profiteroles filled with blue cheese. Lobster and Michigan white beans are an unlikely, but superlative, combination in a soup. The white beans are cooked in lobster stock, then puréed and served with a garnish of sweet lobster meat. Richly flavored pheasant consommé is garnished with tiny, tender, mushroom-filled dumplings. A heady lobster broth has as its garnish a barquette, or boat-shaped mound, of oysters encased in lobster mousse, all wrapped in spinach, then lovingly cooked so that the oysters and mousse, along with the accompanying dollop of caviar, just melt on the tongue.

Entrees are as remarkable as appetizers. The foods are complex, involving many colors and textures, and do not always lie flat on the plate. Timbales and tarts might be garnished with additional taste treasures layered on top. A grilled porgy is served with a flan of caramelized leeks baked in a delicate pastry shell, which is then piled high with chunks of sautéed lobster and finally surrounded with a very light chive sauce. Grilled swordfish is presented with a rich poultry broth, tiny cheese dumplings, and a mélange of grilled vegetables. For an added treat, there is a tart of layers of delicate baked phyllo pastry richly buttered and sprinkled with herbs: just before serving, sautéed scallops are carefully arranged on top of the phyllo, and the whole wonderful creation is placed on the swordfish as an extraordinary garnish. On the same menu is a luscious fillet of Norwegian salmon, seared just to doneness and served with a ragoût of baby squash, onions, and peppers, garnished with crunchy fried pasta and finished with a sauce of Maine soft-shell clams, white wine, garlic, and basil. Another night's fish dish is striped bass broiled inside scallop mousse, served with a warm sauce of pepper and herb vinaigrette, and garnished with puffy shrimp beignets, sweet corn, leeks, red pepper, and baby green beans. This plate is a veritable riot of color.

Equally colorful and flavorful is the plate of Coleman's Natural Beef tenderloin, seared, poached to pinkness, presented on a plate of tiny asparagus, baby yellow squash, roasted shallots, and julienned red peppers, and accompanied by small and delicate herbed spaetzle. Each beef slice is topped with a small sautéed morel stuffed with foie gras. The sauce is a reduction of stock and sherry liberally laced with fresh thyme. Sometimes diners are offered a combination plate of grilled veal flank steak, stuffed lamb loin, a veal sweetbread, and a lamb chop, all with a sauce of lemon, roasted garlic, shallots, and basil. Another combination plate includes roast prime rib of veal and lobster-stuffed veal medallions served with a sauce of sweetbreads and mushrooms. We were especially tempted by the plate featuring Michigan El-Bow Farm's fabled quail, stuffed with a nutty short-grained-rice dressing, roasted until crisp and moist, and accompanied by sliced rare breast of Barbary duck and a roasted mallard leg. Delicate squab-filled ravioli are tucked between the birds, along with a variety of roasted vegetables. A luscious sauce of reduced natural juices and red wine finishes the platter.

This is one of the few restaurants we visited that offers a cheese course. One look at the tray of treasures inspires you to save a little of the red dinner wine as an accompaniment. And for dessert, you can choose from a number of tarts and small cakes, which change daily. A frozen chocolate soufflé is exquisitely smooth and the chocolate-orange sauce adds another fillip of pleasure. A confection called Cashew Annie is a chocolate lover's delight, with its chocolate chiffon and chocolate ganache studded with cashews. Local summer fruits become the inspiration for flaky tarts and airy tortes, along with fruity ice creams and sorbets. Desserts are wonderfully presented on plates that frequently have intricate designs painted in chocolate, crème anglaise, and framboise. And, to gild the lily, a tray of tiny pastries and cookies comes along with the coffee.

Chez Raphael was originally housed in a motel next door. When the neighboring automobile showroom became available, the Wisne family bought it and in 1986 created a beautiful new setting for their restaurant. It is a big space, divided into three rooms. There are only eighty-eight seats at twenty-two tables, with plenty of room between them. The ceilings are high, with dark beams and pillars. One wall is wonderfully crafted of fieldstone, the other walls are painted a comfortable rose. An elegant piano complements the handsome bar. There is a huge fireplace and a superb French buffet and hutch. Everyone sits in an upholstered armchair. It is gracious and stylish, but not pretentious, with the look and feel of a Michelin three-star restaurant, complete with a formal "cocktail" garden that is open in summer. The staff is as competent as any we have seen. Achille Bianchi's wine list is also one of the best, and fairly priced.

While we might not find much food like this in France, any fine French chef would recognize and celebrate Edward Janos's remarkable talent and creativity. A Midwesterner by birth, and a graduate of the Culinary Institute of America, Janos has spent most of his professional years in Detroit, but travels frequently and participates often in international culinary competitions. How lucky the Wisnes are to have him—and how they should be applauded for bringing together a team of remarkable talent. The food lovers of Michigan are the true beneficiaries of this culinary enterprise.

Chez Raphael

NOVI, MICHIGAN

Steamed Lake Perch Fillets
in Ginger-Lemon Jus-Lié

Navarro Vineyards Gewürztraminer

Escargot-Stuffed Plum Tomatoes
in Poultry Broth

Edna Valley Vineyard Chardonnay

Poached Coleman's Natural Beef
over Baby Lettuces with Herb Vinaigrette

Laurel Glen Vineyards Cabernet

Mallard Duck with Beet Mousse,
Crisped Green Beans, and Roasted Pearl Onions

Lytton Springs Winery Zinfandel

Chèvre Terrine with Black Olive Quenelles

Poached Plums with Port Wine Cinnamon Sauce

Ginger Ice Cream

Rolled Sugar Cookies

J. W. Morris Wineries Port

Wines selected by Donald Patz

Steamed Lake Perch Fillets in Ginger-Lemon Jus-Lié

Serves 4

12 ounces lake perch fillets, skinned
1 medium Idaho potato
2 cups vegetable oil
1 teaspoon minced shallots
4 medium shiitake mushrooms, sliced, stems removed
1 tablespoon grated fresh ginger
¼ cup dry white wine
½ cup Fish Fumet (see page 275)
Juice and zest of 1 lemon
6 tablespoons unsalted butter
12 small whole pea pods, trimmed
2 tablespoons minced fresh chives

Preheat oven to 350°. Peel the potato and cut into julienne strips. Immediately drop strips into a bowl of ice water.

Heat oil in a medium sauté pan until it reaches 325–330°. Remove potato from water, drain, and pat dry. Fry potato in small batches in oil about 5 minutes, or until crisp. Drain on paper towels and keep warm.

Butter bottom of a shallow 8 × 11-inch baking pan. Sprinkle shallots, sliced shiitake mushrooms, and ginger on bottom. Lay perch fillets on top and pour white wine and Fish Fumet over fillets. Cover with buttered parchment paper or foil and bake in preheated oven until fish is just underdone (about 8 minutes).

Remove perch from cooking liquid, cover, and set aside in a warm place. Use a slotted spoon to transfer mushrooms, ginger, and shallots to another plate; cover and keep warm. Pour cooking liquid into a small saucepan and reduce to ¼ cup. Add lemon juice and zest and bring back to boil. Then remove pan from heat and whisk in 4 tablespoons of butter a bit at a time. Keep warm by placing the pan in a larger saucepan filled with hot water.

Quickly sauté pea pods in 2 tablespoons butter and arrange on four warmed dinner plates. Distribute mushrooms, shallots, and ginger onto the serving plates. Carefully arrange perch fillets on top.

Pour sauce over perch, mound the potato on top, and sprinkle with chives.

Escargot-Stuffed Plum Tomatoes in Poultry Broth

Serves 4

60 canned California natural snails

COURT BOUILLON
1 teaspoon salt
2 cups white wine
2 cups water
1 bay leaf
10 sprigs thyme
1 medium carrot, scraped and chopped
1 medium celery stalk, chopped
1 medium onion, chopped
2 garlic cloves, chopped

Chez Raphael

2 cups Chicken Stock, well-strained
　　(see page 276)
3 plump plum tomatoes, peeled,
　　halved lengthwise, and seeded
4 garlic cloves, peeled
1 cup zucchini, julienned
1 cup yellow summer squash, julienned
3 tablespoons olive oil
2 teaspoons minced garlic
1 tablespoon minced shallots
1 cup fresh spinach, chopped
　　Salt and freshly ground black pepper
　　　to taste
1 cup chopped fresh basil

*D*rain snails, rinse well, drain again, and set aside.

Combine ingredients for court bouillon in saucepan, add snails, and simmer 3 hours, or until snails are tender. Drain snails and discard liquid.

Bring stock to a simmer, add prepared tomatoes, and blanch about 1 minute. Do not overcook tomatoes; they should remain firm. Remove tomatoes from stock and set aside in a warm place. Blanch garlic cloves and squash in hot stock. Remove and keep warm.

Heat olive oil in a sauté pan, add snails, minced garlic, and shallots, and cook over medium heat until garlic and shallots start to brown. Add chopped spinach and salt and pepper to taste. Remove from heat and distribute snail mixture among the 8 tomato halves.

Place 2 tomato halves into each of four warmed soup plates. Divide blanched garlic, zucchini, and summer squash among the plates, arranging around tomato halves.

Pour hot chicken stock around tomatoes, sprinkle with chopped fresh basil, and serve.

Poached Coleman's Natural Beef over Baby Lettuces with Herb Vinaigrette

While Coleman's Beef is ideal for this recipe, it is possible to substitute a high-quality, well-trimmed prime beef tenderloin.

Serves 4

MOUSSE

    4 ounces fresh foie gras
    2 ounces boneless and skinless chicken
        breast, minced
    1 large egg white
    ½ cup heavy cream
        Salt and freshly ground black pepper
        to taste
    8 large mushroom caps, stems reserved

HERB VINAIGRETTE

    2 ounces cold-pressed extra-virgin
        olive oil
  1 to 2 teaspoons red wine vinegar
    1 teaspoon Dijon mustard
    1 tablespoon each minced thyme,
        rosemary, sage, and chives
        Salt and freshly ground black pepper
        to taste

    9 ounces Coleman's Natural Beef
        tenderloin, carefully trimmed
        Salt and freshly ground black pepper
        to taste
  1 to 2 tablespoons olive oil
    ½ cup chopped onions
    ¼ cup scraped and chopped carrots
    1 cup Cabernet Sauvignon wine
    1 bay leaf
    4 cups Beef Stock (see page 276)

  3–4 cups assorted baby lettuces, such as
        arugula, mache, oak leaf, young
        curly endive, hearts of romaine, or
        Bibb, raddichio, or any
        combination thereof, washed and
        torn

*P*reheat oven to 350°. In chilled bowl of a food processor, purée the foie gras and chicken breast until smooth. Chill mixture in bowl a half hour, then add egg white and purée again. Chill for another half hour. Return to machine and slowly drizzle in cream while puréeing, then season with salt and pepper. Transfer mousse to a small mixing bowl and refrigerate until ready to use.

In another small mixing bowl, mix all ingredients for vinaigrette together and whisk well. Reserve at room temperature.

Rub beef with salt and pepper. In a saucepan or sauté pan just large enough to hold beef, heat olive oil until smoking and brown beef well on all sides. Remove beef, add onions, carrots, and reserved mushroom stems, and sauté until onions are lightly caramelized. Add wine, bay leaf, and stock.

Bring stock mixture up to 180°, add seared beef tenderloin, and gently poach tenderloin to an internal temperature of 130° (about 15 minutes).

While beef is poaching, stuff mushroom caps with chilled mousse and sear in hot olive oil until cap just begins to brown. Finish cooking in preheated oven about 10 minutes.

Remove beef from stock and let rest in a warm place. Strain stock, return to saucepan, and simmer briskly until stock is reduced to ¾ cup.

Toss lettuces with vinaigrette and divide among four dinner plates. Slice beef into 4 medallions and place over greens. Top with mushrooms and pour stock around the beef.

Mallard Duck with Beet Mousse, Crisped Green Beans, and Roasted Pearl Onions

Serves 4

BEET MOUSSE

    8 ounces beets, cooked, peeled, and
        puréed
    1 large egg
    2 large egg yolks
    ¼ cup heavy cream
        Splash of raspberry vinegar
        Salt and freshly ground black pepper
        to taste

    2 mallard ducks (about 2 pounds each)
    ¼ cup bacon fat
    1 cup chopped onions
    1 750-ml. bottle red Zinfandel
    1 bunch fresh thyme
    1 cup pearl onions, blanched and
        peeled
    32 baby green beans (about ½ pound),
        cleaned and blanched

        Fresh thyme and watercress for
        garnish

Combine all the ingredients for the beet mousse in a bowl and mix well. Pour into four buttered 2- to 3-ounce timbale molds or ramekins. Refrigerate until just before baking time.

Preheat the oven to 350°. Bone each duck and reserve boneless, skinless breasts (see page 274). Cut the leg and thigh sections away from the carcasses at the thigh joint. Leave leg and thigh sections in one piece and do not remove skin. Chop and reserve carcasses.

Heat bacon fat in heavy Dutch oven, add duck legs and thighs, and sear until golden. Remove legs and thighs, add chopped carcasses and onions, and sauté until onions are caramelized.

Pour out fat, but reserve. Add Zinfandel to pot and simmer briskly until liquid is reduced by half. Add duck legs and thighs and thyme. Cover and braise in the preheated oven 1¾ hours, or until tender.

At the same time that the duck goes into the oven, preheat another oven to 325° for the beet mousse. About 1¼ hours after ducks go into the oven, place the timbales in a baking pan that is large enough to hold them without touching each other. Carefully add hot water to the pan until timbales are half submerged. Bake them in this preheated oven 35 to 45 minutes until firm. If you have only one oven, reduce the baking time for the beet mousse to 25 to 30 minutes and put in same oven with duck. Let timbales rest a few minutes, but keep warm.

When duck legs and thighs are tender, remove from Dutch oven and keep warm. Strain sauce, return to Dutch oven, and simmer briskly over medium heat until sauce is reduced to 1 cup. Keep warm.

Just before sauce is finished, put reserved fat into a skillet just large enough to hold breasts. Sauté breasts until medium rare (about 4 minutes on one side and 3 on the other). Remove from skillet and allow to rest 4 minutes, then thinly slice against the grain.

While breasts are resting, reheat the same skillet used for sautéing duck breasts. Add the onions and green beans; sauté until onions are caramelized.

Shake the timbales to loosen the mousse, then invert over the tops of four heated serving plates. Distribute onions around the beet mousse. Place the green beans to one side and put braised leg and thigh over them. Fan the sliced breast around the lower part of the plate. Pour sauce over the legs and thighs and around the fanned breasts. Garnish with thyme and watercress.

Chèvre Terrine with Black Olive Quenelles

We think that this is a spectacular substitute for a cheese course.

Serves 4

2 tablespoons champagne vinegar
¾ teaspoon unflavored gelatin
1 10½-ounce log white Montrachet chèvre
1 tablespoon extra-virgin olive oil
Freshly ground black pepper to taste
½ teaspoon fresh rosemary
1 cup black salt-cured olives, pitted
1 teaspoon minced garlic
8 Belgian endive leaves
4 spinach leaves
1 tablespoon cold-pressed olive oil

Sprigs of fresh rosemary for garnish

*O*ne day before serving, heat champagne vinegar to 110° and dissolve gelatin in it. Purée chèvre in a food processor with the olive oil and the gelatin mixture. Season with pepper and rosemary. Pack into an oiled 1-cup terrine and cover. Chill overnight.

Also the day before, put the black olives in a food processor and pulse until olives are puréed. (This process results in a purée that will later hold its shape when formed into quenelles.) Spoon olive purée into a small container, cover tightly, and chill until needed.

Shortly before serving, scatter the minced garlic on a piece of aluminum foil and place 3 inches below the broiler. Toast the garlic until brown. Be careful not to burn. When the garlic is toasted, remove from broiler and keep warm.

Unmold the terrine by first dipping it into warm water and then inverting it over a plate or board. Slice terrine into ¼-inch-thick medallions.

Carefully wash and dry endive and spinach. Arrange 2 leaves of endive and 1 leaf of spinach on each of four salad plates. Then fan 4 slices of chèvre terrine over the greens. Sprinkle with toasted garlic and drizzle with olive oil. Scoop up one demitasse spoonful of olive purée and press it into a quenelle, or egg shape, by inverting a second demitasse spoon over it and molding with the spoon. Place the quenelle on the plate near the fanned terrine slices. Continue this process, garnishing each plate with 2 olive quenelles and a sprig of rosemary.

Poached Plums with Port Wine Cinnamon Sauce

Serves 4

¾ cup dry red wine
¾ cup port wine
1 cinnamon stick
1 cup wild-grape jelly
4 ripe plums, halved and pitted

Ginger Ice Cream (see below)
Rolled Sugar Cookies (see page 89)

Bring red wine and port to a simmer in a medium-sized saucepan. Add cinnamon stick and jelly. When jelly is dissolved, add plums. Simmer 1 minute and remove from heat. Cool plums in poaching liquid.

When plums are cool, remove from liquid, peel and discard the skin. Return saucepan to heat, bring to a boil, reduce heat, and simmer briskly until poaching mixture is reduced to 1 cup. Cool plums and wine sauce in refrigerator.

To serve, arrange 2 plum halves on each of four dessert plates. Top with Ginger Ice Cream. Spoon wine sauce around the plums, drizzle some sauce over the ice cream, and garnish the plate with Rolled Sugar Cookies.

Ginger Ice Cream

Makes 1 pint

½ cup milk
1½ cups heavy cream
½ cup sugar
2 large egg yolks, beaten
1 tablespoon grated fresh ginger

Scald milk, cream, and sugar in a heavy-bottomed saucepan. Slowly whisk hot mixture into beaten egg yolks, then slowly pour mixture back into the pan, whisking constantly. Cook over very low heat, stirring constantly, until mixture is thick enough to coat the back of a spoon.

Cool custard mixture by placing pan into a larger pan filled with ice water. Stir often. Then pour into an ice-cream maker and freeze according to manufacturer's directions.

Just before ice cream is fully frozen, add grated ginger and blend. Complete freezing, remove, and pack into covered container. Keep frozen until needed.

Rolled Sugar Cookies

Makes about 1½ dozen cookies

> 2 tablespoons unsalted butter, at room temperature
> 2 large egg whites, heated to lukewarm
> ⅓ cup sugar
> 1 drop vanilla extract
> ½ cup minus 1 tablespoon flour

Preheat oven to 425°. Place one shelf in the middle of the oven. In the bowl of an electric mixer, beat butter until fluffy, scraping sides of the bowl at least once during this process. Then beat in heated egg whites, scrape the bowl, and beat again. Then, still beating, add sugar and vanilla. Scrape the sides and beat in flour.

Prepare cookie sheets by greasing and lightly flouring them. (If you use good-quality non-stick cookie sheets, just grease lightly.) Drop 1 very full teaspoon of batter at a time about 5 inches apart on the prepared sheet. Because the cookies cool quickly after baking, do not make more than 6 cookies at a time. Press the batter into very thin 3-inch circles with spatula. Bake in preheated oven until the edges start to brown, about 6 minutes. Remove with a spatula and immediately roll circles tightly into baton shapes. Place on cake racks to cool.

Cousins Heritage Inn

DEXTER, MICHIGAN

We don't think that there is a food lover around who has not had a thought or two of opening a restaurant. But most of us lack the daring, and eventually reason prevails. Paul Cousins, for whom reason did not prevail, taught high-school biology in Dexter for twenty years. His real love, however, was always the kitchen, and he spent many of his leisure hours toiling at a hot oven, making pastries and breads first for his family and friends, and then for a part-time catering business he began. Finally, his passion got the better of him. He and his wife, Pat, bought a turn-of-the-century farmhouse on a main street in Dexter, about ten miles west of Ann Arbor, and began to remodel it into a restaurant, which opened in the spring of 1984. About a year after they first opened, former rock-and-roller Greg Upshur joined them as chef, and Cousins Heritage Inn quickly took shape. In an unpretentious farmhouse, the restaurant serves an array of regional products prepared in a way that would probably be unfathomable to the farmer who built the structure. But today people come from miles around to enjoy the Cousins' gra-

cious hospitality and Greg Upshur's creative cuisine.

Upshur lives some miles out of Dexter, in Stockbridge, or, as he says, "in the salad bowl of Michigan." While his preference is to use Michigan products in season, he also says that his passion for adventure stimulates him to try fine Indian basmati rice, fresh Oregon white truffles, miso from Japan, and ocean fish from the world over. His four appetizers each night vary according to the season and to his mood that day. A salmon terrine is a symphony in pink, with a generous studding of fresh lobster meat one night, crab on another, and punctuations of pistachios or capers, all rolled in a delicate salmon mousseline. Three luscious slices, decoratively placed on a plate, might be served with a light mustard sauce one night, horseradish the next. Generous garnishing with fresh herbs creates a plate that is fragrantly delicious as well as beautiful. Pâté de foie gras will be amply piqued by brandy and Oregon white truffles. Another evening's list might offer a feather-light strudel of wild mushrooms, or a sauté of fresh foie gras accompanied by a sauce of clementines. In morel season, these delicacies appear in a variety of dishes, from a sauté with sherry and cream to homemade fettuccine. House-smoked salmon is often available, as is a wonderful pâté of smoked pheasant, duck, and venison. And, from time to time, the kitchen offers boar with chanterelles, pea pods, and fettuccine, all tossed with a natural pheasant sauce. Cousins also serves at least one soup each night. Potato and Stilton soup is thick and rich, a jaunty scallion garnishing the surface. Thick mushroom-miso soup is filled with paper-thin slices of mushroom, wild rice, and a generous dusting of fresh herbs. Pheasant consommé with shrimp and scallop quenelles is delicious and delicate. A hearty cabbage and tomato soup takes us back to childhood. Wild mushrooms, each in their season, will also appear in the soups. We hope sometime to taste the purée of puffball mushrooms or nutty hen-of-the-woods variety.

There are four entrees each night, each accompanied by a creative potato, pasta, or rice and numerous vegetables to complement each dish. Roasted pheasant and whitetail deer make a special game platter when combined with sautéed slices of foie gras and an Armagnac sauce. A mélange of vegetables includes fresh green beans, braised cabbage, corn, and buttery new potatoes. Another night, the deer is served with its rosy pink slices ringing the plate, accompanied by corn, carrots, sautéed red cabbage, Brussels sprouts, toasty quinoa (a grain from the Andes), and cranberry timbale. A generous handful of fresh rosemary is scattered about and then a delicate sour-cream sauce is carefully spooned around. And to finish it off, a handful of sliced Oregon truffles is sautéed and scattered about the plate. A braised haunch of black bear is served with sour cream and hen-of-the-woods sauce. Michigan

quail often appear on the menu: boned and stuffed with herbs and liver pâté, they are sautéed until crisp and moist, served with a buttery swirl of fettuccine, braised cabbage, pencil-thin asparagus, and sauced with natural juices cooked with dried Michigan cherries. Yet all is not game on this menu. There is at least one fish dish each night. In the spring and summer, the fish come from the cold streams and lakes of the north. In winter, the fish are flown in. A thick swordfish steak is accompanied by a mussel sauce and surrounded with a variety of vegetables and basmati rice with lentils. Another night, poached salmon is presented with seafood bisque, surrounded by bay scallops and mussels, and garnished with pea pods and julienned carrots. Veal or beef is also available each night. And, along with the beautiful vegetable assortment, there is often a delicate potato and cheese gratin.

The desserts are Paul Cousins's personal domain. Diners are offered a tray of about six to choose from. An airy strawberry mousse in a pretty stemmed glass announces that spring has arrived. An inches-high Grand Marnier cheesecake cries out to be tasted. White chocolate mousse has a heavy cloak of fresh raspberries; a strawberry tart, packed with whole berries standing at attention, is a special picture with its sauce of fresh rhubarb. An airy frozen soufflé of Fra Angelico is garnished with raspberries and strawberries; pecan pie, with its flaky shell, has a yummy, gooey caramel top; and Fort Knox, a fudge and caramel tart sporting a huge ripe strawberry, is simply irresistible.

The farmhouse has three intimate dining rooms on the first floor and one upstairs. The walls are papered in shades of pink and beige; the windows have soft rose balloon shades. Antique prints hang on the walls. Bentwood armchairs with comfortably upholstered seats are complemented by the rose linen tablecloths. Other color comes from the beautiful china in a pattern of burgundy and white with gold rims. Most of the servers are college students from the area. They are warm and cheerful, handling the fine food with skill and charm. A small but competent wine list offers some interesting possibilities. Cousins is a thoughtfully and tastefully planned restaurant that is as comfortable as going home. And it welcomes faculty and students alike from nearby Ann Arbor, along with travelers from afar and appreciative locals.

Greg Upshur started working in restaurants at the age of fourteen. The work supported him as he studied art at the University of Michigan and then music. He was reasonably successful as a rock musician, but when he realized that he was not destined to be a star, he yielded to the call of the pots and pans. After working in some of the area's best known places, he joined Paul and Pat in Dexter. Every night after work he makes the nearly one-hour drive home to the rich farmlands that supply his kitchen for the long summer and autumn. In writing to us, he said, "Our local produce in season is unequaled— I don't use tomatoes or baby squash out of season. Have you ever had a Guatemalan baby squash? Yech." His art background is apparent in the richly textured, colorful presentations that he serves, and his passion for the land around him is reflected in earthy menus and a full-flavored, hearty cuisine. If this is heartland food, give us more!

Cousins Heritage Inn
DEXTER, MICHIGAN

Kapusta
Cabbage Tomato Soup

**Sautéed Walleye with
Lobster and Smoked-Trout Sauce
and Fiddlehead Ferns**
Jordan Vineyard & Winery Chardonnay

Roast Pheasant with Prune Sauce
Grgich-Hills Cellar Zinfandel

Roast Venison
Dunn Vineyards Cabernet

Michigan Blueberry Tart
Kalin Cellars Sauvignon Blanc

Wines selected by Dr. Leonard Calabrese

Kapusta
Cabbage Tomato Soup

This is an Upshur family recipe that was brought to the Michigan area when Greg's grandfather emigrated from Poland.

Serves 4

4 strips bacon, diced
2 onions, peeled, trimmed, cut in half lengthwise, and julienned
½ teaspoon flour
4 cups Chicken Stock (see page 276)
1 head cabbage, cored, julienned, blanched, and rinsed
1 bay leaf
1 potato, peeled and diced into ¼-inch cubes
3 tomatoes, peeled, seeded, and diced into ¼-inch cubes
1 heaping tablespoon sugar
1 tablespoon tarragon vinegar
Salt and freshly cracked black pepper to taste

6 sorrel leaves, finely julienned, for garnish

Using a large heavy-bottomed pot over medium heat, cook bacon, turning often. When almost browned, add onions. Cook until onions are nearly transparent. Toss with flour, add 2 cups stock, cabbage, and bay leaf. Simmer 1 hour.

While the soup is simmering, cook remaining stock and potato in another pot until tender, about 20 minutes. Strain stock into pot with cabbage and set potatoes aside. Continue to simmer the soup.

When cabbage is tender (perhaps after 1½

hours of cooking), add tomatoes, sugar, and vinegar. Add salt and pepper to taste.

To serve, distribute potatoes along one side of each of four heated soup plates. Pour soup into soup plate. Garnish with sorrel.

Sautéed Walleye with Lobster and Smoked-Trout Sauce and Fiddlehead Ferns

We love the sauce for this dish and have found that everything can be prepared early in the day up to the addition of arrowroot.

Serves 4

SAUCE
1 lobster, steamed, meat removed and cut into chunks, stomach sack discarded, shells crushed
¼ cup clarified butter
4 shallots, finely chopped
1 bay leaf
2 sprigs fresh thyme
1 teaspoon cracked black peppercorns
2 tablespoons brandy
2 cups Chicken Stock (see page 276)
½ teaspoon tomato paste
½ teaspoon arrowroot mixed with 2 tablespoons water
Salt to taste
2 ounces smoked trout
3 tablespoons heavy cream

½ cup flour
1 teaspoon paprika
2 teaspoons sesame seeds
2 8–12 ounce walleye fillets, skinned, pin bones removed, cut in half
½ cup milk
¼ cup olive oil

1 lemon, cut in half
1 dozen fiddlehead ferns, trimmed and
    blanched

4 sprigs fresh dill for garnish

In a medium-sized heavy-bottomed sauté pan, cook crushed lobster shells and butter over medium heat, stirring often, until shells start to brown. Add shallots, bay leaf, thyme, and peppercorns, and cook 5 minutes. Add brandy, ignite, and continue cooking, stirring until flame expires.

Add stock and tomato paste, and cook another 20 minutes. Strain through a fine sieve into another heavy pot, pushing a spoon against the shells to extract all of the liquid. Set pot on medium heat, bring to a simmer, and stir in arrowroot and salt. Put sauce into blender or food processor, add smoked trout, and purée until smooth. Strain, adjust salt if necessary, add cream, and put sauce in a saucepan inside a larger saucepan filled with warm water until serving time.

Combine flour, paprika, and sesame seeds; dredge walleye fillets in milk, then in flour mixture, to coat well. Place fish on cake rack.

Heat olive oil in large skillet over high heat 1 minute. Add fillets skinned side up. Brown, turn, reduce heat to medium, and sauté approximately 7 minutes, or until fillets are browned and firm to touch. Remove fillets and set on paper towels. Squeeze a bit of lemon juice over them.

Working quickly, wipe out skillet, pour a tiny bit of water into it, and quickly add fiddleheads; toss over high heat until warmed through.

Put lobster meat into hot sauce, stir gently, and ladle sauce over four warm serving plates. Set fillets in middle and distribute fiddleheads around them. Top fillet with sprig of dill.

Roast Pheasant with Prune Sauce

Chef Greg Upshur garnishes the pheasant with sautéed wild mushrooms, braised red cabbage, steamed spring asparagus, wild rice with pine nuts, sautéed julienned red and yellow peppers, and glazed shallots—all seasoned and well buttered. He might tuck some fresh thyme sprigs among the vegetables for added fragrance and color.

Serves 4

MARINADE 1
    1 teaspoon juniper berries
    1 bay leaf
    1 teaspoon dried thyme
    1 teaspoon whole black peppercorns
    1 teaspoon ground allspice

MARINADE 2
    1 medium onion, chopped
    1 stalk celery, chopped
    1 carrot, chopped
    4 strips bacon

    2 pheasants, about 2½ pounds each
    ½ teaspoon salt
    1 gallon cold water
    ½ cup white vinegar
    4 cups Chicken Stock (see page 276)
    ½ cup pitted prunes, chopped
    2 tablespoons water
        Salt and freshly ground black pepper
        to taste
    1 teaspoon dried thyme, rubbed to a
        powder
    ½ teaspoon ground allspice

1 to 2 tablespoons vegetable oil, or butter
    ½ tablespoon arrowroot

    Fresh thyme sprigs for garnish

*P*ound all ingredients for Marinade 1 together with a mortar and pestle. Rub mixture all over the pheasants, then put birds into plastic bag, seal well, and refrigerate for 4 days.

Remove birds from bag and place in a shallow dish. Combine onion, celery, and carrot from Marinade 2 and scatter around pheasants. Lay bacon strips over birds, cover dish and birds with another bag, and seal. Refrigerate for another 2 days.

Preheat oven to 275°. Scrape marinades from birds and reserve. Combine salt, water, and vinegar in a stockpot, add pheasants, and soak a few minutes. Remove, rinse, and pat dry. Remove wings, legs, and thighs in one piece, then remove backs. Also remove wishbone from breasts.

Put stock into a small pot with pheasant wings and backs. Bring to a boil, reduce heat, and simmer 1 hour.

Meanwhile, place reserved bacon in a large, heavy skillet over medium heat and cook until it begins to brown. Remove bacon and save. Add leg and thigh pieces to skillet and cook until golden brown on all sides. Transfer to an ovenproof casserole. Add reserved marinades to bacon fat in skillet and stir over medium heat until mixture caramelizes. Pour this over legs and thighs in casserole. Cover and roast in preheated oven 1 hour. Then turn pieces in casserole and cover with prunes. Continue to roast another 1½ hours, or until tender.

Remove pheasant from casserole, keep warm, and pour remaining contents into the pot with the stock. Cook over medium heat 20 minutes and strain into a clean heavy saucepan.

Raise oven temperature to 375°. Rub breasts with salt, pepper, thyme, allspice, and oil or butter. Cover any exposed flesh with the nearly cooked bacon strips used for the legs. Set on the bottom of a roasting pan skin side up and roast 20 minutes, or until breasts feel firm when squeezed between forefinger and thumb. Internal temperature will be between 130° and 140°. Remove from oven and let rest 10 minutes.

While breasts are resting, skim off fat from top of sauce and discard. Combine arrowroot and water and stir well; then pour into saucepan, heat, and stir. Simmer briskly over low heat 20 minutes.

Separate drumsticks from thighs and discard drumsticks. Carefully twist bone out of thighs and discard. Lightly salt and pepper braised thighs, and dress with some sauce. Keep warm.

Peel skin off breasts, slice against the grain off bone, and fan on heated serving plate, placing the thighs in center. Garnish generously with seasonal vegetables. Spoon remaining sauce over the plates and garnish with fresh thyme.

Roast Venison

No book on food in the Midwest would be complete without a recipe for venison. We have enjoyed it in many restaurants throughout our Midwestern travels, but no one does it better than Greg Upshur. This is Greg's favorite way to prepare red meat. It is not a precise recipe, so it is for the daring among us, but it is worth a try.

Boneless loin of venison, or boned,
    rolled, and tied leg, up to 7
    pounds

MARINADE
    1 tablespoon peppercorns
    1 tablespoon juniper berries
    1 tablespoon whole allspice
    1 teaspoon dried coriander
    1 tablespoon fresh thyme, or 2
        teaspoons dried
    3 bay leaves
    10 mushroom stems
    1 celery stalk
    1 medium onion
    1 carrot
    Chunk of parsley root
    Red wine vinegar

    Fat from honey-cured, apple roasted
        pork, if available
    Fat from roasted pheasant, if
        available
    Salt and freshly cracked black pepper
        to taste
    Clarified butter
    4 bacon strips
    Skin from roasted pheasant, if
        available

Dry-age venison 3 weeks prior to marinating, if you have access to a meat cooler. If meat is already dry-aged, trim away aged fat and any meat that needs trimming. If you do not have access to a cooler, just start with the marinade. Crush peppercorns, juniper berries, allspice, coriander, thyme, and bay leaves with a mortar and pestle. Chop vegetables coarsely, then combine with the crushed herbs and spices in a medium-sized mixing bowl. Add enough vinegar to moisten mixture.

Spread some of the marinade over the bottom of a glass dish that will hold the meat closely. Place meat on top and cover with remaining marinade. Cover with plastic and let stand in refrigerator at least 4 days, turning each day.

Preheat oven to 350°. Remove meat from marinade, brush off, and dry. Melt some of the pork fat and pheasant fat (substitute bacon fat if necessary) in a cast-iron skillet and sear roast on all sides. Rub meat well with salt and pepper. Baste with clarified butter. Cover with strips of bacon and pheasant skin. Place on a rack or directly in a roasting pan and roast just until firm—meat should be medium rare to medium (rare is 120°).

Do not overcook, because venison becomes very dry; too rare and it is very tough. Let rest a few minutes. Slice thinly. Serve with a favorite sauce, perhaps The Phoenix Cabernet-Elderberry Sauce, page 47).

Michigan Blueberry Tart

This is one of Paul Cousins's favorites, and even though fresh Michigan blueberries are not always available, those that have been properly frozen will work nearly as well, and will be almost as delicious.

Makes 1 10-inch tart

PASTRY SHELL
- ½ pound unsalted butter
- ⅔ cup minus 1 tablespoon sugar
- 1 large egg
- 2½ cups minus 2 tablespoons cake flour
- 1 large egg, beaten
- 1 tablespoon sugar

FILLING
- 1⅓ cups sugar
- 3½ pints blueberries
- ⅓ cup cornstarch
- 1 tablespoon unflavored gelatin
- ⅓ cup lemon juice
- ¼ pound unsalted butter, cut into quarters

  Whipped cream and sliced toasted almonds for garnish

To make crust, combine butter, sugar, and egg, and blend well in the bowl of an electric mixer. Scrape sides well and add flour. Quickly blend with your fingers. Gather together in a ball, wrap in plastic, and chill until firm (about 1 hour).

Preheat oven to 350°. Roll dough into a 13-inch circle on a floured board. Place in a 10-inch tart pan with a removable bottom (pan should be about 1½ inches deep) and trim edges. Prick bottom with fork, paint well with beaten egg, and sprinkle with sugar. Bake in preheated oven 20 minutes.

In a small saucepan, combine ½ cup water, sugar, and ½ pint blueberries. Bring to a boil. Remove from heat and let sit 3 to 4 minutes.

Combine ½ cup water, cornstarch, and gelatin, and stir well. Stir into hot mixture and bring back to a gentle boil. Remove saucepan from heat and add lemon juice and butter, stirring until butter has melted.

Put 3 pints blueberries in a large bowl and pour in contents of saucepan, stirring gently until well combined. Pour into prepared tart shell and let tart set for at least 3 hours in refrigerator. Garnish with whipped cream and almonds.

Yoshi's Café

CHICAGO, ILLINOIS

North Halstead is in an area of Chicago that has been enjoying nearly a decade of restoration and renovation. Block after block of old town houses have been remodeled, some continuing as residences while others turn into galleries, offices, restaurants, and stores. Yoshi and Nobuko Katsumura opened their 50-seat restaurant in this neighborhood in 1982. A delicate blend of East and West, it has stayed high on the list of Chicago's best from the very beginning and reservations are at a premium. Yoshi Katsumura is thoroughly grounded in French technique and has developed a style of cuisine that is a mélange of French, American, and Japanese. However, we had no doubt that his cuisine possesses a Midwestern element, too, once we saw some prepared plates passing by; the presentation may be Oriental, but the size of the portions is 100 percent Midwestern!

We happen to adore foie gras, and always try it when we find it available. Yoshi's is thickly sliced and then sautéed and served on a slice of toasted brioche that is garnished with sautéed orange and apple. The presentation is almost a Japanese painting, with tomato ro-settes and long strands of chives creating the illusion of lines and brushstrokes. Another delightful appetizer is lamb-and-eggplant Oriental-style ravioli. Three tissue-thin ravioli are served in a shallow soup plate with a finely minced pesto heavily charged with parsley. The ravioli melt in your mouth. The pesto flavor is long and lasting, with little bursts of flavor coming from the many herbs Yoshi uses. Soups change daily, but there is usually one with cream and one without. We think that the pheasant consommé with matsutake mushrooms and gingko nuts is inspirational, and especially applaud the satisfying woodsy aromas of the mushrooms and nuts.

One must have a special salad at Yoshi's; they are always delicious and beautiful. Being lovers of persimmons, we reveled in a beautifully composed plate that served them sliced, along with pieces of Japanese pear on radicchio and a creamy yogurt dressing. Served on a large glass plate, and garnished with a single pansy, the salad is a wonderful creation that challenges the eye as well as the taste buds. Another satisfying salad is artfully simple: long, plump stalks of fresh green asparagus are peeled and blanched, then served chilled and accompanied by a zippy, creamy lemon vinaigrette.

Such salads set the stage for a number of outstanding entrees. Boned breast of capon, stuffed with a mousse made from the capon legs and chives, roasted until crisp, and then sliced, is served surrounded by a red pepper coulis. Both beautiful and delicious, this dish is made even more appealing by a judicious garnish of green herbs. Lamb is outstanding any way Yoshi serves it, but a boned rack, cut into medallions that are wrapped with bacon, sautéed, then served on a bed of ratatouille and topped with little "hats" of gaufrette potatoes, is sublime. The richly flavored Madeira sauce is a wonderful counterpoint to the ratatouille. Finally, Yoshi prepares a light and tender steamed seafood sausage that is sliced and accompanied by chunks of fresh lobster, sea scallops, and oysters on a rich tomato and basil beurre blanc. This dish is a treat for the senses. And while all of Yoshi's sauces have great depth of flavor, it is in creamy sauces such as this that he really shines.

For dessert one might select a large plate of beautiful slices of fruit, sprinkled with pomegranate seeds and accompanied by a tissue-thin pastry cup of homemade ice cream. If there is green-tea ice cream, try it; perhaps nothing could be more refreshing after dinner than this mint-garnished dish. While Yoshi favors fruit desserts, his pastry is also superb. From a flourless chocolate cake with pistachio pastry cream to a charlotte filled with white and dark chocolate mousse, the range is outstanding. Finally, playing to the Midwestern love of cheesecake, he often offers a light-as-air candied ginger version that dissolves on the tongue, while its accompanying sauces tease you on to bite after bite.

This is a beautiful, peaceful restaurant.

From the pale pink paper on the walls to the delicate dogwood on the gray rim of the china, there are subtle Oriental references throughout. Each table is dressed with heavy linen and silver, and a French flat sauce spoon is served with each course to enable diners to really clean their plates. A black pin on each table holds a stem of tiny orchids. The small serving staff is quiet and efficient, happy to answer questions about the food or about the fine wine list. Despite its black-and-white-tile floor, the room does not reverberate with noise. The crowd is international and chic. Yoshi's is a place to be and to be seen.

A dynamic man with enormous energy, Yoshi bounces from the kitchen to the dining room with great ease. He'll stop at a table or two to greet friends and to make certain that things are under control in the dining room. His warm and smiling face assures everyone that the chef is definitely in charge. The Katsumuras work terribly hard to achieve their fine reputation, but the time has been spent well, despite the humorous statement from Yoshi that "we make everything here except for bread and money." He is reputed to be extremely picky about ingredients, but that is understandable. He now works with some suppliers in the region who plant his produce and supply him with just the right kind of chickens. Today he is also seeking the finest of fish from Japan, persuading other Chicago restaurants to join him in the purchases. One of his frustrations has been his failure to obtain live shrimp, which have far more flavor than those that have been frozen. We have no doubt that the next time we eat at Yoshi's Café there will be fresh shrimp on the menu. This is one chef who will not let simple geographical obstacles get in the way—which is just one of the reasons why dining in his restaurant is such a satisfying experience.

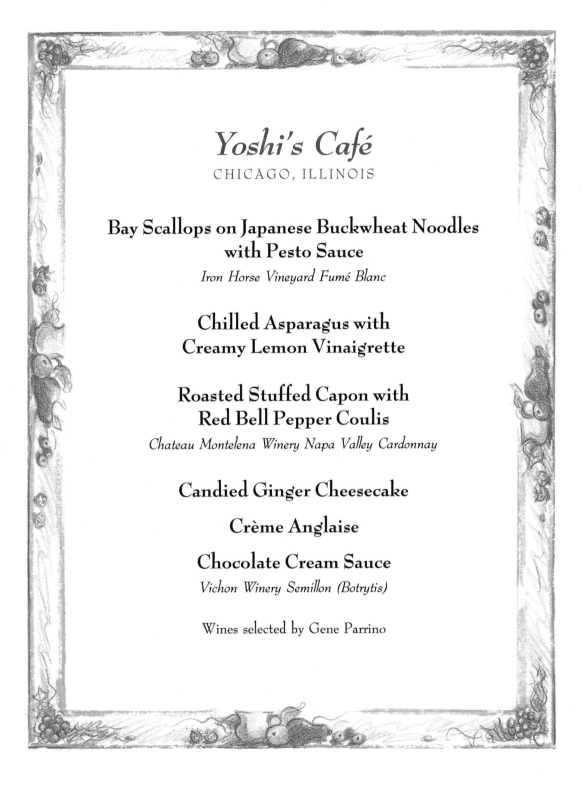

Yoshi's Café
CHICAGO, ILLINOIS

**Bay Scallops on Japanese Buckwheat Noodles
with Pesto Sauce**
Iron Horse Vineyard Fumé Blanc

**Chilled Asparagus with
Creamy Lemon Vinaigrette**

**Roasted Stuffed Capon with
Red Bell Pepper Coulis**
Chateau Montelena Winery Napa Valley Cardonnay

Candied Ginger Cheesecake

Crème Anglaise

Chocolate Cream Sauce
Vichon Winery Semillon (Botrytis)

Wines selected by Gene Parrino

Bay Scallops on
Japanese Buckwheat Noodles
with Pesto Sauce

This buckwheat-pasta recipe works like a charm. Just be sure to let the rolled-out pasta strips dry on towels at least five minutes before cutting. This will make more pasta than you need for four people, so save half, cook it the next day for dinner, and serve with some shiitake mushrooms and butter.

Serves 4

BUCKWHEAT NOODLES
    1 large egg
    14 ounces (2¾ cups plus 2 tablespoons)
        flour
    2 ounces (½ cup minus 2 tablespoons)
        buckwheat flour
    1 cup grated Japanese or Jersey red
        yam
    Pinch of salt

PESTO SAUCE
    2 cups fresh basil leaves
    1 teaspoon fresh tarragon leaves
    1 tablespoon minced garlic
    1 tablespoon pine nuts
    ½ cup olive oil

    ¼ cup olive oil
    ½ pound bay scallops, lightly floured,
        sprinkled with salt and pepper
    1 clove garlic, finely minced
    1 tablespoon grated Parmesan cheese
    Juice of ½ lemon
    1 tablespoon olive oil

    Fresh basil and tarragon leaves for
        garnish

*I*n a medium-sized mixing bowl, prepare the pasta by working the egg into the combined flours. Then add the yam and a pinch of salt. Add a tablespoon of water if the dough seems to be too stiff to knead. Knead on a lightly floured board 20 minutes, then wrap the dough in plastic and refrigerate 1 hour.

Follow instructions on page 274 to knead and roll dough in pasta machine. Cut to spaghettini width and let dry on pasta rack until needed.

Combine ingredients for Pesto Sauce in the bowl of a food processor. Process until smooth and set aside.

Fill a 4-quart saucepan with water and bring to a boil. While water is heating, heat a small skillet to very hot, then add olive oil. When oil is smoking slightly, add scallops and garlic, and sauté quickly, stirring constantly, about 30 seconds. Add 1 tablespoon pesto sauce, cheese, and lemon juice; then set aside. Cook pasta to al dente (about 2 minutes). Drain well and toss with 1 tablespoon olive oil.

On each of four warm plates, make a ring of pasta; mound scallops in center. Garnish with basil and tarragon leaves and serve with remaining pesto sauce on the side.

Chilled Asparagus with
Creamy Lemon Vinaigrette

Serves 4

    20 stalks medium asparagus
    5 large egg yolks
    1 tablespoon Dijon mustard
    1 teaspoon salt
    Pinch white pepper
    2 tablespoons white wine vinegar

2 tablespoons lemon juice
2 cups vegetable oil

*P*eel asparagus and tie into bunches of 5 each with kitchen twine. Cook in boiling salted water for 4 to 5 minutes, or until tender but crisp. Remove bunches from boiling water and immediately refresh by plunging them into a bowl of ice water. When chilled, remove from ice water and pat dry. Arrange on four chilled salad plates and refrigerate.

Whisk remaining ingredients except oil together. Continue whisking and gradually add salad oil until completely incorporated. If dressing is too thick, add a touch of lemon juice. Drizzle vinaigrette over chilled asparagus and serve immediately. Reserve extra vinaigrette in refrigerator, but let come to room temperature before using.

Roasted Stuffed Capon with Red Bell Pepper Coulis

Serves 4

1 7-pound capon, boned from the back, breast left whole, carcass reserved
1 large egg
2 tablespoons Cognac
2 tablespoons heavy cream
  Salt and freshly ground black pepper to taste
1 bunch chives, minced
1 tablespoon vegetable oil
1 carrot, scraped and coarsely diced
1 onion, coarsely diced
2 stalks celery, coarsely diced
2 cloves garlic, peeled

RED BELL PEPPER COULIS
1 quart Chicken Stock (see page 276)
5 large red bell peppers, seeded and cut into large dice
1 cup heavy cream
  Salt and cayenne pepper to taste

Chives for garnish

*R*emove leg meat from capon and put through meat grinder twice, until finely ground. (If you do not have a meat grinder, coarsely dice the meat with a sharp knife and then place meat in the bowl of a food processor and pulse several times.) Place ½ pound ground leg meat in food processor bowl along with egg. Blend until smooth. Add Cognac and heavy cream, and blend again. Add salt and pepper to taste. Put into another bowl, blend in chives, cover tightly, and refrigerate for 6 hours. Wrap whole, boned breast and refrigerate. Make stock from carcass and remaining leg meat.

Remove capon breast from refrigerator and open it, skin side down, on work surface, spreading the tenderloin portions evenly over the breast. Spread chilled mousse down center and fold sides back up. Tie with string at 1-inch intervals from top to bottom.

Preheat oven to 325°. In heavy skillet, sear capon in vegetable oil until nicely browned. Add carrot, onion, celery, and garlic. Roast in the preheated oven 45 minutes.

Meanwhile, bring stock and peppers to a boil in a large saucepan and simmer 20 to 30 minutes, until peppers are very soft. Purée mixture in a food processor or blender, then force purée through a sieve. Discard remaining skin and reserve red pepper purée.

In a medium-sized saucepan over medium heat, briskly simmer heavy cream until it is reduced to ¼ cup. Add strained stock and pepper purée. Season to taste with salt and cayenne.

Remove capon from oven and let rest in a warm place 15 minutes. Discard string, slice, and arrange decoratively on serving plates. Ring with red bell pepper coulis and garnish with chives.

Candied Ginger Cheesecake

This is a silky smooth, delicate dessert that you can actually begin to prepare a week ahead. Prepare the candied ginger and store in the refrigerator. Make the pâte sucrée and freeze. The Chocolate Cream Sauce can also be made a week ahead, and the Crème Anglaise will keep well for several days.

Serves 10 to 12

CANDIED GINGER
>   4 ounces fresh ginger, peeled and diced
>   2 cups water
>   1 cup sugar

PÂTE SUCRÉE
>   ½ cup sifted flour
>   1 tablespoon superfine sugar
>   3 tablespoons unsalted butter, cut into pieces
> 1 to 2 tablespoons ice water
>   Granulated sugar

FILLING
>   22 ounces cream cheese, softened
>   1 cup superfine sugar
>   1¾ cups heavy cream
>   4 ounces (½ cup) lemon juice
>   2 tablespoons unflavored gelatin, softened in cold water
>   Dash of orange liqueur

Grated rind of 1 lemon
Crème Anglaise (page 107)
Chocolate Cream Sauce (page 107)

Half pint raspberries for garnish

*I*n a small saucepan, blanch ginger in plain boiling water 25 minutes. Drain, rinse, and repeat. Then cover blanched ginger with 2 cups water and sugar, and cook over medium heat. Let sugar dissolve and cook the mixture over medium high heat until it begins to caramelize. When liquid is reduced by two-thirds, remove from heat and set aside to cool. Reserve ⅓ cup drained candied ginger for the cheesecake. Store remaining ginger and liquid in a tightly covered container in the refrigerator and serve on ice cream as a garnish.

Next, make the pâte sucrée: Combine flour and sugar in a mixing bowl, add the butter, and rub between your fingers until mixture resembles very coarse cornmeal. Slowly add the water, mixing lightly with your fingers. Using only one hand, gather the dough to mix evenly. Turn mixture out on a pastry board, and use the heel of your palm to rub a tablespoon at a time away from you to evenly distribute the butter. When all the dough has been blended, use a pastry scraper or spatula to gather it up, then press it into a ball. Wrap in plastic and chill for an hour.

Preheat oven to 400°. Lightly flour a small work surface; then, using a floured rolling pin, roll the pastry into a thin circle. Place the pastry on an ungreased cookie sheet and sprinkle with a scant tablespoon of sugar. Bake about 20 minutes, or until light brown. Cool and crumble. If you make this ahead, store the crumbs in an airtight container.

Into the bowl of a food processor, with the motor running, place a small bit of cream cheese and purée until smooth. Add the rest of the cream cheese bit by bit, scraping sides occasionally and processing with the motor running continuously until completely smooth. Add sugar and process until incorporated. Add heavy cream, scrape sides of bowl to remove lumps, and process until smooth.

Heat lemon juice in a small saucepan until very hot and add softened gelatin. Stir until gelatin is dissolved. Remove from heat and add orange liqueur. With food processor running, add lemon mixture to bowl and process until incorporated. Transfer to a mixing bowl, add lemon rind and ⅓ cup candied ginger. Set this bowl in a larger bowl filled with ice water and cool until quite thick. Transfer to a well-buttered 6-cup rectangular terrine (Yoshi lines his terrine with plastic wrap to facilitate unmolding), smooth top with a spatula, and sprinkle with pâte sucrée crumbs, pressing crumbs in to help them adhere. Refrigerate at least 4 hours (overnight is better). To unmold: Rap terrine on a hard surface, then run a sharp knife around the edges. Invert onto a serving platter.

Carefully spoon some of the Crème Anglaise on one side of each of four dessert plates and some of the Chocolate Cream Sauce on the other side. Place a cheesecake slice in the middle. Scatter a few raspberries over the top and let one fall into the sauce.

Crème Anglaise

Makes 4 cups

> 6 large egg yolks
> ½ pound (1 cup plus 2 tablespoons) sugar
> 2 ounces (½ cup minus 2 tablespoons) flour
> Dash vanilla extract
> 1 quart milk, scalded

*I*n a large mixing bowl, combine egg yolks, sugar, flour, and vanilla, and beat well. Slowly add the milk, whisking constantly.

Pour mixture into a heavy-bottomed saucepan and cook over low heat, stirring constantly, until mixture thickens and just begins to bubble. Cover with wax paper resting directly on the surface of the sauce and refrigerate at least 4 hours.

Chocolate Cream Sauce

Makes about 2 cups

> 6 ounces bittersweet chocolate, chopped
> ½ cup heavy cream
> ½ cup half-and-half
> ½ cup milk
> 1 tablespoon vegetable oil
> ½ teaspoon vanilla extract
> 1 tablespoon orange liqueur

*P*lace all the ingredients except the liqueur in the top half of a double boiler. Cook over simmering water until melted, stirring occasionally.

Remove from heat and strain mixture into a mixing bowl. Stir in liqueur. Set bowl in a larger bowl filled with ice water and stir often until cool. Cover tightly and refrigerate at least 4 hours.

Charlie Trotter's

CHICAGO, ILLINOIS

If Charlie Trotter is this good when he's under thirty, what will happen when he gets to be middle-aged? Charlie Trotter is surely one of the very finest talents on today's American food scene. He and his wife, Lisa, run a restaurant that is as good as it looks, and it happens to be smashingly beautiful. Not even the raves that sent us there really prepared us for the excitement that came with each new dish. Or, as Fred so often says, "The hits just keep on coming!" Charlie and Lisa Trotter are Midwestern by birth, coming from the Windy City itself. Charlie, trained both in the United States and in France, could have opened his restaurant anywhere, but he and Lisa have a genuine love for Chicago. They also believed that Chicago would be supportive of their plans and would respond well to Charlie's highly sophisticated style, a cuisine that is American/French with strong touches of the Orient. Their instincts were right. Since the restaurant opened in 1987, it has been filled to capacity each night, and the waiting list keeps getting longer.

Food just cannot get better than this. We sip a drink and nibble on the evening's *amuse-gueule,* a little palate teaser that might be a bit of foie gras, or some crabmeat with lobster, garnished with herb flowers, red and yellow pepper, and alfalfa sprouts. We try to select from perhaps six extraordinary appetizers. Delicate pasta squares are filled with small mussels, sauced with saffron cream, and drizzled with squid ink. A tender cannelloni is filled with a dice of quail and foie gras, water chestnuts, and woodears. The crisp legs of the quail serve as garnish, as does a single fried quail egg. Delicate puff pastry forms a melt-in-your mouth mille-feuille layered with wild mushrooms and potato with spinach-escargot butter. Shad roe with caramelized fennel is served with ginger sauce. Squab and eggplant terrine is garnished with a coarse beet vinaigrette and peppered pecans. And what could be more appealing than sautéed foie gras with sweet corn, rhubarb glaze, and ginger-scallion pancakes! The difficult problem of decision making is made even more complicated by the fact that the soups are equally outstanding. There are usually two each night. A creamy oyster soup garnished with small, tender oysters and a generous dollop of sevruga caviar is sublime. Rich duck stock is combined with wild mushrooms to create a luscious consommé garnished with herb croutons. Another menu might offer the lobster consommé with sweetbreads and tiny beggar's purses filled with wild mushrooms, or roasted-eggplant soup that is richly garnished with eggplant "croutons" and strips of smoked tenderloin of lamb. The variety seems to be limitless from this kitchen.

Between appetizers and entrees, there are always a number of salads available. Perhaps we might share some Belgian endive, Japanese pear, black walnuts, and chèvre en croute. Or we might select limestone lettuce, radicchio, pears, and Stilton with port vinaigrette. Before the entree we opt for a sorbet intermezzo. We may never again have anything more intensely flavored and fragrant than the sorbet of passion fruit and port wine. Served in an elegant long-stemmed goblet, it is a terrific way to set the stage for the next course!

One wonderful night, there were enough people in our party to enable us to try almost every entree—a food lover's dream come true. Rack of lamb with properly creamy and al dente Gorgonzola risotto is garnished with a sauce of olives and tomato; an entire head of roasted garlic is there to spread on superb bread. Fleshy turbot, firmly tender and tasty, is accompanied by a galette of slices of potato and artichoke, the creamy lobster sauce accented by a generous portion of beluga caviar. Rosy-pink slices of roasted buffalo loin are accompanied by sautéed foie gras; a ginger-cranberry reduction is the accompanying sauce, while brilliant green haricots verts and a twirl of peppery buckwheat pasta complete the plate. Partridge with sweetbreads and rabbit sausage ragoût, served with herbed and buttered spaetzle, are another delight. On the same menu are stuffed duck thigh, braised beans, white carrots, and truffled butter, or, should you prefer, steamed skate, aromatic vegetables, and smoked polenta. Then again, we cannot neglect a sliced saddle of lamb caressed by white truffle oil and garnished with richly truffled couscous and tiny tarts filled with vegetable purées.

It is impossible to do the desserts justice merely by describing them. Chocolate Satin on rose cream is a sight to behold: a shiny chocolate confection is surrounded by a pale pink rose sauce, with a delicate candy rose sitting on top and a fragrant real rose casually placed on the plate. Cascading Confection is a pastry cornucopia filled with crème fraîche, a wealth of berries, passion fruit, tiny cookies, some heavenly candies, and small scoops of ice cream and sorbet all tumbling over the plate. Zinfandel granita with orange and berries is still another amazing mélange of frozen ices, berries, and sauces. Baked chocolate mousse, with its banana surprise in the middle, is on a heavenly caramel cream sauce. Ginger pecan cheese strudel and hot pear compote with ice cream are some of the most extraordinary dishes ever to pass our lips.

The wine list is splendid. The restaurant offers about fifteen fine wines by the glass each night, making it possible to accompany the *menu dégustation* (a tasting menu of eight small courses) with a variety of interesting wines. Everyone there is remarkably knowledgeable about good food-and-wine combinations, something not found very often. Recently the Trotters persuaded wine expert Larry Stone to join their staff. He was the first American to win the prestigious annual International Best Sommelier in French Wines and Spirits award in France. His presence will allow Lisa Trotter to resume her doctoral work in comparative law, specializing in the international crazy quilt of wine laws.

Furthermore, the old brownstone on West Armitage boasts one of the most skillful renovations we have seen. One enters a reception area that soars up to the second-floor dining room, which, like its first-floor counterpart, seats about thirty-four people. A small bar to one side of the reception area is backed with wine bins that nearly reach the stratosphere. A gorgeous Brazilian cherrywood parquet floor in the reception area gives way to the stunning gray-and-burgundy carpet of the dining rooms. Inspired by the designs of early-twentieth-century Vienna, architects accented the covered walls with tables and fabrics designed by Josef Hoffmann, period sconces, and fine artwork. Halogen lights illuminate the tables, creating soft shadows.

Heavy silver and a vast array of elegant china complete this carefully planned setting. People have good reason to feel beautiful in this warm and soothing environment.

While the public areas are small, intimate, and soothing, the kitchen here is enormous, brightly lit, and frenetic. We were charmed by the long line of Trotter-created herbal oils and vinegars that perch atop the cupboards. The variety they represent is a flavorful summary of the rich range of tastes and fragrances to be found any evening in the dining room. Always experimenting and creating, Charlie Trotter draws inspiration from everything he does; there is no simple way to define his style, since it is an amalgam of all he reads and tastes. With the boundless energy that the Trotters bring to this project, we know that great things are still ahead.

Charlie Trotter's
CHICAGO, ILLINOIS

**Black Bass Tartare with Buckwheat Blini
and Asian Vegetables**

Flora Springs Wine Co. Chardonnay

**Chilled Tomato Soup with
Basil-Avocado Sorbet**

**Lasagne of Quail, Foie Gras,
and Wild Mushrooms**

Calera Wine Company Pinot Noir

**Chocolate Marquise with
Sauternes-Infused Sultanas**

Quady Essencia

Wines selected by Donald Patz

Black Bass Tartare with Buckwheat Blini and Asian Vegetables

Serves 4

BLINI
2 tablespoons active dry yeast
¾ cup water
¾ cup all-purpose flour
¾ cup buckwheat flour
2 tablespoons butter, melted
¾ cup milk
1 large egg yolk
2 large egg whites
Clarified butter

⅓ cup sesame oil
2 tablespoons peanut oil
1 tablespoon miso
1 tablespoon soy sauce
3 tablespoons rice wine vinegar
Freshly ground black pepper to taste
8 snow-pea pods, blanched and finely
    julienned
½ cup finely julienned Napa cabbage
½ yellow bell pepper, seeded and finely
    julienned
4 shiitake mushrooms, finely julienned
3 ounces enoki mushrooms
24 chives, cut into 2-inch pieces
¼ cup dried seaweed, reconstituted in
    water and drained
⅓ cup alfalfa sprouts, rinsed
8 ounces black sea bass fillets, skinned,
    boned, and finely chopped
1 garlic clove, finely chopped
2 teaspoons peeled and finely chopped
    fresh ginger
1 tablespoon finely chopped cilantro
1 tablespoon rice wine vinegar

1 tablespoon soy sauce
1 tablespoon Hoisin sauce

*T*o make blini: Dissolve yeast in water in a large mixing bowl and let stand 15 to 20 minutes in a warm place. Stir in all-purpose flour, cover bowl with plastic wrap, and let rise in a warm place 1 hour. In a small mixing bowl, combine buckwheat flour, butter, milk, and egg yolk, and add to yeast mixture. Blend well, then cover again, and let rise another hour in a warm place. In a medium-sized mixing bowl, beat egg whites until stiff peaks form. Fold into risen dough. Cover with plastic and set aside.

Just before making the blini, combine the oils, miso, soy sauce, vinegar, and pepper in a large mixing bowl and whisk well. Pat vegetables dry and toss with the vinaigrette in the bowl. Arrange the vegetables on four serving plates.

Then prepare the bass: Combine remaining ingredients in a mixing bowl and blend well. Divide into 4 servings and attractively mound on vegetables in the center of the plates.

Then make the blini: Brush a large skillet with clarified butter and heat. When hot, drop batter a scant tablespoon at a time into the skillet; make 1-inch blini; do not crowd. Reduce heat to medium and cook about 1 minute, or until brown. Turn blini gently and cook until brown. Turn out on a tea towel and keep warm; repeat until all the batter is used. Add butter to pan only if necessary. Makes about 24 blini.

Serve 6 blini on each plate. You can ring them flat around the rim of the plate or fan them out to one side of it.

Chilled Tomato Soup with Basil-Avocado Sorbet

Serves 4

SORBET

  1½ tablespoons sugar
   4 tablespoons water
   2 ripe avocados
    Juice of 1 lemon
  1½ tablespoons chopped fresh basil
    Salt and freshly ground white pepper
     to taste

  1½ tablespoons olive oil
   2 shallots, finely chopped
   6 cloves garlic, finely chopped
   2 pounds plump vine-ripened
    tomatoes, chopped
    Salt and ground white pepper to
    taste

   6 Niçoise olives, pitted and coarsely
    chopped, for garnish
   4 small basil leaves for garnish

Make a simple syrup by combining the sugar and water in a small saucepan. Boil until the sugar is dissolved. Set aside. Combine avocados, lemon juice, and simple syrup in the bowl of a food processor. Purée. Thin with a little water if too thick. Fold in basil and season with salt and pepper to taste. Freeze in an ice-cream maker according to manufacturer's directions.

Meanwhile, heat olive oil in a large, heavy saucepan; then add the shallots and garlic. Cover with wax paper directly touching the shallots and garlic and sweat over very low heat 5 minutes. Remove paper, add tomatoes, and simmer 15 minutes. Purée in food processor; then push through a strainer to re-move skin, seeds, etc. Transfer to a mixing bowl. Add salt and pepper to taste and chill thoroughly.

To serve, ladle equal portions into four soup plates. Top each with an egg-shaped scoop of sorbet (use two oval spoons to shape), scatter chopped olives across the top, and garnish with a basil leaf.

Lasagne of Quail, Foie Gras, and Wild Mushrooms

Serves 4

LASAGNE

   ½ cup puréed wild mushrooms (e.g.,
    shiitake)
   1 large egg
   1 teaspoon salt
  1½ cups flour
   ½ cup cornmeal

   2 tablespoons butter
   1 small onion, chopped
   1 carrot, scraped and chopped
   1 fennel bulb, chopped
   6 cloves garlic, minced
   1 tomato, chopped
   ½ cup aged sherry vinegar
   ½ cup Pinot Noir wine
  1½ quarts Duck Stock (see page 278)
    Salt and coarsely ground black
    pepper to taste
   3 tablespoons extra-virgin olive oil
   4 quail, boned (see page 274) and cut
    into bite-sized pieces
   ½ pound duck foie gras, cut into 8
    1-ounce slices
   4 ounces shiitake mushrooms, sliced
   4 ounces cremini mushrooms, sliced

4 ounces chanterelle mushrooms,
sliced

Fennel fronds for garnish

*I*n a small bowl, mix egg with mushroom purée. In another bowl, mix salt with flour. Then knead both mixtures together. Wrap with plastic and let rest 1 hour in a cool place. Then follow instructions on page 274 to roll dough in a pasta machine. Then, using a sharp knife, cut dough into 2 × 3-inch sheets (16 all together). Place lasagne strips on cookie sheets that are sprinkled with cornmeal, cover loosely, and set aside.

Melt butter in a 2-quart saucepan. Sauté onion, carrot, and fennel until lightly browned. Add garlic and tomato. Stir for a minute or two. Add vinegar, stir briskly to scrape loose browned particles from the bottom of the pan, and simmer briskly until liquid is reduced by half. Add Pinot Noir and stock, and simmer over medium heat until reduced to 1½ cups. Strain, season with salt and pepper, and keep warm.

Bring a large pot of water to a raging boil. Pour 1 tablespoon olive oil into 3 sauté pans (you may need an extra pair of hands for this final step) and heat over medium flame. Sauté quail in one, foie gras in another, and mushrooms in the third. Sauté quail 2 minutes per side. Foie gras will cook in less than 1 minute per side, and the mushrooms will take 4 to 5 minutes total. Keep warm while pasta cooks.

Plunge pasta into the boiling water and cook about 3 minutes, or until al dente. Drain well.

Arrange a single sheet of cooked pasta on each of four heated serving plates. Layer some quail, then another sheet of pasta, then a slice of foie gras, then a sheet of pasta, then more quail, then one more pasta, then a second slice of foie gras, and finally a last piece of pasta.

Distribute mushrooms around the lasagne and drizzle sauce over all. Garnish with fennel fronds.

Chocolate Marquise with Sauternes-Infused Sultanas

Serves 4 to 8

1½ cups sultanas (golden raisins)
¾ cup Sauternes wine
11 ounces bittersweet chocolate
  (preferably Valrhona)
6 ounces unsalted butter
5 large egg yolks
¾ cup confectioner's sugar
5 large egg whites

Edible flowers and petals (such as
  nasturtiums, miniature roses,
  pansies, and geraniums) for garnish

*C*ombine the sultanas and Sauternes in a small bowl and macerate 12 hours. Drain and reserve the sultanas.

Melt chocolate with butter in the top of a double boiler over barely simmering water. Remove from heat.

Whisk egg yolks and ½ cup sugar together thoroughly in a small bowl, then fold into melted chocolate mixture.

Beat egg whites with the remaining sugar until stiff and glossy. Fold into the chocolate mixture. Fold in the drained sultanas. Pour into a 6-cup terrine lined with plastic wrap, smooth top with a spatula, cover, and chill overnight.

To serve, invert terrine onto a serving platter and slice with a warm, wet knife. Garnish plates with some pretty edible flowers and petals.

Frontera Grill

CHICAGO, ILLINOIS

Eat your hearts out, Texans and Californians! The best Mexican food north of the border is a little farther north than it used to be. You have to go all the way to Chicago now. We realized just how sophisticated the Midwest had become when we learned of the popularity of Rick and Deann Bayless's new restaurant in a downtown Chicago storefront, not far from the Loop. For those of us who long for something other than standard and boring gringo-style dishes, this place is Mecca. From the lines of people waiting for tables and the raves we hear from all kinds of sources, including national food magazines, we know there is an appreciative audience in the Windy City, and we are delighted. We are only sorry that Rick, who had set up the kitchen for López y Gonzáles in Cleveland in 1981, didn't return to Cleveland when he set up the Frontera Grill. But at least we can all enjoy the Baylesses' highly acclaimed book *Authentic Mexican: Regional Cooking from the Heart of Mexico,* published in 1987. And for those lucky enough to be able to visit the restaurant itself, many of the wonderful dishes described within the book's covers can be sampled directly.

The Baylesses know how to do it right. The menu has something for both the timid first-time eater and the hot-food aficionados. The appetizer sampler gives a taste of many different things: crisply fried taquitos, filled with good-tasting chicken and a zesty seviche are among the treats. Guacamole is perfectly made here, not smoothed into a paste, but chunky and spicy, with lots of lime and cilantro. Small quesadillas are crisply fried on the outside, with tender masa cheese on the inside; each bite is a burst of rich flavor. We love chile chipotle, a smoke-dried chile that adds a marvelous smoky flavor to any dish, especially the Baylesses' salsa with chipotles. And what could be better than Chiapas-style tamales untados, with a delectable filling of pork, raisins, olives, and sweet mole, all steamed in banana leaves? Our passion for soup also includes those of the Mexican variety. These change weekly at the Frontera, but we are sure that we would never meet a soup there we wouldn't like. Tortilla soup is a rich chicken stock blended with fried tomatoes, onions, and garlic, ladled over toasted tortillas and Mexican cheese and enlivened with a spritz of lime and a sprinkling of dried chiles. There are soups with corn and soups with fish and shellfish. There are clear soups and thick soups. And then there is pozole. Pozole here is made with Mexican hominy— very large dried kernels of corn with the hull and germ removed. Chunks of pigs' feet and pork simmer for hours with the hominy, some garlic, and onion; then a variety of dried peppers—toasted, soaked, and puréed—are added to the mixture. Another variety is made with pumpkin seeds and tomatillos, small Mexican green tomatoes with husks. Pozole is for the serious eater, for cold winters, and for warming the soul.

The best tortillas we have ever eaten are also served here. We could make a meal on them alone. Rick Bayless's delicate white tortillas are made from superfine white masa (a fresh corn dough specially prepared for tortillas) and often served with meats grilled over the hardwood fire and garnished with peppers and black beans. We also like to try the extraordinary specials, which represent Mexican regional cuisine at its best. From marinated fish baked in banana leaves, to shredded marlin served in a creamy sauce of tomatillos and chiles, to heavenly snapper that is grilled and superbly sauced with chiles poblano and sour cream, one is offered a unique culinary tour of Mexico. On the poultry side, there is also great variety, although one of our old favorites is from Rick's Cleveland days—a game hen rubbed with a variety of spices, grilled, and served with a zesty sauce.

Since the Baylesses' book has a whole chapter on moles, those gorgeous rich sauces that are made from ground nuts, chiles, seeds, herbs, spices, and sometimes chocolate, there often are moles on the list of specials. Generally, but not always, served with fowl, properly made moles are, we believe, heaven's gift to food lovers. In fact, when created by Rick Bayless, they really do become manna from heaven. But then, whether it be grilled pork chops, pork tenderloin, skirt steaks, or roasted meat, whatever this wonderful kitchen offers is of enormous satisfaction to the taste buds. Even the garnishes are intriguing, ranging from charcoal-grilled green onions to fried plantains in sour cream.

All these meals need to complete them is a touch of sweet. The texture of satin, Rick's flans are kissed by delicate caramel and often flavored by exotic puréed fruit. While we confess to wanting nothing else when such flan is available, we would be remiss if we did not mention that the Baylesses make some of the best pies ever to cross our tongues. Not terribly Mexican, perhaps, but terribly Midwestern for sure. Delicate flaky crusts that might be filled with fruit one day, and heady and creamy chocolate cream the next, these are pies for dedicated pie lovers.

A visit to the Frontera Grill is always an experience. Lines form early and last late, but the delicious margaritas can do much to soothe the impatient, and besides, we feel a certain camaraderie standing with a crowd, waiting our turn. Deann Bayless is there to lend personal cheer to the hungry with words of encouragement. And we find that the funky atmosphere alone can make time pass quickly. Servers are enormously helpful and enthusiastic about the food. Once seated, you can be certain that the service will be unrushed but prompt. Baskets of delicious fresh tortilla chips and bowls of salsa help to stave off hunger pangs while you sip.

The Baylesses allowed their creativity to range freely in planning the Frontera. The large storefront space is casually divided into two dining areas. The pale gold and rust walls are decorated with both temporary art installations and a permanent collection of col-orful, often humorous, folk art, mostly originating south of the border. The colorful tiles and bustling employees in the bar and open kitchen area in the back complete the visual excitement. Rick and Deann have incorporated their passion for Mexico into a highly successful, very personal restaurant. Since their presence is so keenly felt, we know that it is a real challenge to work in new trips to Mexico for continued research. And so, their success with Frontera Grill speaks well, not only of their energy and creativity, but also of Chicagoans, who know a good thing when they see it and are willing to support it, especially when it offers something unfamiliar.

Frontera Grill

CHICAGO, ILLINOIS

Tlacoyos
Oval Masa Cakes with Fava Bean Filling
and Green Tomatillo Sauce

R. H. Phillips Vineyard Chenin Blanc

Pez Espada en Mole de Cacahuate
Swordfish Baked in Spicy Peanut Mole

Qupe Syrah

Flan de Coco
Fresh Coconut Flan

Hidden Cellars Late Harvest Riesling

Wines selected by Sandra Jordan Earl

Tlacoyos
Oval Masa Cakes with Fava Bean Filling and Green Tomatillo Sauce

Luckily, tortilla presses are inexpensive and now easily available in most gourmet shops, because mastering the art of hand-patting the tortillas is more than most of us will ever be able to accomplish.

Makes 12 tlacoyos, serving 6 as first course

- 1½ cups hulled fava beans (preferably the hulled yellow Mexican variety)
- 3 cups water
- Salt to taste
- 1 pound fresh masa, or 1¾ cups masa harina mixed with 1 cup plus 2 tablespoons water*
- 8 ounces (5 to 6) fresh tomatillos, husked and washed
- 1 to 3 hot green chiles, to taste
- ⅓ cup finely chopped onion
- 2 tablespoons finely chopped fresh cilantro
- ½ teaspoon salt
- 2 tablespoons lard or vegetable shortening
- ½ cup crumbled fresh Mexican queso fresco cheese, pressed farmer's cheese, or feta that has dried in the kitchen for 24 hours
- ¼ cup finely chopped onion
- 4 leaves romaine lettuce, shredded
- 8 to 10 radishes, thinly sliced

*Masa harina is not just cornmeal but a powdery meal that is made from fresh masa that has been force-dried and ground superfine. Along with fresh masa and all the other Mexican ingredients in this section, masa harina can be purchased in any Mexican or Puerto Rican market.

Combine beans and water in a small saucepan and bring to a boil. Simmer, uncovered, until beans are very tender and begin to fall apart, at least 3 hours. The liquid should be very nearly consumed at this point; if it is not, pour off excess. Mash beans with a fork and season with salt. The mixture should be the consistency of refried beans—a thick purée that will hold its shape when scooped with a spoon. Chill while you prepare the tlacoyos.

If using masa harina, mix with hot water in a large bowl, cover, and let stand ½ hour.

Meanwhile, boil tomatillos in salted water until tender, about 10 minutes. Cool and purée in blender or food processor with chiles. Stir in onion and cilantro. Season with ½ teaspoon salt and thin with enough water to achieve a medium-thick consistency. Then add the lard and ¼ teaspoon salt to the masa harina, kneading to combine the ingredients thoroughly. If necessary, add a little water to give the masa the consistency of soft cookie dough. If using fresh masa, mix with the lard and salt and knead as described above.

Divide dough into 12 equal portions; lay them on a small plate and cover with plastic. Using a tortilla press lined with plastic, flatten one of the portions of masa into a thick, 4-inch round; lift off the top piece of plastic. Spread 1 tablespoon cold mashed bean filling in a 1-inch strip down the center, leaving a ½-inch space at the top and bottom. Slip your two hands under the plastic beneath the tortilla, paralleling the strip of filling. Fold in the two sides of the tortilla to meet in the center, and roughly cover the filling. Now, working the two ends (with plastic between you and the dough), lift and mold the masa from both sides up over the filling to completely cover it at the ends, creating an oval cake. Peel the plastic open to expose the tlacoyo, lay another piece of plastic over it, and pat gently with your fingers to flatten the top. Unmold the tlacoyo from the plastic and set aside. Repeat with the remaining 11 portions.

As the tlacoyos are formed, lay them on a griddle over medium heat. Cook a total of 10 to 15 minutes, turning periodically to ensure even cooking. When they are done, the sides will have lost their soft, moist feel and the tops and bottoms will be nicely browned. Remove to a wire rack; when cool, cover lightly.

About 15 minutes before serving, heat the lard in a medium-sized skillet over medium heat. When oil is hot enough to make the edge of a tlacoyo really sizzle, begin frying them a few at a time for about 2 minutes per side, to heat them through and make them more tender. Drain on paper towels and keep warm in a low oven while finishing the rest.

Line a decorative serving platter with the tlacoyos. Spoon tomatillo sauce over top and sprinkle with crumbled cheese, chopped onion, shredded lettuce, and radish slices. Serve immediately.

Pez Espada
en Mole de Cacahuate
Swordfish Baked in Spicy Peanut Mole

Serves 6

2 dried chiles anchos, stemmed and seeded
2½ tablespoons lard or vegetable oil
½ small onion, peeled and sliced
2 cloves garlic, peeled
1 cup toasted peanuts, plus more for garnish
2 slices firm white bread
2 canned chiles chipotles en adobo, seeded

7½ ounces canned tomatoes, drained
4 whole allspice, ground (about ⅛ teaspoon)
½ cinnamon stick
3½ cups Fish Fumet (see page 275)
1 tablespoon cider vinegar
½ cup red wine
2 bay leaves
1 generous teaspoon salt
1 tablespoon sugar
6 swordfish steaks, totaling about 3 pounds

Toasted peanuts and flat-leaf parsley for garnish

*T*ear chiles anchos into flat pieces, then toast on an ungreased griddle or skillet over medium heat, pressing flat with a metal spatula until they blister and change color slightly. Then flip and press again. They should never give off more than the slightest whiff of smoke. Place toasted chiles in a medium bowl, add boiling water to cover, and weight with a plate to keep submerged. Let soak ½ hour. Drain.

Heat 1 tablespoon of lard in a medium skillet over medium heat. Add onion and whole garlic cloves, and fry until well browned, about 10 minutes. Scrape into blender or food processor. Add peanuts, bread, chiles chipotles, tomatoes, and chiles anchos. Pulverize allspice and cinnamon in a mortar and pestle. Add spices along with 1½ cups fumet. Blend to smooth purée, and strain through a medium-mesh sieve.

Warm remaining lard or oil in a large saucepan over medium-high heat. When hot enough to make a drop of purée sizzle sharply, add purée all at once. Stir for several minutes as mixture thickens and darkens. Add remaining stock, vinegar, wine, and bay

leaves. Cover partially and simmer over medium-low heat about 45 minutes. Season with
salt and sugar.

Preheat oven to 350°. Pour half the warm
sauce into a large baking dish. Place swordfish
in a single layer on top. Cover with remaining
sauce, then bake in preheated oven until fish
just flakes when firmly pressed with the back
of a fork, about 5 minutes for ½-inch steaks.
Garnish with peanuts and parsley.

Flan de Coco
Fresh Coconut Flan

Serves 8 to 10

⅔ cup sugar
¼ cup water
1 fresh coconut
1½ cups milk
2 cups half-and-half
1 cup sugar
8 large eggs
1 teaspoon dark rum
1 teaspoon vanilla extract

*P*ut sugar into a small, cold, heavy saucepan
or caramel pot. Dribble the water into the
pot—first around the side, then over the
sugar—and stir. Bring to a boil, wash down
the sides of the pan with a pastry brush dipped
in water, and simmer over medium heat, without stirring, until the syrup begins to color.
Swirl the pan continually over fire until syrup
is an even deep amber. Immediately pour caramel into a 2½-quart soufflé dish and, wearing

oven mitts, carefully swirl and tilt to distribute
caramel over bottom and sides. Set aside.

Using an ice pick, hammer into the three
black "eyes" on one end of the coconut and
drain coconut liquid through a fine-mesh
strainer into a 2-cup measure. Add milk to
bring measure to full 2 cups and pour into a
medium-sized saucepan. Add half-and-half
and sugar, stir, and set over medium-low heat.

Crack coconut with a hammer until it splits
lengthwise. Remove meat from shell and cut
into 1-inch pieces. (There is no need to peel
off the dark, thin skin.) Place pieces in a
blender or food processor, pour in hot milk
mixture, cover, and process until coconut is
finely chopped. Let stand 30 minutes.

Preheat oven to 350°. In a large bowl, beat
eggs with rum and vanilla, and whisk in coconut mixture. Strain through a fine-mesh
sieve, pressing on coconut to extract all the
liquid; then pour into caramelized mold. Set
mold in a deep baking pan, pour about 2
inches of very hot water around mold, cover
lightly with foil, and bake in preheated oven
until custard has just set (a knife inserted near
center will come out clean), about 40 to 50
minutes. Remove from oven and let cool in
the water bath.

Remove soufflé dish from water bath and
chill thoroughly in refrigerator. Shortly before serving, run a non-serrated knife between the flan and the dish, penetrating to
the bottom; then twist mold back and forth
to ensure that the custard is free. Invert a deep
serving plate over the top, turn upside down,
and listen for the flan to drop. Scrape out any
remaining caramel and spoon it over the flan.

The Everest Room

CHICAGO, ILLINOIS

This may be haute cuisine in more ways than one. Perched atop One Financial Plaza in Chicago, with a spectacular fortieth-floor view of the city, The Everest Room is one of the country's most stunning restaurant settings. To the good fortune of all who dine here, the food surpasses the view! Jean Joho, executive chef, came to Chicago from his native Alsace in 1984. While his style of cuisine reflects his superlative classical training, he is not a chauvinistic Frenchman. Rather, he has created a menu that responds to America's interest in lighter food, encourages the sophistication of his patrons, and reflects his own interest in exploring the wide range of American regional ingredients. And he offers food that stimulates all our senses.

Joho's talents are enormous. *Amuse-gueule* are a delicious touch at The Everest Room, and Joho changes them according to the daily market. A tiny pot of cauliflower mousse, garnished with a bit of tomato concasse, was feather-light. A crisply fried smelt melted on our tongues. A *menu dégustation* offers the enthusiastic diner a nine-course meal that reflects both the regular menu and specials of

the day. Appetizers range from delicate pasta filled with frog's legs to homemade smoked salmon served with Chinese beluga and garnished with a sauce of fresh horseradish, a dab of intensely flavored tomato coulis, and batons of brioche. Black squid carnerole risotto, made with calamari and fresh basil, warms the soul. There is a remarkable crispy packet of phyllo filled with shrimp and a julienne of leek and watercress that demonstrates, again, the range of Joho's creativity. Soups are outstanding and change daily. We were tempted by one of smoked herring with caviar, and also by a cold one of almond and garlic cream, garnished with delicate balls of summer melon and salmon roe. A cream of wild mushroom soup the texture of satin, garnished with paper-thin slices of white truffle and chanterelles, is a truly inspired mélange of flavors and textures.

Joho elevates the lowly monkfish to new heights. Exquisitely grilled, the thick fillet is served with a generous dusting of fresh tarragon on a bed of finely julienned carrots and leeks, and is punctuated by a piquant green sea bean, its slight saltiness adding still another dimension of taste. The fabled Everest Room lasagne is a marvel. An Art Deco rectangle of tricolored diagonal stripes of pasta covers meaty chunks of lobster. This is then surrounded with a delicate sauce of green asparagus butter and garnished wth the lobster carapace. Venison never tasted better than Joho's rosy pink slices, blessed by a sauce of fresh currants and accompanied by "mother's own" knoepfl (spaetzle), richly buttered and sprinkled with parsley.

Salad takes on a new meaning at The Everest Room. Would that we could have had seconds of the splendid roasted potato that was slashed across the top and filled with hot and creamy Alsatian Munster cheese, heavily sprinkled with caraway and spears of chives, and served on a bed of corn lettuce dressed with fragrant walnut oil.

Desserts are light, luscious, and elegant. There is a meringue-like cheesecake with a caramelized top, a white chocolate mousse served on a dark chocolate sauce, and a fragrant chocolate-and-ginger soufflé, rushed to the table while it is still hot and puffy. A deft server immediately takes a spoon filled with chocolate-ginger sauce, inserts it under the soufflé's crown, and deposits the lush dollop of sauce into the center of the steamy soufflé. And we shall always remember the rich flavor and perfume of the silver-gray licorice ice cream, unlike any we had ever tasted before.

A rapid elevator ride from the lobby of the Midwest Stock Exchange takes you to the thirty-ninth floor and the special car for The Everest Room. The long corridor with its leopard-print carpet does not prepare you for the spaciousness of the airy, two-story dining room with its mirrors and huge bay windows. In the center of the room is an enormous crystal chandelier. Several murals of leopards and other exotic African fauna accent the walls. Reminiscent of the fifties, the woods are blond, the draperies light in color, and the linens peach. A tiny lamp and a small bouquet of flowers on each table complement the fine china and crystal. Servers are quietly attentive; they are knowledgeable about the food as well as the wide-ranging wine list. At night you feel you are in fairyland, as the city sparkles below.

It is the perfect setting for a chef who describes his own signature style as characterized by freshness, the finest ingredients, lightness, simplicity, and a sense of design. This style did not come overnight. After completing his formal training in France, Chef Joho spent many years apprenticing at many of the finest French restaurants. He returned to L'Auberge de l'Ill in Alsace, where for a year and a half he worked with his mentor, the fabled chef Paul Haeberlin, before moving to Chicago in 1984. In Europe, Joho was an avid painter, capturing the beauty of the countryside in watercolors. Today his canvas is a bit different, but his aesthetic sense remains the same. He writes: "When you dine, it is to give pleasure to all the senses." He sets his standards high and achieves them superbly.

The Everest Room
CHICAGO, ILLINOIS

Mosaic of Wild Maine Salmon and
Osetra Caviar en Gelée
Iron Horse Vineyard Brut Sparkling Wine

Radicchio Cream Soup with Semolina Quenelles

Fillet of John Dory with
Michigan Chardonnay Sauce and Red Cabbage
*Madron Lake (Michigan) Chardonnay or
Matanzas Creek Winery Chardonnay*

Lamb Loin in Potato Crust
Spottswoode Winery Cabernet Sauvignon

Chocolate Terrine with Mocha Sauce
Joseph Phelps Vineyards Late Harvest Johannisberg Riesling

Wines selected by Donald Patz

Mosaic of Wild Maine Salmon and Osetra Caviar en Gelée

There are lakes and streams in northern Michigan that are filled with wild, or landlocked, salmon—especially in the fall. If you are unable to obtain these, use coho fillets rather than the coarser Atlantic or Pacific salmon. Chef Joho makes generous use of a variety of caviars. For this dish he prefers Osetra, which is usually a deeper color than beluga, has a somewhat firmer grain, and is stronger in flavor. It is also less expensive than beluga. American sturgeon caviar would make a good substitute, or even natural salmon caviar, although it is larger-grained than Osetra and a different color as well.

Makes about 10 servings

> 1 pound wild Maine salmon fillets
> 4 ounces carrots, scraped and diced
> 4 ounces zucchini, peeled and diced
> 1 ounce leek, diced, plus 1 small leek, whole
> 2 pounds tomatoes, plus 1 whole tomato
> 2 cups Fish Fumet (see page 275)
> 4 large egg whites
> 1 medium onion, peeled
> 1 ounce Pernod
> 2 whole star anise
> 2 teaspoons tarragon vinegar
> 2½ tablespoons unflavored gelatin
> 2 tablespoons water
> 4 ounces Osetra caviar
> 1 cup Crème Fraîche (see page 275)
> Salt to taste
>
> Fennel sprigs and caviar for garnish

*B*utter and lightly salt a baking pan. Cut salmon into ½-inch strips. Arrange strips on pan and place under broiler until fish is medium-done, about 1 to 2 minutes. *Do not overcook fish.* Let cool.

Blanch diced carrots, zucchini, and leek for 2 to 3 minutes in salted water. Drain and pat dry.

Chop 2 pounds tomatoes, purée in a food processor, and pass through a fine strainer into a heavy 3-quart saucepan. Mix in fumet and egg whites. Add whole tomato, onion, whole leek, Pernod, anise, and vinegar. Simmer 6 to 8 minutes. Do not boil. Strain through cheesecloth and discard vegetables.

Dissolve gelatin in cold water and stir into fumet mixture. Cool to room temperature.

Oil a 6-cup terrine and place it on a bed of ice. Ladle in enough fish gelatin to coat the bottom about ¼ inch deep. Then add half the blanched vegetables. Allow the gelatin to set.

Place one layer of salmon and then one layer of caviar over the gelatin and vegetables. Next, add the remaining salmon, then the remaining vegetables. Cover with remaining gelatin. Let set in refrigerator at least 2 hours.

Mix Crème Fraîche with a bit of salt. Put a spoonful of the cream on the bottom of each serving plate. With an electric knife, cut a 1-inch slice of the terrine and place on top of sauce. If you do not have an electric knife, use a very sharp chef's knife dipped into very hot water. Garnish with a sprig of fennel and a dollop of caviar.

Radicchio Cream Soup with Semolina Quenelles

Serves 4

QUENELLES

> 3 ounces semolina
> 4 tablespoons butter
> 1 large egg
>> Salt and freshly ground black pepper to taste
>> Grated nutmeg to taste

> 4 cups Chicken Stock (see page 276)
> 1 cup red wine (Cabernet Sauvignon or Pinot Noir)
> 4 heads radicchio (reserve 4 leaves)
> 8 tablespoons unsalted butter
> 1 clove garlic, peeled
> ½ shallot, peeled
> 1 cup plus 1 teaspoon heavy cream

> 4 radicchio leaves for garnish

To make quenelles: Cream butter with egg and semolina. Season with salt, pepper, and nutmeg. Transfer to a small heavy saucepan and cook slowly over low heat 30 minutes, stirring constantly. Form mixture into quenelles (egg shapes) by scooping a small amount of the mixture into a demitasse spoon. Invert another demitasse spoon over the first and press gently to form small ovals. Cook the quenelles in boiling salted water about 6 minutes, turning once. Drain. Just before serving, warm quickly with some hot water and drain again.

In a heavy saucepan, briskly simmer the stock until it is reduced by half. Meanwhile, in another saucepan, briskly simmer the wine until it is reduced to 1 teaspoon.

Wash and coarsely chop the radicchio. Melt 2 tablespoons butter in a heavy saucepan. Add radicchio, garlic, and shallot, and toss in melted butter to coat. Cover with wax paper directly touching the vegetables and sweat over low heat 2 to 3 minutes. Remove garlic and shallot and discard.

Add stock and 1 cup cream to radicchio mixture, and cook 10 minutes. Add 6 tablespoons butter, transfer to a blender or food processor, and purée until smooth. Pass through a strainer into another saucepan. Add reduced wine and teaspoon of cream; season to taste and keep warm.

Julienne 4 radicchio leaves and blanch in salted water. Drain well and reserve for garnish.

To serve, divide soup among four heated soup plates. Garnish each plate with radicchio and 3 quenelles.

Fillet of John Dory with Michigan Chardonnay Sauce and Red Cabbage

Serves 4

> 8 ounces red cabbage
> ¼ cup red wine vinegar
> 2 tablespoons olive oil
> 1 tablespoon cranberry juice
>> Pinch of salt
>> Pinch of sugar
> ¼ cup plus 3 tablespoons Madron Lake Chardonnay
> 2 tablespoons dry vermouth
> 1 shallot, minced
> 1 to 3 cups Fish Fumet (see page 275)

½ cup heavy cream
2 tablespoons butter
2 tablespoons whipped cream
2 tablespoons red wine
1 cup water
4 fillets John Dory, or very fresh
    halibut
Salt and freshly ground black pepper

Fresh chervil for garnish

*S*eparate leaves from cabbage, remove white vein, and cut leaves into coarse julienne. Combine next 5 ingredients in a shallow dish and marinate cabbage in this mixture 1 hour.

Meanwhile, combine Chardonnay (except 1 tablespoon), vermouth, shallot, and 1 cup fumet in a small saucepan and simmer briskly until reduced by three-quarters (to about half a cup). Add cream and butter and simmer 10 minutes. Pour into a blender or food processor, add whipped cream and 1 tablespoon Chardonnay, and purée until smooth. Return to a saucepan and keep warm.

Preheat the oven to 400°. Drain the cabbage and discard the marinade. Combine the red wine and water in a small saucepan, cover, and steam the cabbage 10 minutes. Drain again.

Meanwhile, arrange the fillets in a sauté pan that is just large enough to hold them. Pour in enough of the remaining fumet to braise the fillets. Amount will vary with size of fillets and size of pan, but you do not want them to be covered with stock. Sprinkle with salt and pepper. Braise in oven 4 minutes, or longer if the fillets are thick. This should be just enough to cook fish to rare.

Remove fillets from pan and pat dry. Arrange cabbage on four heated serving plates and place fish on top. Surround with sauce and garnish with fresh chervil.

Lamb Loin in Potato Crust

Serves 4

2 lamb loin strips, completely trimmed
    (about 2 pounds)*
Salt and freshly ground black pepper
    to taste
Olive oil
2 large baking potatoes, peeled
4 tablespoons butter, melted
1 tablespoon minced fresh thyme
1 tablespoon minced fresh rosemary
1 tablespoon minced fresh chervil
1 tablespoon minced fresh parsley
1 tablespoon minced fresh basil

Steamed or sautéed seasonal
    vegetables
Fresh herbs, including chives, for
    garnish

*P*reheat oven to 475°. Set oven rack in upper third of oven. Season lamb strips with salt and

*The lamb strip is a very specific cut that is not commonly available in supermarket meat counters. Have your butcher bone a whole lamb loin. This will yield 2 strips that weigh about a pound each and 2 tenderloins that are just a few ounces each. Have him remove the silverskin on the tenderloins and the strips; use the tenderloins for salad (see recipe from Café Provençal, page 150).

pepper. In a large cast-iron skillet, heat just enough olive oil to coat the bottom of the pan. When the pan is hot, quickly sear the loins for a few seconds on all sides. Then remove them from the pan until you are ready to complete the dish. Reserve the skillet.

Slice the potatoes lengthwise as thinly as possible. Either use the finest slicing blade of your food processor or a mandolin. (Do not slice potatoes in advance or hold in water—this crisps them.)

Return the strips to the skillet. Wrap the potatoes around the strips, overlapping the slices and tucking the edges under them. The potato slices are quite pliable when they are thinly cut. Make several layers of potato slices. Brush well with melted butter and sprinkle with herbs.

Roast in the preheated oven until the potatoes are brown. This should take about 15 minutes. Remove from oven and transfer meat to a carving board that will hold the drippings and let rest in a warm place 5 to 10 minutes.

Arrange seasonal vegetables on four heated serving plates. Slice lamb and arrange on plates. Garnish with lamb jus and fresh herb bundles.

Chocolate Terrine with Mocha Sauce

Serves 8

8 ounces bittersweet chocolate, chopped
4 large egg whites
2 ounces sugar
2 cups whipping cream

MOCHA SAUCE
2 ounces hazelnut nougat*
¼ cup plus 2 tablespoons strong espresso
2 tablespoons dark corn syrup
2 tablespoons dark rum
¼ cup whipped cream

Shaved chocolate and pistachio nuts for garnish

Melt chocolate in the top of a double boiler over simmering water.

Whip egg whites and 1½ ounces sugar until stiff. Fold into chocolate. Whip cream with remaining sugar until stiff, then fold into the chocolate mixture. Pour mixture into a well-buttered-and-sugared 6-cup loaf pan. Rap it on the counter sharply several times to eliminate air pockets, smooth top with spatula, and chill at least 2 hours.

Make the mocha sauce by melting the nougat with the espresso in a small saucepan. Add corn syrup and rum. Cook 10 minutes, then chill thoroughly. Just before serving, fold in the whipped cream.

Rap the chilled terrine once or twice on a hard surface, then invert onto a serving platter. If necessary, carefully loosen sides with a sharp knife. Glaze each dessert plate with mocha sauce. Place a slice of terrine on the sauce. Garnish with shaved chocolate and pistachio nuts.

*To make hazelnut nougat, place equal weights of peeled and chopped hazelnuts and sugar together in a saucepan or caramel pot and caramelize over medium heat. Pour onto a well-oiled cookie sheet and let cool. Grind nougat into a fairly fine powder in a food processor or mortar and pestle, and store, tightly covered, at room temperature.

Jackie's

CHICAGO, ILLINOIS

Can she really be as good as everyone says she is? We wondered if she could live up to the hype. Jackie Shen has been garnering raves for her highly creative cuisine since the fall of 1982, and all that happens is that she gets better and better and it becomes more and more difficult to make a reservation. She is a pioneer. The first chef we know of in the United States to combine Chinese seasonings and cooking styles with local ingredients and French techniques, she comes up with delicious and elegant food that reflects a synthesis of culinary traditions.

So that she can take advantage of the daily market, her fairly short printed menu is amplified by a typed list of specials that change each day. Jackie Shen has become famous for a number of special culinary creations, such as a delicately flaky phyllo pastry cup filled with some wonderful treasures, among them tender, sweet Dublin langoustines, delicate New Zealand green-lip mussels, sautéed chanterelles, and succulent crayfish. A sprinkling of fragrant popcorn adds texture, a scattering of Chinese black beans adds tang. The nest is surrounded by "petals" of a delicate tomato-butter sauce pale rosy-red in color. The final touch is a pansy here, a dollop of minced tomato and beluga caviar there, and a few mushrooms casually scattered around the plate. Sautéed wontons are filled with crabmeat, ginger, sun-dried tomatoes, and goat cheese, or with Wisconsin snails, goat cheese, garlic, basil, and sun-dried tomatoes. The wontons are then folded to resemble butterflies, arranged down the center of a plate, and garnished with sautéed Napa cabbage, shiitake mushrooms, and a light, airy ginger-butter sauce. The final presentation is "casually" dressed by a perfectly tinted sprig of oak-leaf lettuce, a pansy, and a dollop of golden caviar. For the pâté lovers, there are usually at least three available each night, each enlivened by Jackie's creative use of greens, nuts, mushrooms, and edible flowers.

From fish to rack of lamb, there are hard decisions to make when it comes to entrees. Close your eyes and point; you won't go wrong. Imagine a butterflied lamb loin, stuffed with sweetbreads, spinach, carrots, pistachios, truffles, and garlic, then rolled, roasted to perfection, sliced into colorful circles, and sauced with a reduction of red wine and stock generously seasoned with fresh rosemary. For color and texture, the platter is garnished with sautéed shiitake mushrooms and miniature corn. Another splendid dish is roasted game served on a large china plate painted with irises, peonies, and butterflies. Jackie also offers succulent duck, surrounded by slices of pheasant, topped with a crisply plump quail, all resting on top of nutty wild rice and ringed with a rich green peppercorn sauce. And to tempt seafood lovers, there is Jackie's famous lobster and scallops with black pasta. This may sound simple, but it is a dish as beautiful as a painting. The hollow carapace of the lobster is set in the center of a gorgeous china platter, with the whole meat of the claws on either side. The lobster "body" is formed by rosy chunks of lobster meat alternating with grilled sea scallops. Lobster "feelers" are suggested by asparagus. Squid-ink pasta, perfectly cooked and flavored, is swirled and tucked under the hollow shell. And if the dollops of caviar on each of the scallops are not enough, the entire presentation is sauced with a rosy tomato butter on one side and a pale ginger butter on the other. Finally, an orchid adds a colorful accent.

Salads and breads at Jackie's are excellent. We think she must select the lettuce leaves one at a time. Sesame oil adds a delicate flavor to the greens, and other Chinese ingredients are used just as subtly.

A dessert plate changes daily. Cakes are light as air, pastries are delicate and flaky. A must for every first-time dinner is Jackie's signature dessert, one that has been emulated all over the country. It is a small Belgian-chocolate "bag" about 6 inches high, paper-thin, and filled with strawberries, kiwi, and densely flavorful white chocolate mousse, served resting on a puddle of raspberry sauce. We didn't leave a smidgen.

The storefront restaurant is small and simple. Pale gray walls are accented by beautiful floral paintings. Mirrors are judiciously used to create the illusion of greater space. Servers are skilled and move with inconspicuous efficiency. The linens are heavily starched, the wine goblets large, the silverware heavy, and the china exquisite. One can tell that this is the vision of a woman who knows what she wants.

Jackie Shen was born in Hong Kong and came to this country to study at the age of seventeen. She moved to Chicago to pursue a career in hotel management, but became fascinated with the idea of cooking. A lengthy apprenticeship with the fabled Jean Banchet at Le Français gave her a solid foundation in classic French cooking techniques. After a number of years of hard work, she was ready to open Jackie's. She still drives herself tirelessly, working more hours than most humans ought to. And in order to keep in touch with things in the front of the restaurant, she takes reservations herself, speaking directly with the patrons every morning. She sets high standards for her small staff. They, in turn, are devoted to her. Jackie Shen's commitment to excellence is also widely respected by her peers and loyal patrons. We believe that she really is a genius in the exquisite presentation of superbly creative and delicious food.

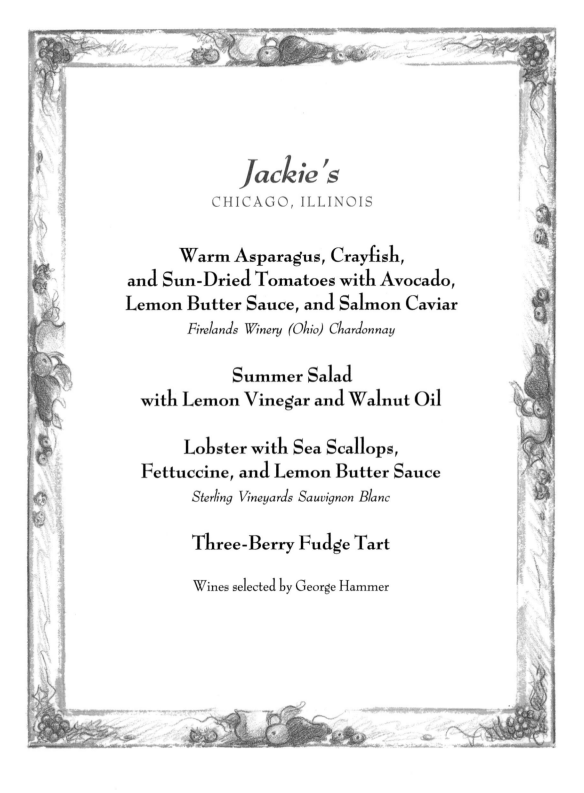

Jackie's
CHICAGO, ILLINOIS

Warm Asparagus, Crayfish, and Sun-Dried Tomatoes with Avocado, Lemon Butter Sauce, and Salmon Caviar

Firelands Winery (Ohio) Chardonnay

Summer Salad with Lemon Vinegar and Walnut Oil

Lobster with Sea Scallops, Fettuccine, and Lemon Butter Sauce

Sterling Vineyards Sauvignon Blanc

Three-Berry Fudge Tart

Wines selected by George Hammer

Warm Asparagus, Crayfish, and Sun-Dried Tomatoes with Avocado, Lemon Butter Sauce, and Salmon Caviar

This is an interesting taste test, since the lemon butter sauce is used in the lobster dish on page 137 as well. You will see how it changes characteristics from one recipe to the next.

Serves 2

LEMON BUTTER SAUCE
1 shallot, diced
¼ cup white wine
1 tablespoon heavy cream
1 pound unsalted butter
Salt and freshly ground black pepper to taste
1 tablespoon lemon juice
Grated zest of 1 lemon

1 pound (about 20) crayfish
1 medium onion, coarsely chopped
1 small carrot, scraped and diced
1 celery stalk, diced
2 tablespoons olive oil
Pinch of thyme
1 bay leaf
1 tablespoon brandy
1 avocado, halved
8 medium asparagus spears, peeled, blanched, and cut into 2-inch lengths, tough stems removed
1 teaspoon chopped sun-dried tomato
1 green onion, trimmed to 2 inches and chopped
2 small cloves garlic, minced

2 rounded teaspoons salmon caviar for garnish

*T*o make the sauce: Combine shallot and wine in a small saucepan; simmer until liquid is reduced to a glaze. Add cream and heat. Whisk in the butter, a little at a time. Add salt and pepper to taste. Strain out shallots and whisk in lemon juice and zest. Keep warm in a larger saucepan filled with warm water while finishing the rest of the dish.

Soak crayfish in a large bowl of cold water 1 hour, transfer to a large colander, and drain well. In a large skillet, sauté onion, carrot, and celery in olive oil with thyme and bay leaf 1 minute. Add whole crayfish and cook, stirring constantly, about 5 minutes. To test if done, remove shell from tail and check to make certain that meat is opaque and tender. Cook 3 more minutes if necessary.

Remove from heat and pour in brandy. Continue stirring until alcohol cooks away. With your fingers peel shells from crayfish just as you might peel shrimp.

Peel and slice the avocado into thin wedges. Fan half the wedges on the right side of each of two serving plates.

In a large skillet, carefully sauté crayfish meat, asparagus (each stalk quartered), sun-dried tomato, green onion, and garlic just to warm (less than 30 seconds).

Arrange crayfish mixture on left side of plate. Garnish with lemon butter sauce and salmon caviar.

Summer Salad with Lemon Vinegar and Walnut Oil

Serves 2

8 red oak-leaf lettuce leaves
1 bunch mache
2 big radicchio leaves, chopped
1 cup frisée (fine curly endive),
    chopped
4 arugula leaves
1 bunch scallions (white part only),
    trimmed to a length of 1 inch and
    chopped
1 tablespoon lemon vinegar
2 tablespoons walnut oil
1 small clove garlic, minced
    Salt and freshly ground black pepper
    to taste

Nasturtium blossoms for garnish

*O*n each of two serving plates, arrange 4 oak-leaf lettuce leaves. In a mixing bowl, toss the remaining greens with the scallions, vinegar, oil, garlic, salt, and pepper. Place a portion in the center of each plate, on top of the oak leaves. Garnish with nasturtium blossoms.

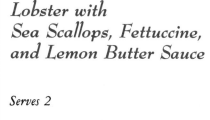

Lobster with Sea Scallops, Fettuccine, and Lemon Butter Sauce

Serves 2

Olive oil
1 celery stalk, chopped
1 medium carrot, scraped and chopped
1 small onion, chopped
1 teaspoon dried thyme
2 bay leaves
1 teaspoon whole black peppercorns
½ cup white wine (Sauvignon Blanc or
    Chardonnay)
2 1-pound lobsters, live
¼ pound egg fettuccine, cooked al
    dente
½ pound medium sea scallops,
    ligaments removed
½ teaspoon finely minced garlic
1 scallion (white part only), trimmed to
    a length of 2 inches and chopped
    Salt and freshly ground black pepper
    to taste

Lemon Butter Sauce (page 136)
Edible flowers for garnish

*I*n a tall stockpot, pour just enough olive oil to coat the bottom and heat. Add the chopped vegetables, herbs, and peppercorns. Sauté until tender, stirring often. Add wine, scrape bottom of pan to loosen any particles, and remove from heat.

Add enough cold water to half fill the pot. Return to stove and bring to boil. Add lobsters and boil until lobsters float to top. This should take 10 to 15 minutes. Remove lobsters, discard broth, and cool.

Remove lobster head, scrape out inside of

head with a spoon, and discard these insides. Wash head well, drain, and set aside. Using a sharp knife, cut body lengthwise down center and remove meat in 2 big pieces. Cut pieces into quarters. Carefully use a cracker to open claws. Try to remove the claw meat in one whole piece. Save lobster legs and keep warm for garnish.

Heat a medium skillet with enough olive oil to coat the bottom. Sauté the fettuccine and season with salt and pepper. Divide pasta between two heated serving plates, placing it in middle of the plate one-third of the way down from twelve o'clock. Place the head above it, at twelve o'clock.

Heat a bit more oil in the skillet and quickly sauté the scallops. Add a bit of salt and pepper, and half the garlic. Arrange scallops in a vertical line below the pasta.

Reheat the skillet, add more oil if necessary, and sauté lobster claws and body meat. Add scallions and remaining garlic. Sauté just until hot. Arrange claw meat on either side of the head (at eleven and one o'clock). Arrange body meat along either side of the scallops. Fan warm legs out from either side of the lobster meat.

Pour the lemon butter sauce on the plate in empty spaces and drizzle some on the lobster meat and claw meat. Decorate with a few edible flowers.

Three-Berry Fudge Tart

Makes 1 9-inch tart

CRUST
- ¼ cup sugar
- ½ cup ground almonds
- ¾ cup unsalted butter
- 100 grams flour (about ¾ cup minus 1 rounded tablespoon)
- 1 large egg

FILLING
- 4 ounces unsalted butter
- 3½ ounces semisweet chocolate
- ¼ cup plus 2 tablespoons heavy cream
- ½ cup sugar
- 2 large eggs
- 1 large egg yolk
- ½ teaspoon vanilla extract
- ⅓ to ½ cup raspberry jam, melted
- ½ pint each raspberries, gooseberries, and blackberries

*T*o make crust: Combine sugar and almonds in the bowl of a food processor; process briefly. Add butter and combine. Add flour and process several times. Then add egg and process until combined. Scrape dough from bowl, form into a ball, wrap in plastic, and chill 24 hours.

Preheat oven to 350°. Using a floured rolling pin, carefully roll dough into an 11-inch circle on a lightly floured board. Because there is so much butter in this pastry, it is often hard to handle. If you have difficulty,

just skip the rolling and press the dough evenly into the tart pan. Transfer to a 9-inch pie plate or to a 9-inch tart pan with a removable bottom. Trim the edges evenly. Line prepared shell with parchment paper and fill with weights or dried beans. Bake in preheated oven 20 minutes. Remove and cool slightly. Remove weights and discard parchment paper.

Melt butter and chocolate together in a small saucepan. Whisk in cream and sugar. Then whisk in eggs, yolk, and vanilla. Pour into the partially baked shell and return to the oven. Bake 10 to 15 minutes, or until set.

After pie has cooled, brush the top with the melted raspberry jam. Arrange alternating rows of fresh berries on top of the glaze to completely cover the pie.

Printer's Row

CHICAGO, ILLINOIS

Long before it was chic, Michael Foley was making corn cakes and wild-rice cakes as entree accompaniments. He combed the heartland for indigenous fruits and berries; he sought regional sources for wild game, and he became an early promoter of native fish from the area's streams and from the Great Lakes. When he opened Printer's Row in 1981, he was setting a trend, not following one. We have followed his career for years in national food magazines and we think that much of the credit for the new interest in Midwestern food must go to Michael Foley. Because of this, it just seemed right to begin our food tour in his restaurant. What we found was fine food, fresh ingredients, intriguing juxtapositions of color, flavor, and texture—food to be taken seriously, and food that was neither silly nor overly cute.

Appetizers are so appealing that choices are tough to make; fortunately, the kitchen will combine small tastes of several dishes when choices cannot be narrowed any further. Perfectly seasoned warm venison sausage with arugula baked in pastry is light and delicious. Salmon gravlax cured with dill and a hint of green peppercorns is accompanied by herb toast points and crisp cucumber salad, which serve as perfect counterpoints to the incredibly fresh-tasting salmon. Cream soups are smooth as satin and heady with flavor and fragrance. On a cold winter's day we long for crayfish bisque with sun-dried tomatoes. Pasta appetizers are equally outstanding. We are especially pleased with the very delicate fettuccini tossed with lemon, cream, and Parmesan cheese. This deceptively simple dish is just heavenly when made as well as it is here. Salads are also appealing. When it is offered, the Chardonnay-poached pear and endive salad with blue cheese and walnuts, lightly bathed in a mellow vinaigrette, is superb. Another fine salad is made with warm crayfish piqued with a grapefruit vinaigrette.

Many of the entrees at Printer's Row come from nearby lakes. Grilled whitefish with red pepper coulis is as delicious as it is beautiful. Garnished with a case of puff pastry filled with green beans, it is also accompanied by buttery spinach, beets, and fiddlehead ferns that make the dish a veritable symphony of colors and tastes. Another of our favorites is the broiled black bass served with the natural juice of seasonal mushrooms. A plate of two varieties of grilled scallops—some from the sea and some from the bay—is equally successful. These are accompanied by spinach in coriander vinaigrette and poached leeks sliced in half, twisted into a spiral, and chilled in a tomato and basil sherry vinaigrette; here you see the chef at his most inventive. Game also appears regularly on the menu. Quail stuffed with wild huckleberries, grilled pheasant accompanied by spaghetti squash and pancetta, and medallions of venison sautéed with golden beets and a cranberry-ginger sauce make our tongues tingle. Shreds of sweet potato fried until crunchy make a great garnish for perfectly grilled duck breast and leg. A Calvados sauce caresses the fan of sliced breast and the crispy leg is surrounded by sautéed apples, a vegetable purée or two, and a twirl of steamed spinach. A barbecued breast of capon might be accompanied by a zesty corn salsa, and a delicate crepe of blue cornmeal. Each entree is garnished individually; no peas and potatoes of the night here.

No discussion of Michael Foley could be complete without mention of his desserts. Since he first opened Printer's Row, he has been applauded for his creative baking. While cobblers and cakes appear frequently on the dessert menu, we must single out the apple strudel with cinnamon ice cream as being especially worthy of praise. The strudel leaves dissolve on the tongue while the rich flavor of the cinnamon ice cream lingers long on the palate. Sorbets are every bit as delicious, and in the summer are served as a garnish in heavenly fruit soups. And both rewarding the taste buds and pleasing the eye is a brilliantly golden passion-fruit soup with pale orange cantaloupe sorbet, garnished with raspberries and pineapple and a sprig of mint. Equally

delightful is scrumptious blueberry cream in a hazelnut meringue base. The nutty and chewy meringue, topped with cassis-flavored whipped cream, is a sublime complement to the luscious berries.

Whether for lunch or for dinner, a meal at Printer's Row will be a fine dining experience. The service staff is quite willing to suggest ways to orchestrate the menu in order that diners may taste more of the chef's creativity. And when it comes to the wine list, sit back and enjoy the fine offerings from both the United States and France. We found Michelot-Buisson's Merseult le Limousin on this wine list; what a grand surprise that was! And it was not served too cold.

The restaurant is a warmly handsome environment that both enhances and harmonizes with Michael Foley's elegant cuisine. Dark wood and lots of leather are especially comforting during Chicago's harsh winters. Tableware has been chosen with great care; heavy silver and fine wine goblets complement the richly starched linens. Oversized Villeroy and Boch china plates add wonderful splashes of color and frame Foley's food quite attractively.

Michael Foley, a third-generation Chicago chef, is a very shy man. After graduating first from Georgetown University and then from the Cornell University School of Hotel and Restaurant Administration, he paid his dues in a number of restaurants before opening Printer's Row. While this is not a restaurant accustomed to frequent perambulations by The Chef, it is clearly one that is guided by a firm hand. All of the parts are in harmony here, and we feel that harmony as we sink back into our very comfortable seats, sip something wonderful from the wine list, and wait to see what new delights will come forth from the kitchen.

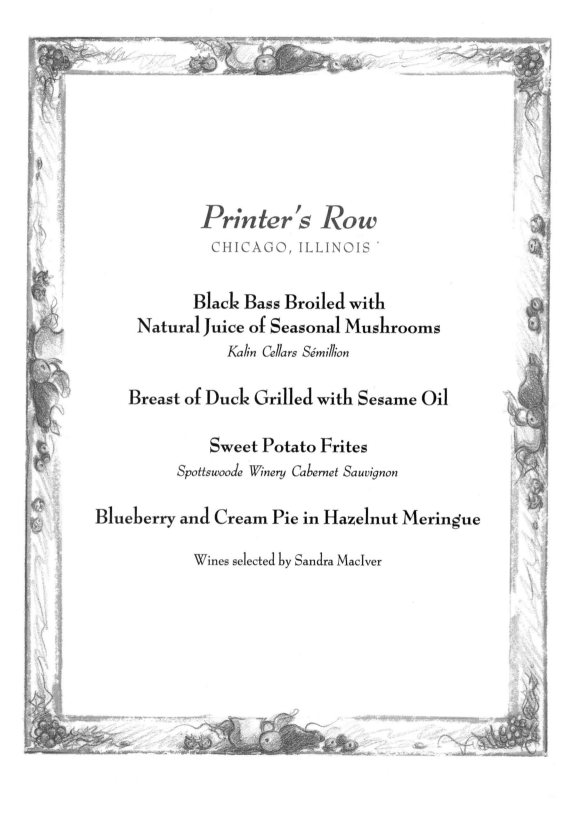

Printer's Row

CHICAGO, ILLINOIS

Black Bass Broiled with
Natural Juice of Seasonal Mushrooms

Kalin Cellars Sémillion

Breast of Duck Grilled with Sesame Oil

Sweet Potato Frites

Spottswoode Winery Cabernet Sauvignon

Blueberry and Cream Pie in Hazelnut Meringue

Wines selected by Sandra MacIver

Black Bass Broiled with Natural Juice of Seasonal Mushrooms

We have made this dish with a wide variety of wild mushrooms. It is outstanding with chanterelles, oyster mushrooms, and shiitakes, but when we can add morels or hen-of-the-woods we are thrilled.

Serves 6

> 3 tablespoons olive oil
> 8 tablespoons unsalted butter
> 6 ounces fresh wild mushrooms, thinly sliced
> 1 cup Fish Fumet (see page 275)
> Salt and freshly ground black pepper to taste
> Juice of half a lemon
> Pinch of cayenne
> 2 tablespoons duck foie gras (optional)
> 2 tablespoons chopped fresh chives
> 1½ pounds thinly sliced black bass fillets
>
> Whole chives for garnish

*H*eat a heavy sauté pan and add the olive oil and 6 tablespoons butter, stirring until butter is melted. Add the mushrooms and sauté until cooked. Add the fumet and simmer briskly until liquid is reduced by two-thirds. Season with salt, pepper, lemon juice, and cayenne. Whisk in the remaining butter, the foie gras, and the chives. Adjust seasonings to taste. Set aside and keep warm.

On a non-stick shallow-sided aluminum cookie sheet wiped with olive oil, carefully arrange the fish fillets so that they do not overlap. Broil about 2 minutes, or until done. Remove from oven and cool about 5 minutes to just above room temperature.

Spoon mushroom mixture among six warm serving plates, place the fillets over the mushrooms, and garnish with chives.

Breast of Duck Grilled with Sesame Oil

Serves 6

> 6 12-ounce duck breasts
> 1 garlic clove, peeled
> ¼ cup sesame oil
> Pinch chopped fresh lemon grass (optional)
> Salt and freshly ground pepper to taste
>
> Sweet Potato Frites (see page 145), sautéed or steamed seasonal vegetables, and fresh herbs, such as chives and watercress, for garnish

*S*plit duck breasts in half. Leave skin on but trim away all excess fat. (If there is too much fat left on the breasts, the meat will dry out before all the fat is rendered.) Remove the little fillets. Rub breasts with garlic clove and then with sesame oil.

Spray a clean grill with Pam and heat it to medium high. Place breasts fat side down and grill 5 to 6 minutes, or until the fat is rendered and the skin darkened. Do not burn, however, as the fat will flame. Turn and sprinkle with some lemon grass. Grill underside about 2 minutes, or until just medium-rare. Don't overcook. Remove breasts to a carving board and let rest 5 to 10 minutes in a warm place. Slice thinly on the diagonal.

Fan duck slices on each of six warmed serving plates. Arrange frites and assorted vegetables around the slices. Brush duck with a bit more oil and lightly season with salt and freshly ground pepper. Garnish with herbs.

The Best of the Midwest

Sweet Potato Frites

The French call them frites; we call them French fries. Whatever the name, fried shoestring potatoes are wonderful. And when they are fried sweet potatoes, they are even better!

Serves 6

> 4 sweet potatoes, peeled
> 3 cups vegetable oil
> Salt and freshly ground white pepper to taste
> Fresh minced parsley (optional)
> Fresh minced thyme (otional)

*U*sing a knife or mandolin, cut sweet potatoes into slivers about ³⁄₁₆ inch thick and 3 inches long.

In a deep, heavy skillet or electric deep-fat fryer, heat oil to 340°. Drop potatoes, a handful at a time, into oil and cook until crisp (5 to 8 minutes). Drain on paper towels. Season with salt, pepper, and herbs to taste.

Blueberry and Cream Pie in Hazelnut Meringue

Makes 1 10-inch pie

PIE SHELL
> ½ cup egg whites, less 1 tablespoon, at room temperature
> ¼ teaspoon salt
> 1 cup sugar
> 1 teaspoon baking powder
> 1 cup graham cracker crumbs
> ½ cup shredded coconut
> ½ cup skinned and chopped hazelnuts
> 1 teaspoon vanilla extract

FILLING
> 3 large egg yolks
> 1 cup sugar
> 3 tablespoons flour
> ¼ teaspoon salt
> 1 tablespoon lemon juice
> Crème de cassis
> 3 cups fresh or frozen blueberries
> 1 cup heavy cream
> 3 tablespoons confectioner's sugar
>
> Candied rose petals, or candied violets, and fresh mint leaves for garnish

*P*reheat oven to 350°. Butter and flour a 10-inch pie plate.

To make crust: Combine egg whites and salt in a mixing bowl and beat until frothy. Continue beating while you slowly add the sugar, and beat until the whites form shiny, stiff peaks. In a small bowl, combine the baking powder, crumbs, coconut, and hazelnuts, then fold into the meringue along with the vanilla. Spread meringue mixture on bottom and sides of prepared pie plate. Bake in preheated oven 20 to 30 minutes. Transfer pie plate to a wire rack and cool completely.

Meanwhile, in a large mixing bowl, beat together yolks and sugar until pale yellow in color. Whisk in flour, salt, lemon juice, and 3 tablespoons crème de cassis. Fold in berries. Place mixture in the top of a double boiler over simmering water and cook, stirring frequently, until it is colored by the blueberries and slightly thickened.

Pour berry mixture into the cooled pie shell and chill at least 2 hours. When ready to serve, whip the cream with the confectioner's sugar until stiff. Whip in 2 or more tablespoons cassis to taste. Spread this mixture over the top of the pie and garnish with candied flowers and fresh mint leaves.

Café Provençal

EVANSTON, ILLINOIS

Mention the word "Provence" to us and we feel warm sunshine on our shoulders, smell the fragrances of wild herbs and olive trees wafting about the hillsides, and taste zesty tomatoes and briny fish grilled over grapevines and herbs. Café Provençal is not a French restaurant, but it offers hearty food that reflects the Provençal love of aromatic herbs, complex sauces filled with flavor, and simple grilled meats and fish. In the dark cold days of winter, Café Provençal brings sunshine and flowers to Chicago's north shore. Menus change with the seasons; daily specials are suggested by local purveyors and the treasures they offer. Owner Leslee Reis was among the earliest devotees of American products. Now she and Chef Kevin Schrimmer make a special effort to work with producers in the region to get the freshest, most interesting produce and game.

We could easily put together a complete meal from the list of appealing appetizers. A superlative quail from Wisconsin is stuffed, roasted, and served on a bed of braised shredded cabbage; a sauce of sherry vinegar and natural jus has a hint of tarragon and a sprinkling of truffles. Small sausages, one of pork

and one of duck, are grilled and served with a warm potato salad. A light vinegar in the salad perfectly complements the spicy, smoky sausages. Smoked salmon is sliced paper-thin, filled with a bit of crème fraîche, American sturgeon caviar, and chives, rolled into long cylinders, and served with heavenly corn pancakes, richly studded with kernels of golden corn or pencil-thin green beans in a mustard vinaigrette. There might be braised rabbit with spinach fettuccine and a mustard cream sauce or New York State foie gras sautéed and served with a small truffle and herb salad with truffle vinaigrette. Every plate is a picture; great thought is given to color and texture as well as to flavor and fragrance.

Beautifully composed salads add to the appetizer possibilities. There might be house-smoked duck breast sliced on a bed of impeccably fresh greens and garnished with sliced pears, toasted walnuts, and chèvre—or roasted lamb tenderloins redolent of thyme and rosemary, accompanied by goat cheese dipped in olive oil and chopped walnuts, baked, and served on a bed of delicate greens dressed lightly with a walnut-oil vinaigrette. And for those of us who love soup, a full-flavored consommé garnished with small chestnut-filled ravioli is a splendid winter treat. A soup for all seasons is the Provence-style fish soup richly flavored with tomatoes, saffron, and fennel. And when the winter winds howl from the lake, Café Provençal offers a hearty and nurturing lentil cream soup.

Kevin Schrimmer's dishes not only are beautiful but are fascinating combinations of tastes. Quickly sautéed striped bass might be presented on a bed of buttery julienned vegetables, surrounded with a light mushroom cream sauce and punctuated with a generous swirl of garlicky spinach—a dish that stimulates all the senses—or it might be lightly dusted with Chinese five-spice powder before it is quickly sautéed, then served on a bed of julienned carrots, celery, and fennel, and gently garnished with a white peppercorn and mustard sauce. Roast saddle of lamb is served with a delicately textured but heartily flavored eggplant and chestnut timbale and a zesty balsamic vinegar sauce. A veal chop perfumed with fresh sage is grilled and garnished with a gratin of artichoke, butternut squash, and caramelized onion. And lightly smoked pheasant, rubbed with a glaze and roasted, is sliced and served surrounded with tender cumin-flavored pasta, a compote of leek and red peppers, and lightly braised cabbage. These are dishes with power!

We cannot resist dessert. Fruit tarts are heavenly here, and a lemon tart with berry sauce is superlative. Little pots-de-crème are a delightful surprise, with vanilla custard garnished with candied chestnuts in one and chocolate custard with a garnish of dried cherries in the other. A caramel trio makes a welcome change from chocolate. It includes a silken crème brûlée as good as we had anticipated. Meringues are always popular, especially when combined with hazelnuts, berries, and cream.

Café Provençal is a gorgeous place that really does feel like the South of France. Dark wood paneling is punctuated by enormous bunches of exquisite fresh flowers, country French pottery, and wonderful green chintz. White lace draperies serve as a backdrop to accentuate the splendidly filled vases. A few dining-room walls are covered with shirred fabric. Seat covers and banquette upholstery are in green-and-white chintz. The tablecloths are deep pink linen, the lighting is soft and flattering, and string music is played in the background. Add to this the highly professional service and an outstanding wine list, and you have all the elements needed for pleasurable dining.

Café Provençal has been among Chicago's finest restaurants since it opened its doors. Leslee Reis was one of the first women restaurateurs to appear in the pages of national food magazines in the late seventies. We imagine that it took courage to open an upscale restaurant in a college town, away from the mainstream of the business community. And although Evanston is a half-hour drive from the Loop, many are willing to make the trip. There have been only two chefs over the years—Kevin Schrimmer became chef late in 1988, and immediately began to get raves from many restaurant critics. A student first at the University of Wisconsin and then at the Culinary Institute of America, he worked in fine restaurants in France and this country before returning to his home area as a sous-chef at Café Provençal. Blessed with a creative mind and a fine palate, he has been able to make his mark in a place already celebrated for the work of his predecessor. It is a wise restaurateur who recognizes such talent and encourages it. Which is, after all, why Café Provençal continues to be among the best restaurants in the Midwest.

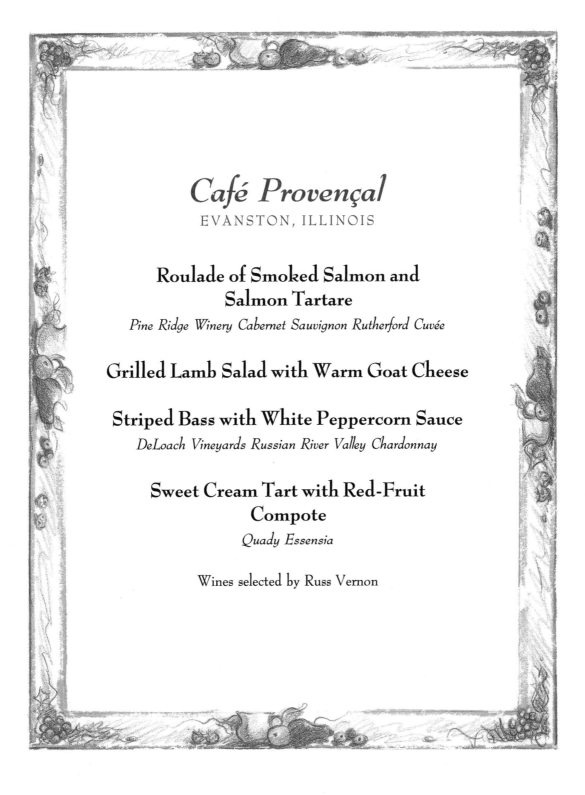

Café Provençal
EVANSTON, ILLINOIS

Roulade of Smoked Salmon and Salmon Tartare
Pine Ridge Winery Cabernet Sauvignon Rutherford Cuvée

Grilled Lamb Salad with Warm Goat Cheese

Striped Bass with White Peppercorn Sauce
DeLoach Vineyards Russian River Valley Chardonnay

Sweet Cream Tart with Red-Fruit Compote
Quady Essensia

Wines selected by Russ Vernon

Roulade of Smoked Salmon and Salmon Tartare

This is simply delicious as an appetizer in any season. It would also make a marvelous brunch dish.

Serves 4

4 1½-ounce slices smoked salmon
1 teaspoon Dijon mustard
1 tablespoon tarragon vinegar
¼ cup extra-virgin olive oil
  Salt and freshly ground black pepper
    to taste
8 ounces fresh salmon, chopped finely
    by hand
1 tablespoon capers, drained
1 tablespoon finely diced red onions,
    soaked in cold water for 5 minutes
    and drained
2 tablespoons finely chopped fresh
    parsley
1 hard-boiled egg, white finely
    chopped, yolk pressed through a
    sieve and reserved
1 tablespoon blanched and diced
    French green beans
1 tablespoon scallions (white part
    only), minced
1 teaspoon cornichons, finely minced

  Sieved egg yolks or sturgeon roe,
    brioche toast triangles or water
    crackers, Crème Fraîche or sour
    cream, whole chives for garnish

*P*lace each slice of smoked salmon between two layers of wax paper and, using a meat cleaver or rolling pin, pound to achieve a 3 × 5-inch rectangle about ⅛ inch thick. Trim edges neatly. Cover with plastic and set aside.

For vinaigrette, combine the next 4 ingredients in a mixing bowl and whisk well. Set aside.

Combine the remaining ingredients in a mixing bowl and mix well with vinaigrette. Adjust seasonings.

Spoon about 2 tablespoons of the tartare mixture along a length of smoked salmon and carefully roll up. Trim edges. Place on serving plate seam side down and top lengthwise with a thin line of either sieved egg yolk or sturgeon roe. Garnish with toast triangles or crackers, a dollop of Crème Fraîche (see page 275) or sour cream, and a few long chives.

Grilled Lamb Salad with Warm Goat Cheese

Serves 4

1 cup olive oil
1 clove garlic, crushed
1 bay leaf
1 sprig fresh thyme, or ⅛ teaspoon
    dried
1 sprig fresh rosemary, or ⅛ teaspoon
    dried
4 lamb tenderloins, silverskin removed,
    well trimmed
  Salt and freshly ground black pepper
    to taste
1 3.5-ounce log goat cheese, cut in 4
    ½-inch slices
⅓ cup olive oil
½ cup finely chopped walnuts
2 tablespoons balsamic vinegar
1 tablespoon finely chopped shallots
6 tablespoons walnut oil

2 lightly packed cups combined mâche, radicchio, Belgian endive, frisée, arugula, red oak-leaf lettuce, and watercress

Combine first 5 ingredients in a mixing bowl and whisk well. Arrange lamb tenderloins in a shallow baking dish and cover with the olive-oil mixture. Let stand in refrigerator, turning occasionally, 1 to 2 days. Drain, dry, and rub with salt and pepper.

Roll goat cheese slices first in olive oil, then in walnut pieces. Place in a shallow baking dish or pie plate.

Spray a clean grill with Pam and heat to medium high. When hot, grill the tenderloins 1 to 2 minutes on each side, or until medium rare. Let rest while finishing greens. Preheat oven to 350°. Combine vinegar, shallots, salt, and pepper to taste in a small bowl. Slowly whisk in the walnut oil. Toss greens with 4 tablespoons vinaigrette. Add more only if necessary. Divide among four serving plates. Then slice tenderloins on an angle and scatter over greens. Heat the goat cheese in a 350° oven 2 to 3 minutes, just until soft to the touch. Place warmed goat cheese slices in center of each salad.

Striped Bass with White Peppercorn Sauce

Serves 4

4 8–10-ounce farm-raised striped bass
    or sea bass fillets
2 small zucchini, scrubbed
2 yellow squash, scrubbed
2 carrots, scraped
2 stalks celery
½ fennel bulb
1 tablespoon olive oil
7 tablespoons unsalted butter
3 tablespoons crushed white
    peppercorns
2 cups white wine vinegar
3 cups dry white wine
2 cloves garlic, unpeeled
½ tablespoon tomato purée
2 teaspoons Grey Poupon mustard
½ cup Crème Fraîche (see page 275)
    Salt
1 teaspoon sugar
4 tablespoons clarified butter
    Freshly ground white pepper to taste
1 tablespoon Chinese five-spice
    powder

Chopped parsley for garnish

Trim fish fillets of the thin outer edges and reserve scraps. Check to make certain that all pin bones have been removed (use a tweezer to remove any remaining ones), then turn fillet skin side up and score with a sharp knife every 1½ inches in a crisscross pattern, just deep enough to break through the skin. Wrap in plastic and refrigerate.

Slice off the outer quarter inch of the squashes and carrots. Trim celery and fennel. Cut into 1½ × ⅛-inch julienne. Set aside.

Combine oil and 1 tablespoon butter in a small skillet and heat until foam subsides. Add 2 tablespoons crushed peppercorns and the fish scraps; sauté until brown. Add white wine vinegar; simmer briskly until liquid is reduced by three-fourths. Set aside.

In a medium-sized heavy saucepan, melt 1 tablespoon butter and sauté 1 tablespoon crushed peppercorns 2 to 3 minutes. Add the vinegar reduction. Add white wine, garlic, tomato purée, and mustard, and reduce to ¾ cup. Add Crème Fraîche and heat through. On low heat, whisk in 5 tablespoons butter, a bit at a time, whisking constantly. Do not let boil. Remove garlic cloves, adjust salt, and whisk in the sugar. Set saucepan in a larger saucepan filled with warm water and keep warm.

Heat 2 tablespoons of the clarified butter in a large Teflon-coated skillet and sauté vegetables just until tender. Season with salt and pepper and divide among four serving dishes. Keep warm.

Lightly season fish fillets with Chinese five-spice powder and salt. Heat remaining 2 tablespoons clarified butter in Teflon skillet over high heat and sauté fish fillets skin side down until browned. Turn fillets and sauté flesh side down 1 to 2 minutes.

Place fillets skin side up on the sautéed vegetables and ladle approximately ¼ cup warm sauce around each fillet. Garnish with finely chopped parsley.

Sweet Cream Tart with Red-Fruit Compote

Serves 4

PÂTE SUCRÉE
  1 cup sifted flour
  2 tablespoons superfine sugar
  6 tablespoons unsalted butter, cut into pieces
2 to 4 tablespoons ice water
  Granulated sugar

  2 cups heavy cream, not ultra-pasteurized
1½ cups sugar
  4 pinches ground cinnamon
  2 cups red wine (Cabernet Sauvignon or Zinfandel)
  1 cinnamon stick
  Zest of 1 orange
  ½ pint fresh raspberries
  ½ pint fresh strawberries, hulled and quartered
  ½ pint fresh sweet cherries, pitted and halved

  Mint sprigs for garnish

First, make the pâte sucrée: Combine flour and superfine sugar in a mixing bowl, add the butter, and rub between your fingers until mixture resembles very coarse cornmeal. Slowly add the water, lightly mixing with your fingers. Using only one hand, gather the dough to mix evenly. Turn mixture out on a pastry board, and use the heel of your palm to rub a tablespoon at a time away from you to evenly distribute the butter. When all the dough has been blended, use a pastry scraper, or spatula, to gather it up, then press it into a ball. Wrap in plastic and chill 1 hour.

Preheat oven to 400°. Cut pastry into 4 pieces. Lightly flour a small work surface; then, using a floured rolling pin, roll the first section of pastry into a thin circle. Carefully fit the circle into a 4-inch tart pan. Repeat this process 3 more times. Prick shells with the tines of a fork and sprinkle lightly with granulated sugar. Line each shell with parchment paper and fill with dried beans or pie weights. Bake about 15 minutes, carefully remove paper and weights, and return to oven until light brown. Remove shells to a wire rack and cool.

In a large heavy-bottomed saucepan, mix cream and 1 cup sugar over medium heat and stir until sugar is dissolved. Bring mixture to a boil, stirring occasionally. Continue boiling 12 to 15 minutes, or until mixture is thickened and a pale butterscotch color. Stir often toward the end of the cooking time—both the sugar and cream can burn easily. Fill prepared tart shells about three-quarters full and sprinkle tops lightly with cinnamon. Let cool completely at room temperature.

In a small heavy-bottomed saucepan, combine ½ cup sugar and wine; bring to simmer. Add cinnamon stick and orange zest, and simmer 10 minutes over medium heat, until syrupy. Allow to cool somewhat. Strain.

Combine berries and cherries in a large bowl. Pour syrup over the fruits and mix gently.

Place tarts on four serving plates. Carefully spoon berry mixture over tarts so that it spills out onto plates. Garnish with mint sprigs.

Old Rittenhouse Inn

BAYFIELD, WISCONSIN

We continue to be astonished at the extraordinary beauty of the northern Great Lakes. Driving along the edge of Lake Superior, near its westernmost corner, we could see the Apostle Islands in the distance. Even in the chill of autumn, we found ourselves thoroughly smitten. Bayfield, Wisconsin, is a tiny community of about eight hundred hardy souls. In summer the whole village thrives on tourism; when the winter snows overwhelm, the villagers turn to each other for companionship and renewal, although hardy tourists pack the inn for a weekend of cross-country skiing and good food. In its heyday Bayfield was the summer playground of the rich and famous in the lumber and shipping industries. Its dark, soil-nurtured brownstone was cut from the hillsides and shipped down through the Great Lakes to permanently affect the architectural faces of cities like Chicago and New York. The decline of shipping and fishing on the lakes took away the economic base of beautiful communities like Bayfield.

Fortunately, however, at least in Bayfield's case, the charm was not ruined. Mary and Jerry Phillips first discovered Bayfield on their honeymoon. Then music students at the University of Wisconsin, they returned each year for vacations. Although they had successful careers as music teachers in Madison, they continued to be drawn by the beauty of the lake and its islands. Then, in 1974, when they heard that the old mansion on the hill was for sale, they moved heaven and earth to buy it. The Phillipses and their son now live there year-round. They have also purchased two more beautiful old mansions in Bayfield for additional guest rooms. And they provide some of the best hospitality in the Midwest.

The Old Rittenhouse Inn began as a bed-and-breakfast. Now it is open nightly for dinner. Mary Phillips had no formal food training before she opened the Old Rittenhouse, but she had always loved cooking. From the very first day, her breakfasts were the talk of Bayfield. Fresh seasonal berries are served on fine china collected by the Phillipses. We enjoyed a first pressing of autumn cider and a crystal goblet of warm applesauce with a hint of cinnamon and a dollop of thick cream. Fresh Lake Superior whitefish, lightly poached, then perfectly broiled, vies for attention with shirred eggs and creamed mushrooms and apple-oat pancakes with their own Swiss pear marmalade. The wonderfully fragrant basket of warm muffins and dishes of homemade berry jellies add to the splendid confusion. Gone at once are the assertions made the night before that we cannot eat another bite for days!

Midwestern cuisine, with its celebration of regional ingredients, may now be in fashion around the country, but it has always been Mary Phillips's fashion. Bayfield is almost three hours from Duluth, the nearest city, and seven hours from Milwaukee, so Mary relies heavily on local foragers, farmers, and fishermen for menu items. Extraordinary things come from the kitchen, but they are usually improvised from whatever is available. Even in times of plenty, the Phillipses feel they must buy whatever a forager brings them, lest they discourage his future efforts. So they use all the mushrooms, wild fruits, and berries that come their way, no matter what the quantity. Mary has become a master of fruit soups and homemade cordials, preserves, and jel-

lies—from a soup of wild plums to choke-cherry preserves. Fruit soups are usually clear, with vibrant, glistening color.

When the winter winds come to stay, there is smoked-trout chowder and cream of almond soup with wild rice. Appetizers include an assortment of tender pâtés, a thin slice of savory cheesecake, or home-smoked salmon. Whitefish and trout are the most common fish on the menu; sautéed or broiled, they are fresh, sweet, and never overcooked. Wisconsin is known for its farms, so meats and poultry are quite fresh. Breast of chicken with a dressing of wild rice from nearby Minnesota is complemented by winter-squash soufflé. A thick pork chop, braised and served with a rich mushroom cream sauce, or tender leg of lamb, fragrant with herbs from the garden, are among the house specialties. Accompanying vegetables often come from nearby farms.

In addition to his evening duty as host and manager, Jerry Phillips is the resident baker, producing all the wonderful muffins, rolls, and desserts. His ethereal ten-layer orange-blossom torte is filled with orange butter cream loaded with Grand Marnier. Lemon cheesecake, topped with fresh berries of the season, and white chocolate cheesecake, topped with a glaze of dark chocolate, are masterpieces. In autumn, there are plenty of apples for pies and cakes, and nuts for tortes. And in every season there is ice cream with thick Rittenhouse sauces, such as hot buttered rum with spiced bananas. Finally, for those with room, Jerry might offer some chocolate truffles with a hint of raspberry cream filling.

The cream-brick and red-shingle Victorian mansion sits high on a hill looking over the lake. In summer, the wrap-around veranda is filled with white wicker furniture and geraniums. The splendid interior has been lovingly restored, and is filled with Jerry and

Mary's superb collection of Victorian furniture and glass. Dining tables are accented by antique lace and porcelain, a vase of flowers, and candlelight. The handsome cherry-wood foyer and staircase, with a gorgeous stained-glass window made by a local artist, serve as a marvelous setting for singers and musicians when the inn presents one of their holiday dinner concerts. Period light fixtures and silver are everywhere. When there is a chill in the air, fires crackle in all the fireplaces. The warmth of the atmosphere is complemented by a delightful and devoted staff. Everything reflects the enthusiastic dedication of Mary and Jerry Phillips, who could not possibly continue their labors if they did not love what they do.

The Phillipses have also created ways to maintain their involvement with music. Many professional musician friends visit the inn and perform "for their supper." And Jerry leads a well-trained choral group drawn from amateur singers from miles around, the Rittenhouse Chamber Singers, who perform at a series of dinner concerts from autumn to springtime. We have to imagine that whatever the long hours and the many difficulties, Mary and Jerry Phillips must really feel it is all worthwhile when the sun dims over the islands, the crackling fire dances over the Victorian wallpaper, every chair is filled with attentive guests, and the Rittenhouse Singers come down the cherry staircase joyously singing "Consider yourself . . . at home."

Old Rittenhouse Inn

BAYFIELD, WISCONSIN

Salsa Cheesecake
Schramsberg Vineyards Crémant Demi-Sec

Apple Consommé

Pork Chops in Cream
Robert Mondavi Winery Pinot Noir Reserve

White Chocolate Muffins

Crabapple Jelly

Watercress Salad

Snow Eggs in Red Raspberry Sauce
Robert Pecota Winery Muscato di Andrea

Wines selected by Gene Parrino

Salsa Cheesecake

There are many good fresh and canned varieties of salsa available in stores today; we use one from the El Paso Chile Company (100 Ruhlin Court, El Paso, Texas 79922). Mary says this cake freezes well. It is not a really tall cake, by the way, but small slices make an ideal appetizer.

Makes 1 9-inch cheesecake

> 2 tablespoons melted butter
> ½ cup very fine bread crumbs
> ¾ pound cream cheese
> ¼ pound Roquefort cheese
> 1 cup sour cream
> 2 tablespoons flour
> 1 cup grated Parmesan cheese
> ½ cup salsa
> 4 large eggs
>
> Leaves of fresh kale, fresh bunches of cilantro, minced cilantro, and minced parsley for garnish

Preheat the oven to 350°. Brush sides and bottom of a 9-inch springform pan with the melted butter and carefully coat with ¼ cup bread crumbs. Tap out excess.

In the bowl of an electric mixer, combine the cream cheese and Roquefort. Add sour cream, flour, Parmesan, and salsa, beating well between additions. Scrape bowl, turn motor to high, and add eggs one at a time. Scrape bowl and beat well to make certain all is blended properly. Pour batter into the prepared pan. Sprinkle with remaining bread crumbs.

Carefully wrap bottom of pan in foil and set in a larger baking dish filled with hot water. Or place pan in oven over another filled with hot water. (Cake will be a bit higher if baked in a water bath.) Bake 1¼ hours. Cool in oven, with door ajar, 1 hour.

Place 1 or 2 leaves of fresh kale on each serving plate. Top with a slice of cheesecake. Then garnish plate with cilantro and sprinkle with minced cilantro and parsley. Serve warm or at room temperature.

Apple Consommé

This can also be served cold; just add the club soda immediately before serving.

Serves 6

> 3 cups rosy pink apple juice*
> 3 cups rhubarb juice†
> 1 3-inch cinnamon stick
> 1 cup sugar
> ½ cup rosé wine
> ½ cup club soda
>
> Paper-thin red apple slices for garnish

*To make 3 cups rosy pink apple juice: Cut, core, and thinly slice 6 cups (about 2 pounds) of unpeeled red-skinned apples. Place in a 3-quart heavy-bottomed saucepan and add just enough water to barely cover. Bring to a boil over medium heat, reduce heat, and simmer until the apples are very tender, 30 to 60 minutes, depending on size of apples. Line a colander with several thicknesses of cheesecloth, rest prepared colander over a large bowl, pour contents of saucepan into colander, and let juices collect overnight. If more juice is needed, return pulp to a saucepan and add several cups of water. Boil ½ hour; then pour mixture back into the lined colander and let juices drain into a large bowl. Discard pulp if used twice; if cooked only once, you can use the pulp for applesauce by forcing it through a strainer to remove skin.
†To make rhubarb juice: Measure 6 cups of rhubarb that has been cut into 1-inch lengths and place in a 3–4-quart saucepan. Add just enough water to barely cover. Bring to a boil over medium heat, reduce heat, and simmer until the rhubarb is very tender, 30 to 60 minutes. Purée rhubarb and liquid in a food processor or blender. Line a colander with several thicknesses of cheesecloth, rest prepared colander over a large bowl, pour purée into colander, and let juices collect overnight. Use remaining pulp for rhubarb mousse or for a cake.

Mix apple and rhubarb juices in a 2-quart saucepan. Add cinnamon stick and sugar and simmer 15 minutes. Remove cinnamon stick; add wine and soda. Heat through. Ladle into heated soup plates and garnish with apple slices.

Pork Chops in Cream

Serves 6

> ½ teaspoon ground white pepper
> ½ teaspoon garlic powder
> ½ teaspoon dried thyme
> ½ teaspoon dried basil
> ½ teaspoon caraway seeds
> 6 2-inch-thick center-cut pork chops
> 4 tablespoons vegetable oil
> 1½ cups Beef Stock (see page 276)
> 1 tablespoon butter
> 1 tablespoon flour
> 3 tablespoons Cognac
> 4 tablespoons chopped scallions
> 3 cups finely chopped fresh mushrooms
> 1 cup light cream
> 3 large egg yolks
> Salt and white pepper to taste
>
> Fresh minced parsley and fresh minced chives for garnish

Preheat oven to 325°. Mix first 5 ingredients in a small bowl. Sprinkle pork chops with the seasoning and rub it in on both sides. Heat vegetable oil in a large skillet until it sizzles. Add the chops and sear until brown on both sides. Set skillet aside and reserve juices.

Arrange chops in a single layer in the bottom of a roasting pan. Pour beef stock over chops, cover pan, and bake in the preheated oven until fork-tender—at least 1½ hours. Save the beef stock in a tightly covered container in the freezer and use for soup or for making pork chops another time.

Melt butter in a small skillet over medium heat. Add flour and whisk until smooth. Continue stirring over medium heat for 2 minutes, then whisk in Cognac; set aside.

Reheat the skillet that was used to brown the chops. Then add scallions and mushrooms. Heat through, then add ½ cup cream. Cook slowly over medium heat until mushrooms yield some juice. Bring just to a boil. Slowly whisk in the flour-Cognac mixture until sauce is well combined and slightly thickened.

Combine egg yolks and remaining cream in a small bowl. Whisk well to blend. Temper by adding some hot sauce to the bowl, then slowly pour mixture back into the skillet containing the scallions and mushrooms, whisk-

ing steadily. Be careful not to curdle the egg yolks. Taste and adjust seasonings. Place a pork chop on each of six heated serving plates. Spoon sauce over and around chops. Dust with parsley and chives.

White Chocolate Muffins

Jerry makes these in huge quantities. While we were astonished at the large amount of baking powder he calls for, we found that it is really needed to add lightness to these muffins. They are delicious with Crabapple Jelly (page 162).

Makes 15 large muffins

> 2 large eggs
> ¼ cup vegetable oil
> ½ cup frozen orange-juice concentrate
> ½ cup milk
> 1¾ cups flour
> ¼ cup sugar
> 2 tablespoons baking powder
> ⅓ cup (2½ ounces) grated white chocolate
> ¼ cup ground almonds

*P*reheat oven to 400°. Combine first 4 ingredients in a medium-sized bowl and mix well.

Combine remaining ingredients in a large bowl and mix well. Make a well in the center and add the wet ingredients all at once. Stir just to blend. *Do not overmix.*

Fill well-oiled muffin tins about three-quarters full. Bake in preheated oven about 20 minutes, or until a toothpick inserted into the middle is dry and tops are golden brown.

Crabapple Jelly

There are so many wonderful fruits and berries growing outside Mary's door that she could be a full-time jelly maker. In season, she is in the kitchen before dawn to make certain that no berry goes to waste. You can buy these treasures at the inn, or order them by mail if you wish (Old Rittenhouse Inn, P.O. Box 584, Bayfield, Wisconsin 54814).

Makes 6 10-ounce jars

> 3 pounds fresh whole crabapples
> 6 cups cold water
> 1 package (1¾ ounces) powdered
>   pectin
> 6 cups sugar

Remove stems from crabapples. Place them in a large kettle and add the water. Bring to a rolling boil, reduce heat, and simmer until the apples split (about 15 minutes).

Line a colander with a double layer of cheesecloth and stand it over a large mixing bowl. Pour the contents of the kettle into this colander and let juices drip for several hours. This should yield 4 cups of juice.

Clean the kettle and return the juice to it. Add pectin and heat until juice begins to boil. Add sugar and stir constantly for 75 seconds.

Remove from heat and skim off foam with a spoon. Immediately pour into sterilized jars and seal according to manufacturer's directions.

Watercress Salad

Serves 6

> 1 head romaine lettuce, washed, dried,
>   and torn into bite-size pieces
> Fresh tomatoes, sliced
> 1 cucumber, washed and cut in
>   julienne strips
> 1 zucchini, scrubbed and cut in
>   julienne strips
> 1 green bell pepper, washed and finely
>   chopped
> 6 scallions, finely chopped
> 2 bunches fresh watercress, washed,
>   dried, tough stems removed
> Vinaigrette of your choice (Yoshi's
>   Creamy Lemon Vinaigrette, page
>   104, or Phoenix's Balsamic
>   Vinaigrette, page 48)
> Salt and freshly ground black pepper
>   to taste

Place romaine on each salad plate and arrange 3 slices of tomato, slightly overlapping, in the center of the romaine.

Top the tomatoes with alternating strips of cucumber and zucchini. Sprinkle with chopped green pepper and scallions. Surround the plate with the watercress.

Dress with vinaigrette, salt, and freshly ground pepper.

Snow Eggs
in Red Raspberry Sauce

Makes 12 to 14 snow eggs (6–7 servings)

1 tablespoon unflavored gelatin
¼ cup cold water
1 cup boiling water
¾ cup superfine sugar
¼ cup strained lemon juice
1 tablespoon grated lemon rind
3 large egg whites
½ pint heavy cream
   About 2 tablespoons walnut or
      hazelnut oil
16 ounces top-quality raspberry jelly
½ cup honey

   Whole fresh raspberries and mint
      leaves for garnish

*I*n a medium-sized mixing bowl, sprinkle gelatin over cold water and let stand 5 minutes. Add boiling water, sugar, lemon juice, and rind. Blend well. Chill in refrigerator, stirring occasionally, until mixture thickens (about 30 minutes). Then beat with electric mixer until fluffy.

Beat egg whites until stiff and shiny. Then, in another bowl, beat cream until stiff. Gently fold both into gelatin mixture.

Brush muffin tins with oil. Using two large spoons, form the cream mixture into 12 egg shapes. Place in muffin tins and chill at least several hours.

Meanwhile, prepare raspberry sauce: Combine jelly and honey and heat just until softened. Do not overheat. Let cool to room temperature.

Ladle a small amount of raspberry sauce in each of 6 wide soup plates, and top with 2 chilled eggs. Garnish with raspberries and mint.

L'Étoile

MADISON, WISCONSIN

Located on the second floor of an office building across from the state capitol, L'Étoile has, since 1976, offered a seasonal menu that is completely dependent upon what is fine and fresh. It is a restaurant that does not distort the ingredients or overly manipulate them. It is a restaurant that celebrates its roots and those of its neighbors. Owner Odessa Piper has led it steadfastly upstream, against the tide of fast food, against the preference for frozen fish and pre-prepared sauces, struggling to educate her constituency and to develop a broader range of purveyors. And she is winning. Yesterday she was ahead of her time; today she represents what is best about the Midwest. And her fame is spreading.

The menu changes daily; the only constant is the note at the bottom identifying the wonderful table butter as being produced locally by Bleu Mont Dairy from a Swiss culture. Among the appetizers are a pâté, several soups, and some fish and pasta. In autumn, the kitchen preserves duck and goose in the traditional French confit. The well-stocked larder enables them to offer duck confit with Wisconsin Brie on toasted garlic croutons—moist chunks of duck, redolent of herbs and garlic, marry well with the creamy, nutty Brie.

Or the duck confit might be served with buckwheat pasta and accented with fresh rosemary. We were also intrigued with the chicken terrine garnished with pear chutney and mustard seed. With a large Scandinavian population in Wisconsin, it is not surprising to find gravlax on the menu with some frequency. Briny fresh fillets of salmon are cured with a mixture of salt and sugar, then packed with dill for several days to absorb its flavor. From silky carrot with hazelnut butter to corn chowder with shiitake mushrooms, soups are highly creative and tasty. The variety and quality of ingredients which come from some of the nation's finest farms are extraordinary. Fantome Farm in Ridgeway, Wisconsin, produces phenomenal goat cheese, which is showcased magnificently at L'Étoile. Whether marinated in some extra-virgin olive oil and herbs, spread between two sautéed slices of eggplant, or stuffed in sweet red peppers baked and sprinkled with pecans, the chèvre is one of the highlights of the menu. Salad, however one has it, is of the freshest of greens, seemingly minutes from the garden. When tomatoes are in season, thick slices rich in fragrant flavor are served, simply drizzled with olive oil and sprinkled with herbs.

165

The real jewels here, however, are the entrees. Farm-fresh chicken, untouched by steroids and chemicals, might be roasted and served with wild morels from surrounding woodlands, or skinned, sautéed, and garnished with a cream sauce studded with fabled Door County cherries and local black walnuts. Trout comes right out of ponds just a few miles down the road. Northern pike is quickly sautéed and served on a bed of spinach, garnished with Moroccan olives and sun-dried tomatoes. Beef and lamb are from farms nearby; game might be local or obtained through a purveyor in Chicago. Odessa Piper will buy only foods that are free of chemicals and additives. And while the emphasis is on regional products, L'Étoile offers superb ocean fish and shellfish, always in keeping with her demanding standards.

When we first went to Wisconsin, so fabled as a dairy region, we expected to see cows tethered at every milepost! We just knew that there were probably wonderful cheeses being made that never left the state. We must applaud Odessa Piper for doing her best to promote these treasures. Besides the superb chèvre, we had several other varieties, along with crisp apples and wonderful walnut bread, served as a separate course following dinner. Then we were ready for dessert. Delicate crème caramel, bourbon-and-peach ice cream, and decadent chocolate cake are all beautifully made from superb ingredients. Accompanied by a glass of dessert wine, and followed by the best coffee in Wisconsin, dessert is the sublime end to this celebration of our nation's bounty.

L'Étoile has a setting that encourages leisurely dining. The ceiling is two stories high in the front; the walls are exposed brick stripped of years of paint and plaster. Tall windows look out on a view unsurpassed except by a few rare restaurants—the state capitol of Wisconsin, with its elegant dome. Day or night, it is a beautiful sight. Fortunately, Odessa Piper is sensitive to the environment and has created a simple space that evokes feelings of peace and serenity. Colors are soft and muted; a highly architectural suspended grillwork establishes the illusion of a lower ceiling toward the back of the restaurant. A cozy bar in the back welcomes visitors with its comfortable chairs.

Odessa Piper has worked hard for her dream. While she has no formal training in food, her New England childhood revolved around celebrating the land's bounty and sharing it at the table. Discovering the wealth available in Wisconsin's farmer's markets, she determined to develop a restaurant that would act as its proper showcase. Jim Spaeth, chef since 1987, is her match for enthusiasm and dedication. Trained in food service at Western Wisconsin's Technical Institute, he honed his skills in Denver working for Michael McCarty and Jimmy Schmidt at the Rattlesnake Club. He is highly skilled in the kitchen and sensitive to the fact that fine raw materials need only simple enhancements. There is real artistry in his simplicity. One story that must be shared is that of the first annual benefit dinner for the Dane County Farmer's Market, held at L'Étoile in July 1988. Among the guests that night were some of the growers themselves. For many, it was the first time that they had seen their products married with chèvre, or fine Italian olive oils, or garnished with edible flowers. For many, it was the first time they had tasted a fish served rare or a duck confit. For all, it was a feast of love and celebration as they shared the fruits of their labors together. And this is why we applaud L'Étoile.

L'Étoile

MADISON, WISCONSIN

Baked Chèvre with
Marinated Mushrooms and Olive Paste

Flora Springs Wine Co. Sauvignon Blanc

Capitol Beer-and-Cheddar Soup

Charles F. Shaw Vineyard and Winery Gamay Beaujolais

Free-Range Chicken with Door County Cherries

Amity Vineyards (Oregon) Pinot Noir Reserve

Spring Salad

R. H. Phillips Vineyards Chenin Blanc

Walnut Bread

R. H. Phillips Vineyards Cabernet Sauvignon

Chèvre Coeur à la Crème
with Raspberry Sauce

Quady Essencia

Wines selected by John Giguirre

Baked Chèvre with Marinated Mushrooms and Olive Paste

Serves 6

1½ pounds chèvre
Kosher salt

MARINADE

2 cups extra-virgin olive oil
1 tablespoon fresh rosemary,
    or 2 teaspoons dried
1 tablespoon dried thyme
1 tablespoon dried basil
3 bay leaves
4 garlic cloves, peeled
10 whole black peppercorns

3 ounces lemon juice
⅔ cup plus ¼ cup extra-virgin olive oil
3 garlic cloves, peeled and bruised
    Salt and freshly ground black pepper
        to taste
2 bay leaves
1 pound small cultivated mushrooms,
    stemmed
2 cups pitted Niçoise olives
    Freshly cracked peppercorns to taste
24 ¼-inch-thick slices French bread
1 large clove garlic, peeled and cut in
    half
6 leaves Boston lettuce

Sprigs of rosemary for garnish

*D*ivide the chèvre into 6 4-ounce portions. Roll each portion in kosher salt. Cut 6 10-inch squares of cheesecloth and make 3 packages out of the 6 squares. Put 2 portions of chèvre in each package, tie with household string, and hang over a drain or pan for 24 hours. Remove chèvre from cheesecloth and place in a deep container that will hold all the pieces easily. Pour in olive oil to cover; sprinkle with herbs, garlic, and peppercorns. Set aside. This can marinate at room temperature all day, or in the refrigerator for at least 2 days. (After cheese is removed, this oil can be used for salad dressing or as a sauce for vegetables.) To serve, put 1 piece of cheese into each of six 4–6-ounce ramekins. Set aside.

Mix together lemon juice, ⅓ cup olive oil, garlic cloves, salt, pepper, and bay leaves in a saucepan. Bring to a boil, then simmer over low heat 10 minutes. Add mushrooms and simmer 5 to 10 minutes. Let cool in liquid and set aside.

Put olives in food processor and, with motor running, slowly add ⅓ cup olive oil and purée into a paste. Add freshly cracked peppercorns. Set aside.

Shortly before serving time, arrange slices of French bread in a single layer on a baking sheet. Lightly toast in the oven. Then brush with ¼ cup olive oil and rub with garlic clove. Sprinkle with salt and pepper. Return to oven 3 to 5 minutes to blend flavors.

Bake chèvre in hot oven 10 minutes. Set

ramekins on six serving plates. Distribute drained mushrooms among lettuce "cups" and set on plate. Add 4 warm slices of toast per person, a large dollop of olive paste, garnish with rosemary, and serve. We think the best way to eat this is to put some of the chèvre and some of the olive paste on each slice of toast and to eat the mushrooms separately, alternating a bite of toast, cheese, and olives with a bite of mushroom.

Capitol Beer-and-Cheddar Soup

Serves 6

¼ pound unsalted butter, softened
2 tablespoons Pommery mustard
1 12-ounce can beer
⅓ cup chopped shallots
1 tablespoon minced garlic
2 quarts heavy cream
¾ pound aged Wisconsin Cheddar, grated
Salt and freshly ground white pepper to taste

*P*ut butter into bowl of electric mixer and beat with paddle until smooth. Add mustard and beat well. Scrape mixture from bowl and spread on wax paper. With the paper still wrapped around the mound, roll and shape mixture into a cylinder that is about 1 inch in diameter. Seal the ends of the wax paper tightly and chill thoroughly.

Combine beer, shallots, garlic, and cream in a heavy saucepan; cook over medium heat until almost a thick soup. Slowly add the grated cheese and stir until it is completely melted. If soup needs more thickening, just cook a bit longer over low heat, stirring often. Strain.

Add salt and white pepper to taste. Ladle into heated soup plates. Garnish with ¼-inch slices of the mustard butter placed in the center of each serving.

Free-Range Chicken with Door County Cherries

L'Étoile uses dried tart cherries from Door County in Wisconsin, but thanks to American Spoon Foods (P.O. Box 566, Petosky, Michigan 49770), tart dried Michigan cherries are available in specialty food stores across the country. This delicious chicken dish is even better when served with Goodfellow's Wild-Rice Compote (see page 202) and asparagus garnished with lemon butter.

Serves 6

½ cup dried tart cherries
½ cup Kirsch
½ cup black walnuts
3 12-ounce skinless and boneless free-range chicken breasts
⅔ cup flour
4 tablespoons clarified butter
2 tablespoons minced shallots
2 cups heavy cream
2 tablespoons chopped fresh parsley
Salt and freshly ground black pepper to taste

Whole chives for garnish

Soak dried cherries in 2 tablespoons Kirsch.

Place the walnuts on an ungreased cookie sheet and toast about 3 inches below a hot broiler about 1 minute. Stir walnuts well and put back under the broiler. Watch carefully and make certain that the nuts brown but do not burn. The whole process will take less than 4 minutes. Remove walnuts from the cookie sheet, place in a large strainer or sieve, and toss until skins are loosened. Carefully remove nuts from strainer and set aside. Discard skins.

Divide chicken breasts in half and dredge in flour. Heat butter in a large skillet and sauté breasts about 2 minutes a side (another minute if the breasts are thick). Remove chicken from skillet and keep warm.

Add shallots, walnuts, cherries, and remaining Kirsch to the skillet. Flame the Kirsch, then add the cream and simmer until sauce is slightly thickened. Add parsley, salt, and pepper. Place a half chicken breast on each of six heated serving plates. Spoon sauce over the chicken. Garnish with chives.

Spring Salad

We like to serve L'Ètoile's walnut bread (see below) sliced thinly and lightly toasted along with this course if we include Brie with the salad. Otherwise, we serve walnut toast and a few cheeses following the salad, using the same plate in order to get the remaining vinaigrette mixed in with the cheese and bread.

Serves 6

½ cup nasturtium vinegar
1 cup extra-virgin olive oil
2 tablespoons finely chopped shallots

1 teaspoon finely minced garlic
¼ teaspoon salt
   Coarsely ground black pepper to taste
35 nasturtium blossoms
1 head radicchio
1 head Bibb lettuce
1 bunch watercress or arugula
1 head red oak-leaf lettuce
2 cups asparagus tips, blanched and refreshed in cold water
1 pound Wisconsin Brie, cut into 6 or 12 wedges (optional)
1 cup red radishes, julienned
1 cup cucumber, peeled, seeded, and julienned

*P*ut the vinegar into the bowl of a food processor or blender. With motor running, slowly add olive oil until all is incorporated and a stable emulsion is established. Whisk in shallots, garlic, salt, and pepper. Remove petals from 5 nasturtium blossoms, coarsely chop petals, and add them to the vinaigrette.

Carefully wash remaining nasturtiums and greens; spin greens dry. Set nasturtiums on paper towels to drip dry. Toss greens and nasturtiums with vinaigrette and distribute among six large salad plates. Arrange asparagus, Brie, radishes, and cucumber decoratively on top of the greens. Grind a bit more pepper over salad and serve.

Walnut Bread

To serve thin slices of walnut bread with cheese has been quite popular in France over the last five or six years. We have sampled many loaves and have tried for years to replicate them in our kitchen. We feel that this particular recipe is truly delightful, and we now manage to keep a few loaves of it in our freezer most of the time. And on a cold Sunday evening, we enjoy bowls of Capitol Beer-and-Cheddar Soup (see page 169) and thick slices of toasted Walnut Bread. That's all you need!

Makes 3 9 × 5-inch loaves

    2 cups milk
    2 tablespoons active dry yeast
4 to 5 cups all-purpose flour
    1 cup rye flour
    2 tablespoons sugar
    1 tablespoon salt
    ¼ teaspoon freshly ground black pepper
    ½ cup walnut oil
    8 ounces chopped walnuts
    2 tablespoons finely chopped fresh rosemary

In a medium saucepan, heat milk to 105°. Put yeast in a small bowl, pour in ½ cup warm milk, and set in a warm place until mixture begins to froth and bubble, about 15 minutes.

Combine flours, sugar, salt, and pepper in a large mixing bowl. In another bowl, mix remaining milk, walnut oil, and yeast mixture. Combine wet ingredients with flour mixture. Mix until well moistened. Stir in walnuts and rosemary. Knead in the bowl of an electric mixer with dough hook for 10 minutes, or by hand on a lightly floured board until smooth.

Put dough into a large, well-oiled bowl, cover with plastic wrap, and let rise in a warm place until doubled in volume, about 3 hours. Then divide dough into thirds. To shape loaves, pat each third into a flat oval, fold in half, turn over so that seam side is down, tuck ends under, and form into a flat loaf shape.

Put into well-greased loaf pans. Cover pans with plastic and let rise in a warm place 1 hour. Bake in a preheated 375° oven for 45 to 55 minutes.

Chèvre Coeur à la Crème with Raspberry Sauce

Serves 8

    12 ounces cream cheese
    12 ounces mild chèvre
    ¼ cup confectioner's sugar
    1 cup heavy cream
    2 12-ounce packages frozen raspberries, thawed
    2 teaspoons fresh lemon juice
    ⅔ cup sugar

    Fresh raspberries for garnish

One day before serving, combine cheeses and sugar in food processor and purée until smooth. Add heavy cream and process until thoroughly incorporated.

Line an 8-inch coeur à la crème mold with two thicknesses of slightly dampened cheesecloth. Fill the mold with cheese mixture and set inside a shallow pan to catch drippings. Cover and refrigerate 24 hours.

Purée the frozen raspberries in a blender or food processor and, over a small bowl, pass through a fine strainer to separate the juice from the seeds. Whisk in lemon juice and sugar. Ladle into an attractive serving vessel.

Unmold dessert on a serving platter and garnish with fresh berries. Serve the raspberry sauce on the side.

River Wildlife

KOHLER, WISCONSIN

Whenever we hear the term "heartland food" we think of River Wildlife. It is unlike any other restaurant we have visited. No chrome or polished granite here. River Wildlife is a log cabin deep in the woods, accessible only by footpath and invisible from the road. Kohler, Wisconsin, a couple of hours north of Milwaukee and just west of Sheboygan, is an attractive town, the home of the huge Kohler Company, manufacturer of plumbing fixtures and owner of River Wildlife. The Kohler Museum is here, and so is the American Club, a company-owned resort situated in a beautiful cluster of Tudor-style buildings. Originally built as a dormitory for the company's immigrant employees, it is now an artfully renovated complex offering fine dining, beautiful rooms, and outstanding recreational facilities. A private hunting, fishing, and dining club, the nearby River Wildlife serves its superlative meals not only to lucky members but to anyone staying at the resort who wishes to purchase a daily membership and dine in a truly bucolic setting.

The food writer Bill Rice told us not to miss this place. He was so enthusiastic that we really worried as we drove there about being disappointed, since our expectations were so high. The country road, splashed with the russets and golds of autumn, drew us farther into the woods. We parked the car and crunched along a narrow path through the forest until we came to a wonderful log cabin with a huge stone chimney. The scent of dried leaves commingled with the welcoming fragrances of a crackling fire and baking bread. Ah, heartland!

The menu appears on a chalkboard near the fireplace; it changes daily, according to the availability of fresh products from nearby farms, forests, and waters. A rich autumn soup is often made from cauliflower, further enriched by a generous helping of Maytag blue cheese, and punctuated with marjoram and thyme and a zip of Tabasco. The chill of winter is banished by a steaming bowl of smoked turkey and sweet-potato soup, with generous additions of provolone cheese and spicy garlic sausage. Skilled hands in the kitchen make heavily saged croutons for the garnish. Another season might be welcomed with a delicate berry soup, or one from spring's first mushrooms. All the soups are hearty, filled with a complexity of flavors reflecting the bounty of surrounding lands. With chunks of warm, freshly made wheatberry French bread and gobs of fresh Wisconsin butter, one could be fully satisfied after the appetizer.

Fish is usually right out of nearby streams and lakes. Gently battered, pan-fried trout is irresistible; Lake Michigan whitefish is sweet and delicious; almond-and-millet-coated walleye with a Brie sauce is extraordinary. Salads are rarely commonplace. The woods and fields are combed daily for edible wild greens, flowers, nuts, and berries used in the salads and entrees. We, who are happy with tasty, simple greens, especially enjoy a julienne of smoked chicken combined with sliced green apples, purple onions, greens, garlic, and mustard vinaigrette.

Game also is outstanding here. Pheasant and venison have never tasted better. Whether roasted and sauced with dried berries or served in a rich, flavorful stew, these meats are always moist and succulent. Duck comes in many guises, but our favorite is the luscious lunchtime duck hash with pan-fried eggs, accompanied by a toasted Cheddar-and-beer brioche. Kohler beef, bred to be low in cholesterol, is often on the menu. But we prefer the locally bred veal, and still rave about a splendid veal roast in a spicy ginger sauce, accompanied by light-as-air potato dumplings. And speaking of accompaniments, they are exactly what we think of as "heartland"—a hearty pilaf of wheatberry, rice, and barley, or buttery mashed potatoes, or chunks of seasonal vegetables quickly sautéed and sprinkled with fresh herbs and nuts. Pies are out of this world, and we scraped the chilled pewter plate clean of every crumb of rich brownie served with homemade vanilla ice cream. The restaurant's cheesecakes are the equal of the best we have tasted anywhere.

River Wildlife serves dinner only on weekends, but it does offer lunch during the week. Thick sandwiches on homemade breads might feature local Wisconsin cheeses as well as meats smoked right behind the cabin. Whatever the meal, the two-story log cabin is a wonderful setting for hearty dining. A spacious reception room with a huge fireplace and comfortable chairs is just the place for a pre-dinner drink. Denim-dressed servers make guests feel right at home. All pretensions are left in the car. A glass of good wine, a crackling fire, the occasional fragrance of meats roasting in the ovens, all set the proper mood.

Members of the staff describe their kitchen style as "kamikaze cookin'," and with only a few exceptions, no recipes are written down. Never formally trained as chefs, the kitchen staff has learned to develop their senses of taste and smell and to trust their instincts. Frequent trips to fine restaurants in the Midwest have further developed their palates. Aina Suthard, manager at River Wildlife for about ten years, boasts that her very young staff has not become inhibited by formal training. "We've never learned," she says, "what we can't do." The log they keep is fascinating reading. It really shows the enormous creativity of the staff. We long to try the Cognac-and-hazelnut-battered onion rings and cranberry mint lamb shanks. How about pheasant Stroganoff with wild mushrooms, or drunken rabbit, or pork tenderloin with blue cheese, Swiss cheese, and pecan stuffing and Cognac-onion gravy? For lunch we would love the grilled pumpkin-battered sandwich with ham, Granny Smith apples, and Brie. Shari Peterson-Havlik, Mary Bayens, Suzanne Majerus, Sandra Wassink, Kathy Schwinn, and their fearless leader, Aina Suthard—here's to you! Don't ever take a cooking class!

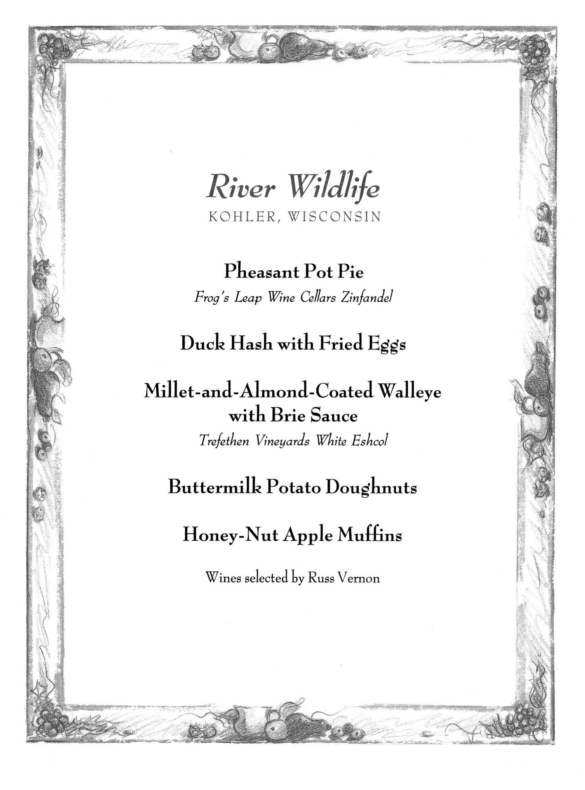

River Wildlife

KOHLER, WISCONSIN

Pheasant Pot Pie
Frog's Leap Wine Cellars Zinfandel

Duck Hash with Fried Eggs

Millet-and-Almond-Coated Walleye
with Brie Sauce
Trefethen Vineyards White Eshcol

Buttermilk Potato Doughnuts

Honey-Nut Apple Muffins

Wines selected by Russ Vernon

Pheasant Pot Pie

Serves 12

2 pheasants, about 2–2½ pounds each
   Salt and freshly ground black pepper
    to taste
2 quarts Chicken Stock (see page 276)
2 cups flour, sifted
1½ sticks unsalted butter, chilled, cut
    into pieces
1 large egg
1 tablespoon heavy cream
2 pounds bulk pork sausage
6 tablespoons butter
¼ cup plus 2 tablespoons flour
1½ pounds carrots, scraped and cut into
    1-inch chunks
24 pearl onions, dipped into boiling
    water, drained, and peeled
8 celery stalks, cut into 1-inch pieces
2 cups half-and-half
   Salt and coarsely ground black
    pepper to taste
2 teaspoons dried thyme
1 teaspoon dried marjoram
½ teaspoon dried rosemary
½ teaspoon poultry seasoning

Remove giblets from pheasants if they are still inside. Rub pheasants with salt and pepper. Place side by side in a 5-quart Dutch oven. If giblets are available, scatter them around the pheasants. Add the stock and bring to a boil over medium heat. Cover pot, reduce heat, and simmer 1 to 1½ hours, or until the pheasants are tender.

Meanwhile, combine sifted flour and butter in the bowl of a food processor. Using the metal blade, pulse on and off 15 times. Then add egg and cream, and pulse 10 more times. Turn mixture out on a pastry board and use the heel of your palm to rub a tablespoon at a time away from you to evenly distribute the butter. When all the dough has been blended, use a pastry scraper or spatula to gather it up, then press it into a ball. Wrap in plastic and chill for an hour.

When pheasants are done, remove them from the pot and set aside to cool just enough to handle. Strain braising liquid and skim to remove fat. When pheasants have cooled, remove meat and cut into small chunks. Reserve in a large bowl.

Sauté sausage meat in a large skillet over medium heat until the pink is gone and all fat is released, about 8 to 10 minutes. When sausage is cooked, drain and discard fat. Combine cooked sausage with pheasant meat.

Then make a roux by melting butter in a small skillet over medium heat. Slowly whisk in flour and blend well. Lower heat and continue to cook, whisking constantly, until flour mixture is a nutty brown. Set aside.

Pour skimmed stock into the Dutch oven and bring to a boil over medium heat. Add carrots, onions, and celery, and cook vegetables in stock until tender, about 12 minutes. Add half-and-half, seasonings, pheasant, and sausage. Slowly add roux, stirring between additions. You may not need to add it all. Simmer 5 minutes and add remaining roux if mixture has not thickened. Adjust seasonings if necessary. Pour into a pretty 4–5-quart overproof ceramic, enamel, or cast-iron casserole.

Preheat oven to 425°. Remove pastry from refrigerator 10 to 15 minutes prior to rolling. Lightly flour a work surface, then, using a floured rolling pin, roll and turn the pastry, adding more flour as needed. Keep rolling the pastry until it is the right size and shape for your casserole. The crust should be ⅛ to 1/16 inch thick. Carefully roll it up onto the rolling pin; then roll it back out over the casserole. Trim and flute edges. Cut some decorative vents on top. Bake at 425° until top is brown and done, about 20 to 30 minutes.

Duck Hash with Fried Eggs

If this is served as part of a larger buffet, it ought to be enough for 12 people. Just fry enough eggs for each person to have one.

Serves 6

> 2 4–5-pound ducks
>   Salt and freshly ground black pepper
>   to taste
> 3 pounds potatoes, peeled
>   Up to 2 sticks butter
> 1 cup green bell pepper, seeded,
>   deveined, and coarsely chopped
> 1 cup red bell pepper, seeded,
>   deveined, and coarsely chopped
> 1 cup carrots, scraped and coarsely
>   chopped
> 2 stalks celery, chopped
> 1 tablespoon poultry seasoning
> 1 tablespoon Worcestershire sauce
> 2 to 3 tablespoons margarine, oil, or butter
>   6 eggs
>
>   Fresh herbs, including chopped
>   parsley, for garnish

*P*reheat oven to 375°. Rub ducks with salt and pepper. Prick the skin with a sharp trussing pin so that the fat will release more easily, and roast, breast side up, in preheated oven

1½ to 2¼ hours, or until the leg bone turns easily and the meat is tender. Remove from the oven and let cool; when cool enough to handle, remove the duck meat with skin attached and shred into bite-sized pieces. Set aside.

Cook potatoes in boiling water until almost done. Cut into ½-inch dice. In a large cast-iron skillet, melt 1 stick of butter over medium heat; add potatoes, peppers, carrots, and celery, and sauté until peppers are tender. Add more butter as necessary.

Add duck meat and seasoning and Worcestershire sauce and mix very well. Add more of remaining butter if needed. Fry until a crispy crust develops on the bottom side of the hash.

While the hash is frying, melt 2 tablespoons of margarine, butter, or oil in another large skillet over medium heat. When skillet is hot, break 3 eggs, one at a time and away from one another, into the hot pan. Lower heat and fry eggs until edges are crispy. If you wish, you can tilt the skillet as eggs are frying and baste yolks with some of the hot fat, using a large cooking spoon. When eggs are done, remove from skillet with a spatula and hold on a heated platter in a warm place. Repeat process for remaining eggs.

It is nice to serve the hash right from the skillet, garnishing the top with herbs and chopped parsley. Serve a fried egg on top of each portion.

Millet-and-Almond-Coated Walleye with Brie Sauce

This is another dish that will serve up to 12 if it is part of a larger buffet.

Serves 6

2 large eggs, beaten
2 tablespoons milk
1 cup millet, toasted or pan-browned
1 cup finely chopped almonds, toasted or pan-browned
1 cup bread crumbs
2 tablespoons flour
¼ teaspoon garlic powder
1½ tablespoons seasoned salt
2 teaspoons freshly ground black pepper
2½ pounds fresh walleye fillets
3 cups clam juice
1½ cups Chicken Stock (see page 276)
½ cup dry white wine
Juice of ½ lemon
1 clove garlic, finely minced
1 cup heavy cream
½ cup buttermilk
8 ounces Brie, rind removed, cut into small cubes
1 tablespoon flour
1 stick unsalted butter, softened
Zest of 1 lemon
⅓ cup watercress leaves
Up to 1½ cups vegetable oil

Combine eggs and milk in wide bowl; blend well. Combine millet, almonds, crumbs, flour, and seasonings in a wide bowl and mix well. Dip walleye fillets first into the egg mixture and then into the grain mixture and coat well. Let fillets rest on a rack or on wax paper.

Combine clam juice, stock, wine, lemon juice, and garlic in large saucepan and boil 8 minutes. Add heavy cream and boil another 8 minutes. Add buttermilk and reduce heat. Slowly stir in Brie, a bit at a time. In a small dish, mix 1 tablespoon flour with 2 tablespoons butter until well blended. Stir this into cheese sauce to thicken. Continue to simmer the sauce. If not thick enough, mix more flour with some of the remaining butter and repeat. Add remaining butter, a bit at a time. Stir in lemon zest and watercress. Keep warm.

Pour oil ⅛ inch deep in the bottom of a large cast-iron skillet and fry fillets until brown (about 4 minutes); turn and brown on other side. Drain well. Arrange fillets on serving plates and ladle sauce over each fillet.

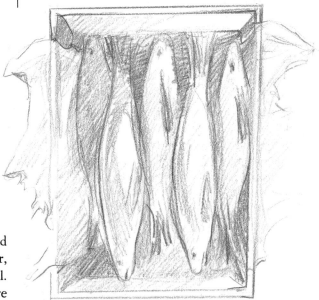

Buttermilk Potato Doughnuts

Makes about 2 to 3 dozen

3 large eggs
1 cup sugar
1 teaspoon vanilla extract
⅓ cup cream
⅔ cup buttermilk
1 cup mashed potatoes
1 teaspoon baking soda
1 teaspoon baking powder
1 teaspoon salt
½ teaspoon ground nutmeg
4 to 5 cups flour
Vegetable oil
Confectioner's sugar

*B*eat eggs well in a large mixing bowl. Blend in sugar, vanilla, cream, and buttermilk. Add mashed potatoes, then dry ingredients, and blend. Turn out on a lightly floured surface and knead lightly. Place dough in a large mixing bowl, cover tightly with plastic, and chill 2 hours.

Heat about 4 inches of oil in deep fat fryer to 350–360°. Roll dough on lightly floured surface to about ½ inch thick. Using a floured doughnut cutter, cut into doughnut shapes. Lightly knead scraps and holes together and roll and cut again. Fry about 4 at a time. Turn often and remove when golden (about 5 minutes). Drain on paper towels and sprinkle with sugar.

Honey-Nut Apple Muffins

Makes about 2 dozen

4 cups flour
2 tablespoons baking powder
1 teaspoon salt
2 large eggs
¾ cup honey
2 cups milk
½ cup vegetable oil
2 cups peeled and chopped apples
½ cup chopped walnuts or hazelnuts

TOPPING
1 cup dark brown sugar, firmly packed
½ cup sugar
¼ cup flour
5 tablespoons butter, melted

*P*reheat oven to 375°. Mix flour, baking powder, and salt together in a large mixing bowl.

In a medium-sized mixing bowl, beat together eggs, honey, milk, and oil. Stir in apples and nuts.

Add egg mixture to dry ingredients and gently mix just to combine. *Do not overmix.* Fill well-buttered muffin tins about three-quarters full.

Combine topping ingredients in a small mixing bowl and distribute over the batter. Bake in preheated oven 15 to 20 minutes, or until a toothpick inserted into the middle is dry and tops are lightly browned.

D'Amico Cucina

MINNEAPOLIS, MINNESOTA

Timing may be everything. We are convinced that the celebration of the hearty farm food of the Midwest that began ever so slowly in the mid-eighties made the folks in Minneapolis receptive to other countries' farm-rooted kitchen traditions—especially to the earthy, robust country food of Italy. From its inception in the fall of 1987, people have flocked to D'Amico Cucina, the elegantly contemporary restaurant in the Butler Square Building, a splendidly renovated old warehouse. We wish the D'Amico brothers had stayed in their hometown and opened this restaurant in Cleveland. But to the good fortune of the folks in the Twin Cities, Larry and Richard D'Amico moved to Minneapolis a few years ago and began to shake up the food scene there. It wasn't long before the brothers came to the attention of national food writers as well.

Don't look for spaghetti and meatballs here! The eggplant and red bell pepper terrine is as delicious as it is beautiful, punctuated with a small amount of sun-dried tomato sauce. The venison carpaccio is tender and flavorful, and makes a beautiful presentation on a faux-marble plate, drizzled with pale green mayonnaise and garnished with edible flowers and sprigs of herbs. Gnocchi are always on the menu; we especially enjoy them heavily powdered with a mince of herbs. Risotto, prepared only by special order, is perfectly al dente and creamy with cheese and stock. While the variety changes daily, we are partial to the one studded with dried currants, which is remarkably toothsome. Ravioli and all pastas are made daily. Orecchiette with onion, pancetta, and peas and whole-wheat spaghetti with lamb ragoût are just a few of the dishes that might be available on the frequently changing menu.

We enjoyed one of the most heavenly fish dishes of our lives at D'Amico Cucina, thanks to chef Greg Westcott. Imagine a thick fillet of red snapper delicately seasoned with lemon and garlic, wrapped in paper-thin slices of eggplant, sautéed until the eggplant is a rich nutty brown, and graced with a flavorful tomato-orange sauce. What a treat! And, as in an Italian *cucina,* this kitchen usually offers several roasted meats. Pan-roasted venison with a slightly sweet Valpolicella sauce is outstanding, as are pork loin with Gorgonzola sauce and lamb loin with garlic mashed potatoes. Sautéed medallions of pork are splendid, with their silky Marsala cream sauce. Don't miss the accompaniments, either. We like the risotto cakes with porcini mushrooms or basil and pine-nut bread pudding. And if you happen to see sautéed spinach, rich with garlic, on the menu, grab it.

We doubt that farm food is often presented as beautifully as it is here. Fabulous faux-marble china in black or rust certainly enhances even the simplest dish. And a lavish use of herbs and flowers makes it even more appealing. But don't think that the inventive presentation is meant to distract attention from ordinary food. While the dishes are richly flavored, they are never heavy. Portions are very Midwestern, so you won't go away hungry. And if you have room for dessert, be sure to try the chocolate bread pudding—it is a must. There is also a fine wine list, and the excellent staff will guide you through it if necessary. This is a fine place to learn, since the selection is broad and the prices fair.

Larry and Richard D'Amico grew up in the restaurant business just outside Cleveland, where D'Amico's is still flourishing in the hands of their father. Wanting to build their own business and attracted by the opportunities offered in a revitalized Minneapolis, they moved in the early eighties. Today they also own Primavera, another fine restaurant, and a catering business in their new community. Their consulting business also has them involved in numerous restaurant projects around the country. Larry is responsible for the kitchen side of the business. It is he who brought Greg Westcott to D'Amico Cucina. Richard D'Amico designed the restaurant, and he created a space that is at once sophisticated and warm. Thanks to the inventive menu, delicious food, and outstanding service, D'Amico Cucina is an all-occasion place. From just a dinner out to a special celebration, from a business meeting to simply a glass of wine and a snack, this is a place you will really love. We do!

D'Amico Cucina
MINNEAPOLIS, MINNESOTA

Red Snapper Wrapped in Eggplant with Tomato-Orange Sauce
St. Francis Winery Merlot

Risotto Cakes with Porcini Sauce
Sebastiani Vineyards Zinfandel

Sautéed Pork Medallions with Marsala Cream Sauce

Basil and Pine-Nut Bread Pudding
Duckhorn Vineyards Cabernet Sauvignon

Chocolate Bread Pudding with Red Wine Sauce

Wines selected by Dr. Leonard Calabrese

Red Snapper Wrapped in Eggplant with Tomato-Orange Sauce

This dish does not require much in the way of accompaniments. We do, however, like to serve some flash-grilled radicchio as a nice counterpoint.

Serves 6

> 6 tablespoons unsalted butter, softened
> 2 cloves garlic, finely minced
> Zest of 1 lemon
> Olive oil
> 3 large, long eggplants, peeled
> Salt and freshly ground black pepper to taste
> 6 4-ounce red snapper fillets, cut thick and square
> ½ cup tomato juice
> 1½ cups strained purée of fresh tomatoes
> ½ cup fresh orange juice
> 1 tablespoon finely julienned orange zest
> ½ cup white wine
> 1 teaspoon minced shallots
> ½ pound unsalted butter, cut into small pieces
> 4 tablespoons clarified butter
>
> Nasturtium blossoms for garnish

Combine the first 3 ingredients in a small mixing bowl. Beat well and roll into a log. Wrap in wax paper and chill while you complete the remainder of the recipe.

Preheat the broiler and put a rack just below the heating element. Rub two cookie sheets with olive oil. Slice the eggplant as thinly as possible, arrange the slices close together on the sheets, wipe the eggplant with more olive oil, and sprinkle with some salt and pepper. Put one sheet at a time under the hot broiler for about 1 minute, turn, and broil the other side for a few seconds. Repeat with remaining eggplant until all the slices are done.

On a sheet of wax paper, arrange a few overlapping slices of cooked eggplant to make a "sheet" that will wrap around the edges of each fish fillet. Place a fillet in the middle, and top fish with 1 tablespoon of the garlic-lemon butter. Top with more overlapping slices so that it forms a neat package that is completely covered with eggplant on all sides, with the ends of the eggplant tucked under the package. Repeat the process until each fillet is covered with several layers of eggplant. Using a large spatula, carefully move the fillets to a flat dish. Cover with plastic wrap and chill.

Combine the tomato juice and purée in a food processor or blender and blend. Measure out 2 cups of the blended liquid.

Combine the 2 cups tomato mixture with the orange juice, orange zest, wine, and shallots in a saucepan. Simmer briskly over medium heat until mixture is reduced to about 1 tablespoon, or just enough to coat the bottom of the pan. Whisk in the ½ pound of butter a little at a time. Adjust seasoning. Keep warm by placing the saucepan in a larger saucepan filled with hot water. If the sauce breaks down, you can save it by whisking in about 1 tablespoon of heavy cream.

Heat the clarified butter in a large non-stick skillet. Sauté the wrapped fish fillets 5 minutes over medium heat. Carefully turn with the help of two spatulas and sauté 5 minutes on the other side.

Place fillets on heated serving plates and garnish with some of the sauce either by spooning it around each "package" or by spooning it over one side of the fish and drizzling the rest onto the plate. Garnish with nasturtium blossoms.

Risotto Cakes with Porcini Sauce

Serves 6

2 tablespoons olive oil
1 cup finely diced onions
3 large eggs
3½ cups heavy cream
   Salt and freshly ground black pepper
      to taste
1 cup Taleggio or Italian fontina
      cheese, grated
4 cups arborio rice, cooked in Chicken
      Stock (see page 276)
7 tablespoons butter

2 teaspoons minced shallots
2 dried porcini mushrooms, soaked in
      boiling water until soft, and
      drained
½ cup Chicken Stock
2 tablespoons dry Marsala wine

   Fresh chives and flat-leaf Italian
      parsley for garnish

*H*eat olive oil in a small skillet and sauté the onions over low heat until they are tender but not brown.

In a medium-sized mixing bowl, combine eggs, 1½ cups cream, salt, pepper, and cheese; blend well. Then stir in onions and fold in the rice until mixture reaches a semi-thick consistency. Add more salt and pepper if necessary. Mold into 12 round or oval cakes and set aside.

Melt 2 tablespoons butter in a small saucepan. Add shallots and cook 1 minute. Add porcini, stock, and Marsala. Simmer briskly until liquid is reduced by half.

Add remaining cream to reduced mixture and simmer until liquid is reduced by half again. Whisk 1 tablespoon more butter into the pan, a bit at a time. Season with salt and pepper.

Heat 4 tablespoons butter in a large skillet. Add rice cakes and sauté until brown on each side, about 5 minutes a side. Place 2 cakes on each serving plate and spoon some of the sauce over the tops. Garnish with chives and parsley.

Sautéed Pork Medallions with Marsala Cream Sauce

This delicious dish is especially good when accompanied by the outstanding Basil and Pine-Nut Bread Pudding (see below).

Serves 6

> 2 cups Veal Stock (see page 276)
> 1 cup heavy cream
> ¼ cup dry Marsala wine
> 2 teaspoons minced shallots
> 12 3-ounce pork medallions, cut from the tenderloin
> ½ cup clarified butter
> Salt and freshly ground black pepper to taste
>
> Fresh basil, chives, and nasturtium blossoms for garnish

*I*n a small saucepan, briskly simmer stock over medium heat until reduced by half. At the same time, in a second saucepan, simmer cream until it, too, is reduced by half. Simultaneously, in a third saucepan, combine Marsala and shallots and simmer until reduced by half. Add reduced stock to reduced Marsala mixture and reduce a little more. Whisk in reduced cream, increase the heat, and simmer briskly until sauce is slightly thickened. Keep warm by placing saucepan in a larger saucepan that has been filled with hot water.

Slightly flatten the pork medallions with your hand.

Melt half the butter in a large skillet. When skillet is hot, sauté a few medallions at a time over medium-high heat 2 minutes per side. Add more butter as necessary. Sprinkle with salt and pepper. Transfer to a baking dish and keep warm in a 200° oven while you finish the remaining medallions.

Arrange 2 slices of tenderloin per person on heated serving plates and surround with some of the Marsala cream sauce. Garnish with fresh basil, chives, and nasturtium blossoms.

Basil and Pine-Nut Bread Pudding

This is an extraordinary dish that became a huge hit in Cleveland at Thanksgiving when we prepared it on Fred's *Morning Exchange* television program. It is the texture of a fine soufflé and has a marvelous aroma while baking.

Serves 6

> 1 cup half-and-half
> ¾ cup heavy cream
> 4 large eggs, beaten
> 4 cups Italian bread, torn in pieces
> 1 stalk celery, finely diced
> 1 small onion, finely diced
> 1 tablespoon chopped basil
> ⅓ cup pine nuts
> Salt and freshly ground black pepper to taste

*C*ombine all ingredients in a mixing bowl and blend well. Mixture should be very creamy, so, if too dry, add a bit more half-and-half. Pour mixture into a buttered 2-quart baking dish and let rest at room temperature at least 2 hours.

Bake in preheated 400° oven 45 minutes. Remove from the oven and cut into squares.

Or, if you wish to prepare this ahead, you can spoon the baked mixture into six buttered ramekins and reheat ramekins in a 325° oven for 20 minutes prior to serving.

Chocolate Bread Pudding with Red Wine Sauce

While this can be served cold, it is yummiest when still warm. The red wine sauce is a perfect complement, but it is also luscious with homemade vanilla ice cream.

Serves 10

> 4 apples, peeled, cored, and quartered
> 2¼ cups Valpolicella wine
> 4 cups heavy cream
> 3¼ cups half-and-half
> 10 ounces bittersweet chocolate, chopped
> 2¾ cups sugar
> 4 large eggs
> 1 tablespoon vanilla extract
> 1 loaf French bread
> 6 large egg yolks

*P*reheat oven to 375°. Place apples in a small baking pan and add 2 cups of the red wine.

Cover pan with foil and bake in preheated oven 20 minutes. Remove pan from oven and set aside.

Mix 2 cups of the cream and the half-and-half together in a large saucepan and heat to near-boiling. Place the chocolate in a large mixing bowl. Pour cream mixture over chocolate and stir until melted.

In a medium-sized mixing bowl, combine 2¼ cups sugar, eggs, and vanilla, and beat well.

Tear bread into small pieces and put into a large mixing bowl. Pour chocolate cream mixture over the bread and toss until well coated. Add sugar and egg mixture and toss again.

Preheat oven to 375°.

Put half the bread mixture in a well-buttered 3-quart baking dish. Drain the apples and spoon them evenly over the surface, then add the remaining bread mixture. Bake 1 hour, or until firm.

Meanwhile, to make the sauce, combine 2 cups cream and ¼ cup wine in a medium-sized heavy saucepan. Heat until hot, not boiling.

Mix egg yolks and ½ cup sugar in a small mixing bowl. Slowly whisk a small amount of the hot cream into yolks; then slowly pour yolk mixture into hot cream, stirring constantly. Continue to cook and stir over low heat until cream coats the spoon or spatula. If the sauce overcooks, it will be lumpy.

Tejas

MINNEAPOLIS, MINNESOTA

We first saw Tejas on a summer day, when the sunshine was pouring down through the windowed wall of The Conservatory on Nicollet, one of Minneapolis's newest architectural jewels. Sunlight covered the huge umbrellas and shimmered over the floor and off the tiled walls. We looked over the balustrade and rushed down the sweeping staircase. We knew we just had to eat there. We could imagine, too, how inviting that sight would be on a Minnesota winter day, forgetting that the wind-chill factor can make the outside temperature feel about −35°F. In planning this café, Stephan Pyles and John Dayton made it possible for Minnesotans to have a sunny holiday without leaving town. By responding so enthusiastically, their patrons show how receptive the Midwest has become to food ideas far from the familiar.

Pyles and Dayton had already tasted success in Dallas—Routh Street Café and Baby Routh have achieved national reputations. But Minneapolis, John Dayton's hometown and that of his famous Dayton-Hudson family, has been a city on the move. Gaining in affluence and sophistication, it seemed to be a city ready for the culinary developments that were being experienced in other parts of the country. And when The Conservatory was in the planning stages, with locations available for two outstanding restaurants, the men accepted the challenge of owning restaurants in both cities. Today, the elegant, sophisticated Goodfellow's (see page 197) occupies the top floor space, while Tejas, the comfortable Southwestern café, is across the building in the atrium below.

Our only regret is that we were not able to taste everything. Salads and soups, for starters, are outstanding. A Southwestern Caesar salad gets a hint of piquancy from the tamarind vinaigrette and a bit of zip from cayenne croutons. A luscious black-and-white bean soup, garnished with red jalapeño cream, is wonderful just to look at and smell. Appetizers, like everything else, change with great frequency. The venison tamale with cranberries and chipotles has a delicate cornmeal exterior encasing a filling of delicious venison chili. We love the chipotles' smokiness, which is a terrific contrast to the tart cranberries. There were fat poblano peppers, with a hint of heat, roasted and peeled, and filled with roast pork, apricots, and pumpkin seeds. For the more timid among us, Tejas offers smoked-chicken nachos with roasted peppers and pungent Asiago cheese, served with avocado and chile sauce on the side. All the smoking is done on the premises, and all of it is done very well.

The brunch at Tejas can get your day off to a really lively start, whether you have a little tequila in your orange juice or a little lime juice in your tequila. We love any combination of eggs, tomatoes, and chiles; so do the folks at Tejas. The sausage might be made of venison; the pancakes might be made from blue cornmeal. All the menus at Tejas are wonderfully inventive and appealing, combining something familiar with something new. They do marvelous things with pork chops. A pork-filled meat pie, an empanada, is garnished with a picante relish of tomatillos. The pioneer's traditional spoon bread takes on a new look when it has a green chile or two folded into it. Flank steak, a family favorite, is delicious when it is char-grilled, sliced diagonally, and used to fill freshly made flour tortillas garnished with wonderful salsa. And to chase away the winter's chill, there is venison chili, garnished with Texas goat cheese, black beans, and grilled onions. Servers frequently replenish a basket of addictive blue-cornmeal corn sticks, so it is often difficult to save room for dessert. Our favorite in that area by far is the chocolate ancho chile cake. It is a flourless cake that has the richness of fine chocolate enhanced by a suggestion of smoky heat, served on a cherimoya crème anglaise with a garnish of strawberry purée. Cherimoya, also known as custard apple, happens to be one of our favorite fruits, and we are delighted to see it available all over the country from late autumn into late spring.

The Conservatory, housing more than fifty fine shops and two major restaurants, is a splendid gift from the Dayton family to their city. It is a gorgeous building, filled with huge windows that welcome the sunshine. The designers of Tejas kept the restaurant design simple and colorful; plain white tables and chairs sit on a tiled terra-cotta floor. All food is served on colorful Fiestaware. Drinks come in Mexican glasses of light turquoise. Diners in the back of the restaurant sit next to deep wall niches filled with extraordinary Acoma Indian pottery. Everywhere we looked, our senses were stimulated—from the colorful murals and wall hangings to decorative baskets and carvings. For added interest, there is an open kitchen; nearby diners are treated to a lesson in tortilla making while they dine. Finally, the dining experience is enhanced by enthusiastic and skilled servers who love to talk about the food while encouraging the first-time diner to be adventuresome.

Stephan Pyles and John Dayton looked to Minneapolis itself for their executive chef. A graduate of the University of Minnesota, Mark Haugen had had sixteen years of cooking experience in Minneapolis when he was hired at Tejas. In preparation, Haugen immersed himself in the new vocabulary of Southwestern food, with months of travel and study. By the time he was ready to open Tejas, he had a good sense of how to present these new ingredients to a very Midwestern city. As a result, the menu has enough of the familiar to make every palate comfortable, but an aficionado of the picante does not have to be disappointed. Altogether, for any palate, at almost any time of day, Tejas will satisfy. And even if it is dark outside, the sparkle of sunshine stays within. Tejas is sand, blazing sun, desert heat; it is a bit of America's Southwest right in the heart of the Midwest.

Tejas

MINNEAPOLIS, MINNESOTA

Grapefruit-Tequila Ice

Blue-Corn Griddlecakes

Venison Sausage

Black Bean and Goat Cheese Relish

Serrano Chile Blue Cornbread

Joseph Phelps Vineyards Syrah or
Dalla Valle Zinfandel

Flourless Chocolate Ancho Chile Cake

Lakespring Winery Cabernet Sauvignon

Wines selected by Sandra Jordan Earl

Grapefruit-Tequila Ice

Makes 1 quart

>   3 cups fresh grapefruit juice
>   1 cup sugar
>   ¼ cup tequila
>   2 tablespoons red wine
>
>   Grapefruit sections and sparkling
>   wine for garnish

Combine all the ingredients in an ice-cream maker and blend well. Freeze according to manufacturer's instructions.

To serve, place 2 scoops of the frozen mixture in each serving bowl, garnish with grapefruit sections, and pour 3 ounces of sparkling wine over the top.

Blue-Corn Griddlecakes

At Tejas, three griddlecakes are served to each person, along with three Venison Sausage patties (see below). Black Bean and Goat Cheese Relish (page 193) is spooned around the griddlecakes. Sprigs of cilantro make the perfect garnish for the whole plate.

Makes about 3 dozen cakes, 3 to 4 inches in diameter

>   2¼ cups blue-corn flour
>   ¾ cup blue cornmeal
>   1 teaspoon baking powder
>   ¼ teaspoon salt
>   5 tablespoons sugar
>   9 large eggs, separated, at room
>   temperature

>   6 tablespoons butter, softened
>   ¾ cup sour cream
>   2½ cups milk
>   1½ cups cooked corn kernels
>   Corn oil
>   Fruit preserves and sour cream for
>   garnish

Mix the first 5 ingredients in a medium-sized mixing bowl and set aside. Place egg whites in the bowl of an electric mixer and beat with whisk attachment until stiff peaks form; set aside.

Cream together butter, egg yolks, and sour cream in large bowl. Blend in dry ingredients. Stir in milk and corn. Fold in egg whites.

Lightly coat a large skillet with corn oil, and warm over medium-high heat until surface is hot. Drop batter from a large spoon to make 3–4-inch pancakes, about 4 at a time. Reduce heat to medium and cook until bubbles appear on surface. Turn carefully with a spatula and continue cooking 2 minutes on other side. Remove from skillet, place on a heated plate, and keep warm in a 200° oven until remaining griddlecakes are made.

To serve, arrange 3 pancakes on each heated serving plate and garnish with preserves and a dollop of sour cream.

Venison Sausage

Makes 4 pounds (32 patties)

>   2½ pounds boneless venison, ground
>   1 pound pork fat
>   ¼ pound bacon
>   2 cloves garlic, peeled
>   2 fresh red jalapeño peppers, seeded

2 fresh green jalapeño peppers, seeded
2 tablespoons chopped fresh cilantro
2 tablespoons chopped onion
1 teaspoon ground cumin
1 teaspoon ground allspice
  Salt and freshly ground black pepper
    to taste
  Vegetable oil

Combine first 8 ingredients in a large bowl. Using a meat grinder or a food processor, grind or process well. Add seasonings to mixture and blend well.

Form mixture into ½-inch-thick patties. Brush a large-sized skillet with a light coating of vegetable oil and heat. When hot, add sausage patties and cook over moderate heat about 4 minutes per side. These will freeze well.

Black Bean and Goat Cheese Relish

Serves 10

1 tablespoon butter
1 small onion, diced
½ cup white wine
1 cup Chicken Stock (see page 276)
2 cloves garlic, minced
1 cup goat cheese
2 cups heavy cream
1 tomato, peeled, seeded, and diced
2 tablespoons chopped fresh cilantro
2 cups cooked black beans
  Salt and freshly ground white pepper
    to taste

Melt the butter in a 2-quart saucepan over medium heat. Add the onion and cook until translucent. Add wine, stock, and garlic, and simmer briskly until liquid is reduced by one-third. Add goat cheese and cream, and simmer until mixture is thick enough to coat a spoon. Stir in the tomato, cilantro, and beans. Add salt and white pepper to taste.

Serrano Chile Blue Cornbread

Serves 10

> 1 cup flour
> 1½ cups blue cornmeal
> 2 tablespoons sugar
> 1 teaspoon salt
> 1 tablespoon baking powder
> 1 tablespoon vegetable oil
> 3 fresh serrano chiles, or 2 jalapeño peppers, stemmed, seeded, and diced
> 1 medium green bell pepper, deveined, seeded, and diced
> 1 medium red bell pepper, deveined, seeded, and diced
> 3 cloves garlic, minced
> 2 jumbo eggs
> ¼ cup plus 2 tablespoons vegetable shortening, melted and cooled
> 6 tablespoons butter, melted and cooled
> 1 cup buttermilk, to which a pinch of baking soda has been added
> 3 tablespoons minced fresh cilantro

*I*n a medium-sized mixing bowl, sift together flour, cornmeal, sugar, salt, and baking powder, and set aside.

Heat oil in a small skillet. Add the chiles, peppers, and garlic, and cook over medium heat 2 minutes. Set aside.

Preheat oven to 400°. Beat eggs lightly in a small bowl. Beat in the melted shortening and butter; blend in buttermilk. Pour this mixture over the sifted flour mixture and beat just until smooth. Fold in the pepper mixture, add cilantro, and mix.

Heat a well-oiled 9-inch cast-iron skillet in oven 10 minutes. Pour batter into hot skillet and bake 30 minutes. Turn out of pan and let cool slightly.

Flourless Chocolate Ancho Chile Cake

Serve this with Crème Anglaise (page 107), whipped Crème Fraîche (page 275), or some wonderful ice cream (try Goodfellow's Vanilla, page 204). If cherimoyas are available, discard the seeds, purée the fruit, and mix with Crème Anglaise for a superlative sauce.

Serves 10

> 6 to 8 large dried ancho chiles
> 4 ounces unsweetened chocolate, chopped
> 4 ounces semisweet chocolate, chopped
> 8 ounces unsalted butter, softened
> 5 jumbo eggs
> 1½ cups sugar

*B*reak the dried chiles into pieces, shake seeds out of the chiles and discard. Also dis-

The Best of the Midwest

card stems. Place chiles in a small mixing bowl and cover with boiling water until soft, about 20 minutes. Place chiles in the bowl of a food processor using a slotted spoon. Purée with the metal blade, adding about 3 tablespoons of the soaking liquid to make a smooth paste. The mixture should be very thick but also able to be forced through a strainer, so add a bit more liquid if necessary. Push through a strainer to eliminate the tough skin bits and any seeds. Set aside.

Preheat oven to 325°. Butter a 10 × 3 × 2½-inch loaf pan, line it with wax paper, and set aside. Melt both chocolates in a double boiler over simmering water. Then add the butter and remove from heat. Stir often until the butter has melted.

Whip the eggs and sugar together in the bowl of an electric mixer until the mixture forms a ribbon when a spoonful is lifted and spilled back into the bowl. Slowly stir chocolate mixture into the eggs and sugar. Then stir in between ½ and ¾ cup of the ancho paste, depending on taste. There should be a sense of heat, not fire.

Spread evenly in the prepared pan and loosely cover the top with some wax paper so that a hard crust will not form. Set pan in a larger baking pan filled with hot water and bake in preheated oven 1½ hours. Remove from oven, remove from water bath, and let cool on a rack in the pan 15 minutes. Then carefully turn cake out of the pan and set upright on the rack to complete cooling.

Goodfellow's

MINNEAPOLIS, MINNESOTA

Minneapolis's Conservatory happens to have two outstanding restaurants, both owned by Stephan Pyles and John Dayton. We ate ourselves silly in Minneapolis, trying to check out the many restaurants that had been brought to our attention. But after making our list and checking it more than twice, we just have to say that in our estimation D'Amico Cucina, Tejas, and Goodfellow's are the three best of all we tried—even if two of them are in the same building and under the same ownership. Besides, New York has its Equitable Building, with Le Bernardin on the ground floor and Palio a few flights upstairs. In any case, Goodfellow's and Tejas are really as different as night and day. One is sleek, elegant, sophisticated, and costly. The other is casual, informal, ethnic, and inexpensive. One is at the top of the building, the other is on the lowest level at the opposite end. One is reached by a swift elevator that whisks you up in a matter of seconds, the other is approached by the kind of grand staircase that brides dream about. Both have fantastic bars in their entrances, but only Goodfellow's has chairs and tables that seem to be out of the twenty-first century. One has a chef from Arkansas in charge, the other is in the hands of a local native. They are both wonderful restaurants.

Goodfellow's offers an enormously inventive range of dishes that blend the seasonings and coloring of hearty Southwestern cuisine with ingredients more common to the Midwest. In the capable hands of executive chef Tim Anderson, Goodfellow's is achieving its own reputation for excellence; it is no one's clone. The menu changes daily at Goodfellow's, according to the seasons and the availability of fresh produce, game, and other ingredients. A starter of golden gazpacho, made from richly flavored yellow tomatoes, is garnished with grilled shrimp and "noodles" of daikon radish and punctuated by a generous sprinkle of minced cilantro. We love the smoked duck salad with warm Wisconsin goat cheese, garnished with crispy fried cayenne noodles. Slices of sweet mango and leaves of peppery arugula add to the complexity of color and flavor. A breaded and fried razor clam makes an exciting appetizer when accompanied by three tomato sauces—one yellow, one green, and one red—and a garnish of julienned red onion. In winter, a soup of baked pumpkin is delicately spiced with cloves, cinnamon, and allspice, and punctuated with a dollop of honeyed crème fraîche and a crunch of apple, chives, red bell pepper, and toasted pecans. And we delight in pan-roasted fillet of Northern pike with ham, leeks, and orange, with a buttery sauce thick with chopped chives.

Selecting a main course is always difficult, because they all sound delicious, especially since each accompaniment is designed to complement that particular dish. A grilled chop and tenderloin of lamb comes with roasted garlic custard and a pecan sauce; South Dakota venison is accompanied by walnut-yam cakes and berry sauce; a sautéed baby coho salmon tastes fabulous with ginger lime sauce and fried maple grits. A grilled Wisconsin veal chop, garnished with fresh wild mushrooms, is superb when combined with creamed corn pudding and tomato-eggplant ragoût. We continue to wax rhapsodic over the grilled king salmon with mango sauce and crisply fried lobster ravioli. A side order of wild-rice fritters, light as air, arrives without a trace of grease. And we may never have a dish to equal the smoked pheasant accompanied by game sausage richly flavored with sage, diced into a compote of wild rice and sweet potato and granished with a tart sauce rich with California cherries.

The bakers at Goodfellow's turn out delicious breads and superlative desserts. There is always a variation of the Tejas blue-cornmeal corn sticks in the baskets and we especially enjoyed them with a slight zip from serrano chiles. We love the flavor of the light and tender sweet-potato rolls. All ice creams

are also made right on the premises. Velvety cardamom ice cream smells as good as it tastes and makes a luscious counterpoint to a warm upside-down pear tart. A lacy tuile makes a crisply flavorful cookie cup for cream and raspberries, all served on a puddle of smoky caramel sauce. And the blueberry-raspberry buckle is a remarkably light and delicious version of a traditional mid-America favorite. But there may be nothing to equal the creamy richness of the banana cream macadamia nut pie with hot fudge sauce.

A sophisticated bar with whimsical tables and chairs possessing certain anthropomorphic qualities greets you at the entrance to Goodfellow's. A special lounge menu, in fact, encourages those who might like to stop just for a drink and a snack. Surrounded by two walls of windows, the dining room possesses simple elegance with Art Deco touches. The blue-gray carpet and light pink walls create an atmosphere of peaceful repose. Tables are well spaced and servers are highly professional. A large, creative wine list offers many plums for the cognoscenti as well as for the novice. Chef Tim Anderson has made a concerted effort to become involved in the Minneapolis community, often taking a leadership role in benefits relating to feeding the hungry and homeless. Caring and generous, he is involved in many charitable activities in the area. He is also a highly talented individual who possesses enormous energy and enthusiasm. Having worked for many years with Stephan Pyles in Texas, Tim Anderson had absorbed the basic skills of Southwestern cuisine before he came to Goodfellow's. But what is presented at Goodfellow's is not a repeat performance of past success; this is why it works so well.

Goodfellow's

MINNEAPOLIS, MINNESOTA

Baked Pumpkin Soup
with Honeyed Crème Fraîche
and Apple-Pecan Relish

Hacienda Wine Cellars Chenin Blanc

Pan-Roasted Northern Pike Fillet with Ham,
Leeks, and Orange Sauce

Matanzas Creek Winery Sauvignon Blanc

Sweet-Potato Rolls

Smoked Breast of Pheasant with Wild-Rice
Compote and Cracked-Pepper Pear Sauce

Saintsbury Pinot Noir

Wild-Rice Fritters

Raspberry-Blackberry Buckle
Vanilla Ice Cream

Wines selected by Sandra MacIver

Baked Pumpkin Soup with Honeyed Crème Fraîche and Apple-Pecan Relish

Serves 8

5 pounds pumpkin, peeled, seeded, and cut into chunks
1 clove garlic, crushed
1½ ounces leek, diced
2½ ounces carrot, diced
1½ ounces celery, diced
6 cups Chicken Stock, plus more if necessary (see page 276)
1 cup heavy cream
¼ cup maple syrup
½ teaspoon ground cloves
½ teaspoon ground cinnamon
½ teaspoon ground allspice
Salt to taste
½ cup Crème Fraîche (see page 275)
3 tablespoons honey
Up to ¼ cup milk
¼ teaspoon lime juice

RELISH

½ cup peeled and finely diced green apple
½ cup fresh minced chives
3 tablespoons deveined, seeded, and minced red bell pepper
¼ cup toasted and finely chopped pecans
3 tablespoons orange juice
1 tablespoon lime juice
Salt to taste

*P*lace first 6 ingredients in a heavy saucepan and cook over medium heat until pumpkin is very tender, up to 1 hour.

Purée contents of pan in a food processor until smooth. Return to the pot and reheat. Stir in cream, maple syrup, and spices. Add more stock if soup is too thick. Add salt to taste.

Stir the Crème Fraîche and honey together in a small mixing bowl. Thin mixture with milk, a bit at a time, to the point that cream will drizzle easily onto soup. A few drops of lime juice will bring out the honey flavor.

Toss all relish ingredients together in a small bowl.

Ladle soup into heated serving bowls. Drizzle cream over the surface of the soup and place 1 tablespoon of relish in the center of the bowl.

Pan-Roasted Northern Pike Fillet with Ham, Leeks, and Orange Sauce

Serves 8

8 4-ounce Northern pike fillets, skinned and boned
Salt
½ cup flour
½ cup vegetable oil
½ cup leeks, trimmed, cut lengthwise, washed, and finely julienned
½ cup finely julienned cooked ham or Canadian bacon
½ cup orange juice
3 ounces Chicken Stock (see page 276)
2 sticks unsalted butter, cut into 2-ounce pieces*
1 cup fresh minced chives

*We find that we are able to use 2 tablespoons less butter and still have a fine beurre blanc.

Season both sides of the fillets with salt and dredge in flour.

Heat the oil in a large sauté pan and cook the fillets top side down until just golden brown. Turn fillets with a spatula, then add the leeks and ham. Toss leeks and ham until coated with oil. Then add the orange juice and stock. Toss pan once or twice, reduce heat, cover, and cook 2 minutes.

Uncover pan and check fish; if not done, leave cover off and cook a little longer. When fillets are done, transfer them to a heated platter and keep warm.

Put pan back on high heat and briskly simmer contents until liquid is reduced to ½ cup. Add butter, 2 ounces at a time, while constantly swirling pan. When all the butter is incorporated, season the sauce with salt and chives.

Divide fillets among eight warm serving plates and spoon sauce over them.

Sweet-Potato Rolls

Makes 2 dozen rolls

> 2 teaspoons active dry yeast
> ½ cup warm water (85°)
> 2 tablespoons butter, at room temperature
> ¾ cup (about 1 large) sweet potato, peeled, boiled, and mashed
> ¼ cup water reserved from boiling sweet potato
> 2 tablespoons molasses
> ¼ cup milk
> 3¼ to 3¾ cups flour
> 1½ teaspoons salt

Dissolve the yeast in the warm water. Set aside in a warm place until mixture bubbles and foams.

Combine the butter with the mashed sweet potatoes while they are still warm. Stir until butter has melted. Then, in a medium-sized mixing bowl, add the yeast mixture, reserved water, molasses, and milk. Blend well.

Sift flour and salt into a large mixing bowl. Add the combined wet ingredients and blend to form a loose, light dough. If too wet, blend in more flour. This is to be a very light, delicate dough.

Place dough in a large greased bowl, cover with plastic wrap, and let rise in a warm place until doubled in bulk, about 2 hours. Punch down and divide in half. This dough should have a silky feel to it. Sprinkle your work surface with a bit of flour and roll each half into a nice fat sausage, so that you can slice it into 12 equal segments. Very lightly flour your palms and roll each of the 24 segments into a ball. Place balls in well-greased muffin tin, cover the tins with plastic, and let rise in a warm place until rolls have doubled in size, about 1 to 2 hours.

Bake in a preheated 425° oven 14 to 18 minutes. Remove rolls from oven and let tins cool on a rack 1 minute, then turn rolls out of the tins onto the racks. These taste best when served warm.

Smoked Breast of Pheasant with Wild-Rice Compote and Cracked-Pepper Pear Sauce

Serves 8

SAUCE
    2 tablespoons vegetable oil
    1 tablespoon scraped and finely chopped carrot
    1 tablespoon finely chopped onion
    1 tablespoon finely chopped celery
    1 tablespoon finely minced parsley
    1 clove garlic, finely minced
    ¼ cup dry sherry
    ½ cup Chicken Stock (see page 276)
    1½ cups Veal or Beef Stock (see page 276)
    ½ ripe pear, baked and puréed
    1 ounce unsalted butter
    ½ ripe pear, cut into ⅛-inch dice
    1 tablespoon coarsely ground black pepper
    Salt to taste

COMPOTE
2 to 3 cups water
    ½ teaspoon salt
    1 medium sweet potato, peeled and cut into ½-inch dice
    1 tablespoon vegetable oil
    1 teaspoon butter
    3 tablespoons soy sauce
    3 teaspoons Chicken Stock (see page 276)

½ teaspoon crushed red pepper
3 cups cooked wild rice
6 scallions, trimmed and thinly sliced
4 smoked pheasant breasts, skinned
Salt and freshly ground black pepper
to taste

To make the sauce: In a medium-sized sauce-pan, heat the oil and sauté the carrot, onion, celery, parsley, and garlic just until tender. Add the sherry and scrape pan to loosen any browned vegetable particles on the bottom, then add the stocks. Cook over medium heat until the liquids begin to simmer briskly. Reduce heat and continue at a brisk simmer until liquid is reduced by half.

Then strain, pressing the vegetables against the strainer. Return the strained liquid to the saucepan and stir in the pear purée and the butter. Stir over medium heat until heated through. Add diced pear and black pepper. Season to taste with salt. Keep warm by placing saucepan in a larger saucepan filled with hot water.

To make the compote: Bring water and salt to boil in a small saucepan, add the sweet potato, and cook just until tender, about 20 minutes. Drain.

Heat oil, butter, soy sauce, stock, and red pepper in a heavy 2-quart saucepan. Stir in wild rice and scallions and toss often over medium heat until compote is hot. Adjust seasonings.

Carefully remove the bone from pheasant breasts and separate each into 2 halves. Rub with salt and pepper.

To serve, slice each half-breast diagonally into about 8 pieces each. Spoon a small amount of pear sauce onto 8 heated serving plates, place a portion of compote on top of the sauce, then fan the pheasant slices around the edge of the compote, with the inner part of each slice touching the sauce.

Wild-Rice Fritters

These are delicious with game and poultry as well as with pork. We have made a smaller version of these for hors d'oeuvres and served them with a melted-butter dipping sauce containing lots of chopped fresh thyme and a splash of Tabasco sauce. When served at Goodfellow's, the fritters are amazingly free of grease. Tim Anderson says, "Don't over-crowd the frying pan when you make them—overcrowding cools the oil temperature and that's what makes the fritters greasy."

Serves 8

3 shallots, chopped
1½ cups cooked wild rice
½ cup scraped and chopped carrots
1½ cups flour
½ teaspoon baking powder
3 large eggs, beaten lightly
1 cup half-and-half
2 tablespoons molasses
Salt to taste
1½ cups vegetable oil

Combine shallots, rice, and carrots in the bowl of a food processor. Pulse several times to make certain that the rice is at least broken in half. Set aside.

Sift the flour and baking powder together into a large mixing bowl. Then add the eggs and half-and-half, and blend well. Add molasses, rice mixture and salt. Mix well.

In a large cast-iron skillet, heat the oil to 350°, then drop batter into the oil 1 tablespoon at a time. Do not crowd, but do turn the fritters constantly. Fry each batch a total of about 5 minutes; check one fritter to make certain that they are cooked in the middle. Drain well on paper towels.

Raspberry-Blackberry Buckle

We think this tastes best served warm with Goodfellow's superlative Vanilla Ice Cream (see below).

Serves 8

CAKE AND FILLING
>1 cup unsalted butter, at room
>   temperature
>⅓ cup granulated sugar
>1 large egg, beaten
>2 cups flour
>2 teaspoons baking soda
>1 cup buttermilk
>1 pint fresh raspberries
>1 pint fresh blackberries

TOPPING
>½ cup granulated sugar
>½ cup dark brown sugar, firmly packed
>1 cup flour
>½ teaspoon grated nutmeg
>½ cup butter, softened
>⅓ cup roasted and chopped pecans

Preheat oven to 350°. In a large mixing bowl, beat the butter and sugar together until light and fluffy. Add the egg and beat well.

Sift together the flour and baking soda. Add to the sugar mixture alternately with the buttermilk. Pour mixture into a buttered and floured 8 × 8-inch baking dish and spread evenly. Then layer berries over the top.

Combine all the topping ingredients in a medium-sized bowl and mix with your fingers. Sprinkle this mixture evenly over the filling and berries.

Bake the buckle in the preheated oven 1 hour. Cool 30 minutes before serving. Cut into squares and serve with Vanilla Ice Cream.

Vanilla Ice Cream

Goodfellow's Vanilla Ice Cream is easily the best vanilla ice cream we have ever tasted. We think that the secret must be in the use of crème fraîche. We now use this particular recipe in our house as a base for most other ice creams. Try it with cinnamon or cardamom and serve it on warm apple pie!

Serves 8

>2 cups milk
>1 vanilla bean, or 2 teaspoons vanilla
>   extract
>6 large egg yolks
>⅔ cup sugar
>¾ cup Crème Fraîche (see page 275)

In a small saucepan, bring the milk and vanilla

The Best of the Midwest

to a boil. Remove from heat and cover. Let stand 15 minutes.

Put the eggs and sugar in a mixing bowl and whip with an electric mixer at high speed until the yolks are pale and form a ribbon when dropped from the beater.

Remove vanilla bean from the milk. With beaters running, gradually pour milk through a fine strainer into the egg-and-sugar mixture. Then pour this mixture into a heavy-bottomed saucepan.

Fill a large mixing bowl with ice and set aside.

Cook the egg-and-milk mixture over low heat, stirring constantly, until it forms a very thick custard (about 185° on a candy thermometer).

Remove from heat and place pan on the bed of ice. Stir in the Crème Fraîche. Let the mixture chill completely. Then freeze in an ice-cream maker according to manufacturer's directions.

Schumacher's New Prague Hotel

NEW PRAGUE, MINNESOTA

From Minneapolis, it's an hour's drive south through cornfields and dairy pastures to New Prague, a small town of three thousand people who are mostly of Czech and German descent. The two biggest buildings in town are a grain-processing plant and Schumacher's New Prague Hotel. Designed by Cass Gilbert, the hotel is a charming building about one hundred years old, with a handsome white porch which runs the width of the building. Its winsome sign, a wonderful variation on the traditional Bavarian hunting sign, depicts a deer resting on two crossed hunting guns, with a pheasant and rabbit resting below—all three very much alive and encircled by a round hunter's horn. We arrived in New Prague (pronounced with a long *a*, so it rhymes with *vague*) well past lunch, but there were perhaps a hundred people still in the hotel, lingering over dessert or touring the building and gift shop. One deep breath was enough to tell us why people were reluctant to leave. Even in mid-afternoon, the air was thick with the aroma of pastries baking, meats roasting, and stocks simmering. For many in the Minnesota countryside, this is food that nourishes the soul.

The cuisine, which shows the influence of its central European origins, is impeccably prepared by John Schumacher, who was raised in the heartland and trained at the Culinary Institute of America. John's pâté is a blend of duck and goose liver, with just the right dash of allspice and bay leaf. Lighter than its peasant ancestor, it is delicious garnished with chopped egg, served with black bread, or eaten just as it is. No one would share a recipe for the splendid Czech sausage that John Schumacher ate when he first moved to New Prague, so he experimented until he came up with his own. It is rich with pork and barley, married with a hint of garlic and spices, and roasted until brown, so that its rich fragrance pervades the kitchen. In winter there are hearty soups on the menu. The old-fashioned Bohemian goulash soup with sour cream has a wonderful flavor that comes from browning the bacon, onions, and garlic together. After adding rich beef stock, tomatoes, carrots, potatoes, and beef, the soup is slowly simmered with caraway until the heady aroma overwhelms even the most timid of appetites.

Kolacky, the slightly sweet Czech yeast

rolls with a bit of fruit preserves in the middle, are made daily at Schumacher's. Every patron is expected to consume at least two of these, slathered with the wonderful unsalted butter that is made nearby. Quails Helenka, named for John's mother, are stuffed with plums, wrapped with bacon, and roasted crisp, then served on a stuffing made from day-old ko-lacky. Other game dishes, such as venison, rabbit, and pheasant, are often available. In fact, for the hearty among us, Schumacher's frequently offers the "Hunter's Feast," a hearty sampler of game. The menu also offers nearly a dozen poultry and fish dishes. Czech duck, stuffed with a sauerkraut and potato dressing and seasoned with caraway, is roasted until every bit of fat is gone. The skin is crack-lingly delicious and each mouthful is a lusty pleasure. There are a dozen different schnit-zels—some of pork, some of veal—all made from the finest ingredients available and fried in rich local butter just until fork-tender. Side dishes number about ten—rich braised red cabbage perfumed with cloves; potato dump-lings sliced and fried until crisp; hash browns gooey with melted Swiss cheese; tender sweet carrots swathed in herbs; spicy and hot Ger-man potato salad. Despite the richness, how-ever, John's food is surprisingly light.

And, of course, there's dessert. Every morning a few farm wives from the area spread a clean bedsheet on the baking table and begin to stretch strudel dough until it is totally transparent. Filled with whatever splendid fruit is in season, the pastry is then heavily buttered, rolled, and baked until golden. (Those of us smart enough to sleep upstairs get to have some right from the oven.) John Schumacher himself makes a me-ringue filled with nuts, bakes it until crisp, then layers it with fresh whipped cream and serves it in huge succulent wedges. And when fresh strawberries are in season, one can treat oneself to a bowl of whole berries sauced with a berry purée blended with thick cream—John's daughter Brandi's favorite dessert.

The decor is ever-changing, as Bavarian craftsmen work with a local craftsman to meld the woods of both worlds. Big Cully's Bar, named for John's father, has hand-painted German glass in the windows and wooden stools at the bar, the bases whimsically carved and painted to look like giant Alpine climbing boots topped by woolen stockings. The dining rooms are paneled in a variety of woods—some rooms are very light and blond, others richly dark and atmospheric. Wonderful Old World paintings abound. John and Kathleen Schumacher also decorate the rooms with their peerless collections of cut glass and china. Upstairs, Pipka, a fabled Wisconsin folk artist, is gradually transforming many of the guest rooms with her charming paintings on walls and furniture.

Schumacher's is always packed, and John sometimes wonders where all the people come from. The answer is everywhere. Dur-ing the week, the dining rooms are filled mostly with people from the local farmlands. On weekends, they come not just from Min-neapolis, St. Paul, and Chicago but from both coasts, and even from Europe, to stay in the eleven charming guest rooms and enjoy John Schumacher's extraordinary food and Kath-leen Schumacher's gracious hospitality. To-gether the Schumachers have brought the charm of a European inn to Minnesota and warmed the hearts of their guests by treating them to a generous helping of Midwestern hospitality.

Schumacher's New Prague Hotel

NEW PRAGUE, MINNESOTA

Schumacher Hotel Pâté

Heitz Wine Cellars Grignolino

Beer-Battered Duck Appetizer

Gundlach-Bundschu Winery Gewürztraminer

Old-fashioned Bohemian Goulash Soup

Stags' Leap Winery Burgundy

Roast Duck with Sweet Kraut Dressing

Lytton Springs Winery Zinfandel

Herbed Carrots

Zelniky
Crispy Czech Bread

Strawberries Brandi

Joseph Phelps Vineyards Scheurebe

Wines selected by Chuck Masterpaul

Schumacher Hotel Pâté

This pâté will be delicious for a week. In fact, the flavors really improve if it is made a day ahead. We prefer to use either goose or duck livers for a richer flavor.

Makes about 3 cups

> 1 quart water
> 1½ pounds duck, goose, or chicken
> 　　livers
> ¾ pound diced onions
> 2 bay leaves
> 1¼ teaspoons ground allspice
> 4 ounces cream cheese
> ½ cup mayonnaise
> 　　Salt and freshly ground black pepper
> 　　to taste
> 2 hard-boiled eggs, finely chopped
> 　　Pumpernickel bread, sliced thin and
> 　　cut into triangles

In a heavy saucepan, combine water, livers, onions, bay leaves, and 1 teaspoon allspice. Cover and cook slowly until onions are tender and transparent, about 10 minutes. Drain and rinse well in a colander. Discard bay leaves and cool.

Purée livers and onions in a food processor. Add cream cheese and mayonnaise; pulse until smooth. Add ¼ teaspoon allspice and purée again. Add salt and pepper to taste. Spoon into serving bowl and smooth the surface. Sprinkle the hard-boiled egg on top and chill. Serve with pumpernickel bread on the side.

Beer-Battered Duck Appetizer

Makes about 36 pieces

> 3 duck breasts, boned, skinned, and
> 　　halved
> 1 cup soy sauce
> 1 large onion, sliced
> 1 cup beer
> 3 to 4 cups flour

SAUCE
> ¾ cup plum preserves
> ¼ cup Pommery mustard
> 1 tablespoon soy sauce
> 1 teaspoon dry mustard

2 to 3 cups vegetable oil

Slice each half duck breast into finger-width strips and place in a glass bowl. Cover with soy sauce and onion slices. Let marinate overnight.

Remove the meat from the marinade, drain, and pat dry.

Make a batter by pouring the beer into a mixing bowl and adding flour a little at a time. Mix well after each addition. Stop adding flour when the batter forms a thick paste. Set aside.

Combine all sauce ingredients in a small saucepan and cook over medium heat, stirring until well blended. Let cool to room temperature and pour into a serving bowl.

Just before serving, pour oil into a wok and heat until a bit of batter bubbles when dropped into the oil. Then roll duck strips in some plain flour and dip into the batter. Fry the strips until brown. Don't overcrowd in the wok or they will stick together. Drain well and serve with the dipping sauce on the side.

Old-fashioned Bohemian Goulash Soup

This tastes even better if you make it one day ahead.

Serves 6 to 8

½ pound bacon, chopped
3 cups chopped onions
4 cloves garlic, finely diced
½ cup diced celery
½ cup scraped and diced carrots
¼ cup flour
1 quart Beef Stock (see page 276)
1½ pounds lean beef chuck, diced
½ teaspoon freshly ground black pepper
1 tablespoon salt
¼ teaspoon caraway seeds
1 cup tomato paste
3 cups diced canned tomatoes, with liquid
½ cup peeled and diced potatoes

6 to 8 tablespoons sour cream for garnish

*I*n a heavy stockpot, slowly brown bacon. Add onions, garlic, celery, and carrots. Cook over low heat until vegetables begin to brown.

Add flour and stir to pick up the bacon fat. Cook slowly 2 minutes, stirring often. Slowly add beef stock, stirring constantly. Then add beef, seasonings, tomato paste, and tomatoes. Simmer slowly until meat is almost tender, about 1 hour. Then add potatoes and continue cooking until potatoes are tender, about 45 minutes.

Ladle into heated soup plates and garnish with a dollop of sour cream.

Roast Duck with Sweet Kraut Dressing

John Schumacher's roasting method is to put the birds into plastic roasting bags (available in the supermarket) and cook in a free-standing broaster-oven at 275° for 4 to 6 hours. Since only a few lucky people have these ovens at home, the roasting instructions below are for a regular oven.

Serves 6 to 8

3 cups sauerkraut
1 cup peeled and grated potatoes
¼ cup sugar
2 tablespoons flour
½ teaspoon caraway seeds
¼ teaspoon dried thyme
3 4–4½-pound roasting ducks, seasoned inside and out with salt and pepper
2 tablespoons butter
1 cup dark brown sugar, firmly packed
6 to 8 apples, cored and sliced in ¼-inch wedges
Pinch of salt

Preheat oven to 450°. Wash and drain sauerkraut. Combine with potatoes in a large mixing bowl.

Mix together the sugar, flour, and seasonings in a small mixing bowl and add to sauerkraut mixture. Blend well. Stuff the birds with this mixture and close the cavity with skewers and string. Prick skin with skewers to release fat.

Arrange ducks back side up on racks in roasting pans. Roast in preheated oven 30 minutes. Drain all fat from the pan. Turn breast side up and roast another 30 minutes. Drain any accumulated fat again. Reduce the heat to 350° and roast 20 minutes more. Let birds rest 10 minutes before serving.

While duck is roasting, melt the butter in a large skillet and add the brown sugar. Stir until dissolved. Add the apples (unpeeled) and salt. Cook, uncovered, over low heat, turning often, for 20 minutes.

Cut the duck into halves or quarters. Making certain that each portion is served with some of the dressing, distribute the duck among heated serving plates. Garnish with the candied apples.

Herbed Carrots

Serves 6 to 8

> 2 quarts Chicken Stock (see page 276)
> ¼ cup butter
> 1½ cups diced onions
> 3 cloves garlic, finely minced
> 2 cups carrots, scrubbed and sliced into
> ¼-inch diagonal slices
> 2 teaspoons freshly ground black
> pepper
> 1 teaspoon salt
> 1 teaspoon minced fresh basil

> 1 teaspoon minced fresh tarragon
> 1 teaspoon minced fresh parsley

Pour the stock into a large saucepan and bring to a boil. Simmer briskly until liquid is reduced by half. Keep hot.

Melt the butter in a large heavy saucepan. Add the onions and garlic, and cook over medium heat until onions are transparent.

Add the carrots and the hot stock, and simmer slowly 10 minutes. Season with pepper and salt. Add the basil and tarragon. Cook until the carrots are tender but still crisp, about 15 minutes. Transfer carrots to a serving dish with a slotted spoon or a large, flat Chinese strainer. Sprinkle with parsley and serve. Save the stock to use as a soup base or for cooking other vegetables.

Zelniky
Crispy Czech Bread

These make a great snack with beer and cheese. For that purpose, we advise sprinkling the strips with a few caraway seeds before baking. However you serve zelniky, if you use cushioned baking sheets, bake the strips at 375°; they will bake better at a slightly higher temperature.

Serves 6 to 8

> 2 cups sauerkraut, undrained
> ½ cup vegetable shortening
> 1¾ cups flour
> Caraway seeds (optional)

Preheat oven to 350°. Put the sauerkraut and its liquid in a large mixing bowl. Add the shortening and blend well. Add the flour, mixing carefully with your fingers. Gather into a ball.

Lightly flour a pastry board and roll out the dough until it is ⅛ inch thick. Cut into 2 × 4-inch strips with a sharp knife. Add caraway seeds if desired.

Place the strips on an ungreased cookie sheet and bake in preheated oven until lightly brown. (If the zelniky get too brown they become bitter.) Remove immediately to a rack and cool.

Strawberries Brandi

Serves 6 to 8

> 1½ quarts fresh strawberries
> 1 tablespoon honey
> 1 tablespoon confectioner's sugar
> 2 teaspoons Cointreau
> 1 pint heavy cream
> 2 tablespoons granulated sugar

Wash the berries and reserve a half pint with stems for garnish. Then hull the rest and purée approximately ½ pint in food processor, until you have ½ cup of purée.

In a medium-sized bowl, combine strawberry purée with honey, confectioner's sugar, and Cointreau, and blend well.

Whip the cream until stiff. Fold the purée into the cream until mixture is well blended.

Sprinkle the remaining hulled berries with the granulated sugar and toss. Put them into either a large crystal bowl or individual serving dishes. Cover with whipped cream mixture. Garnish with the unhulled berries and serve.

Strawtown Inn

PELLA, IOWA

Pella, Iowa, was founded by Dutch immigrants in 1847. Even if the wonderful windmill were not in the center of town, however, you could guess the town's ancestry by looking at the architecture of the charming buildings around the village square. Surrounded by rolling farmlands, Pella is a prosperous community (Pella windows are made there, as well as Vermeer hay balers) that continues to celebrate its roots. Traditional Dutch pastries fill the windows of the two bakeries on the village square. Dutch spiced beef is still the prized secret recipe of local butchers. There is an old-fashioned soda shop in the middle of town serving homemade ice cream and playing 78 rpm records on its old time original jukebox. There is a Tulip Festival every springtime in Pella. And there is the Strawtown Inn just up the road.

People flock from miles around to eat at Strawtown. Many business meetings take place here. Women have a social lunch with their friends before doing some shopping. At night it is filled with couples who enjoy the romantic atmosphere, charming service, wholesome food, and moderate prices. All dinners include Strawtown's famous barbecued meat balls, superb soup, a fresh salad, and a small loaf of their famous Dutch apple bread. These little meatballs have been the traditional opener at Strawtown for a number of years. Light and spicy, dipped in a zippy barbecue sauce, they make a nifty nibble while you wait hungrily for soup. We confess to being partial to cream soups; the cream of cauliflower here is thick and tasty, with lots of fresh cauliflower that is not cooked to mush. The Dutch pea soup has to be a perfect winter chill chaser, with its chunks of pork and smoked sausages. The inn also prepares a lighter version for consumption during the summer.

Strawtown is famous for its Hollandse Rollade, or Dutch spiced beef, and it really is worth a drive to Pella to taste it. A pot-roast cut of beef is marinated in a secret blend of spices by one of Pella's butchers, whose family has been preparing this dish for generations. Then the kitchen at Strawtown braises it long and slowly, serving it with a thick gravy made of its natural juices and creamy potatoes au gratin. Much to our frustration, the entire preparation of this dish remains Iowa's best kept secret. Another menu regular is a thickly cut pork chop with apple-and-apple-bread stuffing, browned and braised in a mushroom wine sauce and served with a side of buttery mashed potatoes. It is not surprising that steaks are popular in this farm country, and Chateaubriand is one of two favorites that can be prepared for a romantic evening for two if ordered in advance. The other classic, roasted pheasant, is actually served under a charming glass dome. Fish and shellfish are not easily obtained in Pella, but are usually available here; jumbo fried shrimp stuffed with crab meat are especially popular.

For dessert, Strawtown makes a delicious cheesecake with an Amaretto cherry glaze. They also offer some outstanding homemade ice creams with a variety of toppings. Pies are outstanding, especially the apple and raisin, with its fine flaky crust. Finally, we must recommend the coffee laced with Vandermint liqueur and topped with whipped cream as a splendid digestive.

The tables are set with heavy white linen, lovely wineglasses, and fresh flowers. And while everything tastes especially good here, we are sure that the charming dining rooms and servers delightfully attired in traditional Dutch costumes add significantly to the quality of the dining experience. Steep, narrow staircases lead to the various dining rooms, many of which were added in recent years as adjacent houses were incorporated into the complex. From the Delft Room to the Rembrandt Room to the Garden Room, one sees fascinating Old Country antique furniture, clocks, tiles, and etchings. There are wallpapers with colorfully flowered designs, wonderfully painted window shutters, and fabulous lace curtains, all adding to the Old World atmosphere. When the evenings are cold, the fires are immediately lit in the Dutch-style fireplaces, sending marvelous shadows up and down the walls.

To learn about the inn's history is to learn about the history of Pella itself. Some of the original Dutch settlers had to build temporary housing right from the sod, weaving roofs out of the indigenous long prairie grasses that so resembled the thatch they used for roofs in their homeland. These original sod shelters were built in a corner of the settlement that became known as Strawtown. Located on that same ground, the original inn was built about 1855 by one G. Hagens, who also used the inn as a bakery. In fact, Princess Juliana of the Netherlands visited Pella in 1942; in honor of that visit, the room that she slept in is now known as Juliana Kamer, or the Juliana Room. While a recent building program added about a dozen rooms to the guest complex, the atmosphere of Old World charm remains the same. It is easy to understand why the buildings were included in the National Register of Historic Places.

At the Strawtown Inn, every thought is given to the comforts of the guests. After a good night's sleep, everyone is served a Dutch-style breakfast of breads from local bakeries, homemade jams, cold meats, and cheeses. But we must confess that we had one treat not usually offered to guests here. Thanks to the incredible generosity of Strawtown's manager, Roger Olson, we received a box of dozens of pieces of Dutch Letters, a kind of flaky pastry filled with almond paste that remains among the greatest discoveries to be made in our wonderful Midwest. Even though we had to share them (at least a little), we made them last a week. But the memory of those heavenly butter-filled confections lingers on and on. And so the Strawtown Inn will always hold a soft spot in our hearts.

Strawtown Inn

PELLA, IOWA

Kaasbolletjes
Cheese Balls

Merlion Winery Coeur de Melon

Bitterballen
Savory Balls

R. H. Phillips Vineyard Chardonnay

Dutch Pea Soup

Hidden Cellars Fumé Blanc

Schol uit de Oven
Fish Fillets with Cheese Sauce

Lambert Bridge Chardonnay

Rollade
Collared Beef

Laurel Glen Vineyards Cabernet Sauvignon

Dutch Letters

Ficklin Vineyards Port

Wines selected by John Giguirre

Kaasbolletjes
Cheese Balls

Serves 8

> 1¾ cups flour
> 1½ cups grated Gouda or Edam cheese
> ½ teaspoon salt
>   Freshly ground black pepper to taste
> 10 tablespoons butter
> 3 large egg yolks

*P*reheat oven to 375°. Combine flour, cheese, salt, and pepper in a large mixing bowl. Using a fork or pastry blender, cut the butter into the flour mixture until it resembles coarse meal. Add the egg yolks and mix. Gather the mixture (it will be crumbly) together with your hands. Knead on a lightly floured board until dough is elastic. Shape into a ball, wrap in wax paper, and chill at least 2 hours.

Shape the chilled dough into ½-inch balls by rolling bits of it between the palms of your hands. Bake in the preheated oven on a lightly buttered cookie sheet for 15 to 20 minutes, or until golden brown. Serve immediately.

Bitterballen
Savory Balls

Serves 8

> 3 tablespoons butter
> 3 tablespoons flour
> 1 cup Chicken Stock (see page 276)
> ½ pound cold cooked veal, shredded
> 1 tablespoon finely chopped parsley
> 1 teaspoon ground nutmeg
> 1 teaspoon Worcestershire sauce
>   Freshly ground black pepper to taste
> 3 cups vegetable oil
> 2 large egg whites
> ½ cup fine bread crumbs
>
>   Dijon mustard

*H*eat butter in a large saucepan. Add flour and cook, stirring constantly, for 2 minutes. Gradually add stock, stirring constantly, until a thick paste is formed. Add veal, parsley, nutmeg, Worcestershire, and pepper. Combine thoroughly and remove from heat. Chill 3 hours.

In a deep, heavy skillet or an electric deep-fat fryer, heat oil to about 350°. Form meat mixture into 1-inch balls. In a small mixing bowl, beat egg whites until foamy. Dip balls into egg whites, then into bread crumbs. Fry in small batches until golden, about 4 minutes for each batch. Serve hot with mustard for dipping.

Dutch Pea Soup

Serves 8

1 pound whole dried green peas
2 pounds pork hocks or country-style
  pork ribs
3 quarts water
  Salt and freshly ground black pepper
  to taste
1½ cups finely chopped celery with tops
3 medium onions, finely chopped
3 potatoes, peeled and diced
¼ cup chopped fresh parsley
4 smoked sausages or hot dogs, sliced

  Sour cream and chopped parsley for
  garnish

*P*ut peas into a large bowl, cover with cold water, and soak overnight. Drain.

Combine peas and meat in a heavy 5-quart pot and add the 3 quarts water. Cook over low heat 2 hours. Add seasonings, celery, onions, potatoes, and parsley, and cook another hour. Add sausages 15 minutes before serving. Ladle into heated soup plates and garnish with a dollop of sour cream and some more parsley.

Schol uit de Oven
Fish Fillets with Cheese Sauce

Serves 6

6 5-ounce fish fillets, such as snapper
  or sole
1 tablespoon fresh lemon juice
1 teaspoon salt

3 tablespoons butter, softened
6 slices bacon
1 cup flour
¼ teaspoon dill seed
¼ teaspoon ground nutmeg
  Freshly ground black pepper to taste
¼ cup grated Gouda cheese
⅓ cup fresh bread crumbs
¼ cup ground and blanched almonds
3 tablespoons chilled butter

  Fresh parsley and lemon slices for
  garnish

*P*at fillets dry, and sprinkle both sides with lemon juice and salt. Let stand at room temperature 30 minutes.

Preheat oven to 500°. Coat the bottom and sides of a shallow baking dish that will hold the fish in one layer with 2 tablespoons softened butter. Cut a piece of wax paper to fit snugly inside baking dish. Remove paper and butter one side with the remaining tablespoon of softened butter. Set aside.

Fry bacon over medium heat until lightly browned and almost crisp. Drain on paper towels. Dry fillets and fold lengthwise in half. Press edges together to hold the shape. Dredge fillets in flour and shake to remove excess. Sprinkle both sides with dill and nutmeg. Arrange in a single layer in the baking dish, lay a strip of bacon on top of each fillet, and sprinkle with freshly ground pepper.

Combine cheese, crumbs, and almonds in a small bowl and mix well. Sprinkle evenly over fish fillets. Dot with bits of chilled butter.

Cover fillets with wax paper, buttered side down, and bake 10 minutes. Remove paper. If top is not brown, or if fish is not done, bake without the paper a few minutes more or put under a hot broiler for a few minutes. Garnish with parsley and lemon slices.

Rollade
Collared Beef

At Strawtown this dish is accompanied by buttery mashed potatoes or richly creamed potatoes au gratin.

Serves 8

2 pounds boneless sirloin steak,
  flattened to a thickness of ½ inch
1 pound filet mignon
½ teaspoon salt
  Freshly ground black pepper to taste
4 tablespoons butter
½ teaspoon dried thyme, or several
  sprigs fresh thyme
1 large onion, finely chopped
1 bay leaf
1 cup heavy cream

Chopped fresh parsley and sautéed
  or steamed seasonal vegetables for
  garnish

Sprinkle sirloin and filet mignon with salt and pepper. Place filet on the sirloin, roll up tightly, and tie securely with a string in several places. Season with more salt and freshly ground pepper.

In a heavy Dutch oven over high heat, melt the butter and brown the steak on all sides. Lower heat and add thyme, onion, and bay leaf. Cover and cook over low heat 1 hour and 10 minutes, turning occasionally, and adding more butter if the meat tends to stick.

Remove meat from Dutch oven and let rest in a warm place for at least 10 minutes. Remove bay leaf, add cream, and place over medium-high heat, stirring the bottom of the pot with a whisk to scrape up all the browned bits from the pan. Cook briskly a few minutes in order to thicken the sauce slightly. Sprinkle with fresh chopped parsley.

Place a few slices of meat on each heated serving plate and spoon a healthy amount of sauce over each portion. Garnish with vegetables.

Dutch Letters

Makes about 8 dozen 2-inch pieces

This wonderful holiday treat freezes very well. Just warm up a bit before serving.

1 pound unsalted butter, softened
4 cups flour
1 cup water
1 pound almond paste
2 cups sugar, plus more for sprinkling
3 large eggs
1 teaspoon vanilla extract
2 large egg whites, beaten

Cream the butter in the bowl of an electric mixer. Gradually add the flour, then the water. Gather dough into a ball with your fingers, wrap in plastic, and chill overnight.

Put the almond paste in the bowl of the mixer. Beat on medium speed until smooth. Gradually add the sugar, then the eggs one at a time. Add the vanilla. Cover with plastic wrap and chill several hours.

Preheat oven to 400°. Divide the dough into 14 parts. Lightly flour a work surface and roll each portion into a 14 × 4-inch strip. Also divide the chilled almond paste mixture into 14 portions, about 3 tablespoons each.

Spread one portion of this filling down the center of a dough strip. Fold one 14-inch side of dough over the filling, then fold the other side; pinch the ends together. Place the roll on a buttered cookie sheet with the seam side down. Continue with the remaining sections in the same fashion.

Brush the tops of the rolls with beaten egg whites, sprinkle with more granulated sugar, and prick with a fork every 2 inches so that steam can escape. Bake in the preheated oven about 30 minutes until golden. Let cool on a wire rack, then cut into sections at the perforation marks.

Lacorsette

NEWTON, IOWA

We owe it all to Dutch Letters. We had learned about this wonderful traditional Dutch pastry from Roger Olson, the manager of the Strawtown Inn in Pella, Iowa, who gave us a huge box of the letters for breakfast one morning. We "graciously" shared the treat with other guests. Mr. and Mrs. Rob Paulson repaid us by urging us to visit their hometown of Newton to try the food at Lacorsette. After their description, we flew to the phone and called for a reservation. We had to beg to get in that night, but gracious owner-chef Kay Owen finally agreed, as long as we were willing to eat on the veranda! This was the beginning of a wonderful culinary adventure and warm friendship. For the record, Newton, a pretty, peaceful community of about eight thousand, is the headquarters of Maytag (appliances and cheese). It is a forty-minute drive east of Des Moines in the heart of farm country—not an area that has a ready selection of the kind of food that a serious chef would want in the kitchen. Therefore, Lacorsette doesn't operate like a "regular" restaurant. The first folk to call for a reservation on any given day select the entree for themselves and the rest of the patrons from about ten that Kay offers them over the phone. Then Kay plans the five other courses according to what makes the best accompaniments for that dish and what is available from her local purveyors, although a dash to Des Moines is often a part of her schedule.

A first course might be a ramekin of creamy cheese custard hiding some farm-made Iowa sausage, a savory dish that is punctuated by a garnish of fresh tarragon from the garden. Or perhaps it could be herbed feta-filled phyllo pastry accompanied by shrimp-tomato butter. A hint of cilantro in the feta package marries well with the zippy shrimp sauce at its side. Or guests could be treated to a tasty country pâté studded with pistachios. The next course is usually a soup. The summer strawberry soup, with just a suggestion of cinnamon and mint, is a favorite of ours. A winter squash bisque, with its garnish of caraway, is a perfect chill chaser. Kay uses the salad course as an opportunity to create combinations of flavors, colors, and textures that might intrigue her diners. She reaches back to old farm ingredients for some of her best recipes. Waldorf salad takes on a new life in her creative hands; tomatoes never taste better than right off the vine, sprinkled with newly picked leaves of basil. And rarely has the humble beet been so well served as in her beautiful mimosa salad. Irresistibly fragrant baguettes, served right from the oven, wrapped in a starched white linen napkin, cry for Kay's delicious Iowa farm butter curls or for some of her seasonal fruit butter.

We have never had more delicious tenderloin tips than those at Lacorsette. Served with a tarragon butter sauce and accompanied by a ramekin of potatoes in cream, the beef was fork-tender and done to perfection. For poultry lovers, there is a heavenly game hen, stuffed with broccoli and served with a Mornay sauce, or roasted breast of chicken with a lemon-mustard sauce. Understandably, in this part of the country, fresh fish is not always available. But in a state famous for its pork, it is not surprising that pork dishes here are outstanding. Kay prepares superb pork loin that is roasted and served with a sweet mustard sauce. She also makes outstanding sautéed medallions of pork with mushrooms and a cognac-cream sauce. But Kay really shines with pork loin accompanied by tomato-prune chutney, with its hint of heat and its touch of ginger.

A cheese course following the main course usually includes some of our favorite Maytag cheese, and it sets the stage for the grand finale. Desserts are easy in the spring and summer, when the farms are in full swing and the weather is gentle. Even autumn and winter see a highly creative use of apples and pears, fruits that store well. It is then that Kay prepares her superlative frozen hazelnut soufflé with hazelnut sauce. We think she surpasses herself, however, with a ginger-poached pear filled with raspberry mousse and accompanied by ginger crème anglaise.

Fine food alone does not a dining experience make, and dinner at Lacorsette is a remarkable event. The Spanish-mission-style house, which is actually Kay's own home, was built by an Iowa state senator in 1909. Its white stucco walls are a foot thick; its enormous expanse of roof is still covered with the original red tiles. There are gorgeous dark woods on the interior walls, and the original Art Deco stained-glass windows and doors are still intact. A large group might sit at the beautiful dining-room table; a party of two will be seated in the book-lined library. When the restaurant is full, tables are set in the elegant foyer as well as in the living room, which, on a quiet evening, is where diners may also relax and chat after dinner. The china is Royal Doulton, the wineglasses are fine crystal, the silverware is Reed and Barton's Francis I sterling, and the beautiful linen tablecloths, with their heavy starch, are the kind we want in our linen closet. Mussel shells, with their

shimmering pearlescent lining, make delightful salt and pepper cellars. Fresh flowers and a silver candelabrum further enhance the table. Tuxedoed servers, superbly trained in the art of gracious service, and a small but excellent wine list complete the event.

Our discovery of Lacorsette was one of the highlights of our Midwestern adventure. Kay Owen used to raise horses nearby, but has always been a passionate cook, collecting cookbooks and food magazines and sharing the fruits of her labors with all her friends. In time, she was persuaded to fill the area's restaurant void by cooking "for a fee" right in her farmhouse. Her following grew; when the house of her dreams right on Newton's main street was for sale, she was ready to move to "the city." With its twenty-one rooms, the house is an enormous challenge to maintain; fortunately, it is a home just right for a bed-and-breakfast. The guest rooms are usually filled, so Kay cooks breakfasts as well as dinners. But she thrives on this pressure, sharing her enthusiasm for the surrounding countryside, with its wonderful antique stores and friendly shopkeepers, with her guests. When time permits, she heads for the cities, where she dines in fine restaurants, takes a cooking class from the area's experts, and renews herself for the season ahead. Kay and Lacorsette are one and the same; one could not exist without the other. We see Kay as a contemporary version of the nineteenth-century pioneer woman, with all her drive, energy, and courage; she typifies for us what is the best of the Midwest.

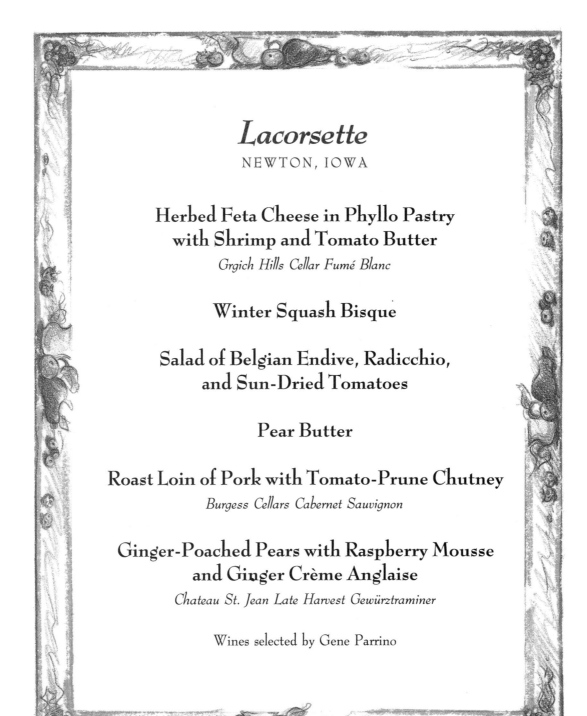

Lacorsette
NEWTON, IOWA

Herbed Feta Cheese in Phyllo Pastry with Shrimp and Tomato Butter
Grgich Hills Cellar Fumé Blanc

Winter Squash Bisque

Salad of Belgian Endive, Radicchio, and Sun-Dried Tomatoes

Pear Butter

Roast Loin of Pork with Tomato-Prune Chutney
Burgess Cellars Cabernet Sauvignon

Ginger-Poached Pears with Raspberry Mousse and Ginger Crème Anglaise
Chateau St. Jean Late Harvest Gewürztraminer

Wines selected by Gene Parrino

Herbed Feta Cheese
in Phyllo Pastry with
Shrimp and Tomato Butter

Serves 8

4 ounces feta cheese
4 ounces cream cheese
1 clove garlic, minced
2 tablespoons minced fresh cilantro
   Up to 1 tablespoon heavy cream
   Salt and freshly ground black pepper
     to taste
4 14 × 18-inch leaves phyllo pastry
1 stick unsalted butter, melted

SAUCE
3 tablespoons butter
½ cup finely chopped onion
1 clove garlic, minced
3 large tomatoes, peeled, seeded, and
   chopped
   Salt and freshly ground black pepper
     to taste
1 tablespoon minced fresh parsley
4 tablespoons coarsely chopped raw
   shrimp
4 tablespoons butter, chilled

   Parsley and cilantro for garnish

Combine cheeses, garlic, and cilantro in a medium-sized mixing bowl and blend well. Thin with a small amount of cream. Add salt and pepper.

Remove the phyllo from the package and cover it with a damp tea towel. Brush one sheet of pastry with a generous amount of melted butter. Cover it with another sheet of phyllo and brush with butter. Then, using a sharp knife, cut layers lengthwise into 5 rectangular strips, and place a rounded teaspoon of cheese mixture about 1 inch from the end of each strip. Fold the top right-hand corner of the pastry over the filling, creating a triangle. Then fold again the other way, as you would fold a flag. Repeat these folds until the entire strip is folded as one triangular package, brushing the triangle top with butter as you go. Make the remaining packages the same way. Store remaining phyllo for another use.

Preheat oven to 400°. Arrange triangles on a buttered baking sheet so that they do not touch each other; bake in preheated oven 20 minutes.

Meanwhile, make the sauce: Heat the butter in a small saucepan; add the onions and garlic, and cook 5 minutes over low heat. Add the tomatoes, cover, and cook 10 minutes more. Remove cover and cook until all the moisture has evaporated, stirring constantly. Add salt and pepper, parsley, and shrimp. Stir.

Add the butter, a tablespoon at a time, until all of it is incorporated. Spoon a small amount of the warm sauce on one side of each serving plate, place a phyllo triangle on the other side, and garnish with parsley and cilantro.

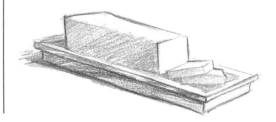

Heat until hot but not boiling. Taste and adjust seasonings. Add more stock if too thick.

Ladle into heated soup plates and garnish with a bit more caraway.

Salad of Belgian Endive, Radicchio, and Sun-Dried Tomatoes

Serves 8

8 large spinach leaves
24 large spears Belgian endive
1 large head radicchio
24 thin strips red bell pepper
8 sun-dried tomatoes
8 small kale leaves

RASPBERRY VINAIGRETTE
2 tablespoons raspberry vinegar
2 teaspoons lemon juice
1½ teaspoons Dijon mustard
8 tablespoons extra-virgin olive oil
Salt and freshly ground black pepper to taste

*W*ash and drain the spinach and lettuces. Place 1 spinach leaf on each of 8 serving plates. Fan 3 endive spears on the spinach and arrange a red pepper strip in the center of each endive spear. Place a radicchio leaf and some shredded radicchio to the lower right of the spinach leaf. Put a sun-dried tomato to the left of the radicchio and a kale leaf somewhere near the middle.

Combine vinegar, lemon juice, and mustard in a small bowl and whisk well. Slowly whisk in the olive oil. Add salt and pepper.

Drizzle salad with raspberry vinaigrette.

Winter Squash Bisque

Serves 8

2 large acorn squash
1 stick unsalted butter
1 medium onion, thinly sliced
2½ cups Chicken Stock (see page 276)
2½ cups heavy cream
Salt and freshly ground white pepper to taste
Caraway seeds

*P*rick squash several times with a fork. Place on baking sheet in 425° oven and cook until tender, about 1 hour. Discard seeds and skin of the squash; set flesh aside.

Melt the butter in a small saucepan, add the onion, and cover with a piece of wax paper pressed directly on the onion. Cook 10 minutes over low heat.

Put onion, squash, and 2 cups stock into the bowl of a food processor and purée until very smooth. Pour the mixture into a heavy saucepan and add the cream, salt, and pepper. Whisk well, then stir in a pinch of caraway.

Pear Butter

Regardless of what season it is, there will always be a wonderful fruit butter served in a pretty dish at Lacorsette. Often garnished with a flower as well as herbs, the fruit butter is a perfect accompaniment to the fragrant warm loaves of bread that are brought to every table. This would still be delicious if made with strawberry preserves and fresh strawberries, raspberry preserves and raspberries, or peach preserves and peaches instead of the pears.

Serves 8

¼ fresh pear, peeled and cored
⅔ cup dry white wine
2 sticks unsalted butter, softened
¼ cup pear preserves

Sprig of cinnamon basil or pineapple mint for garnish

Combine pear and wine in a small saucepan; bring to a boil and reduce heat to a simmer. Poach until the pear is tender, about 20 minutes. Drain pear and dice finely.

Place softened butter and preserves in a mixing bowl and beat until combined well. Fold in the poached pear and blend thoroughly.

Pack into a decorative serving bowl and chill. An hour before serving, let stand at room temperature. Garnish with the cinnamon basil or pineapple mint.

Roast Loin of Pork with Tomato-Prune Chutney

The chutney may be stored for many weeks in the refrigerator. It is good with pork of any kind and also with roasted poultry.

Serves 8

CHUTNEY
3 cups fresh, or 2 cups dried, prunes, halved and pitted
3 ripe tomatoes, peeled, seeded, and coarsely chopped, juice reserved
1 cup dark brown sugar, firmly packed
1 cup sugar
¾ cup red wine vinegar
1 teaspoon mustard seed
1½ teaspoons salt
¼ teaspoon cayenne
¼ cup thinly sliced onion
2 cloves garlic, thinly sliced
2 tablespoons minced fresh ginger
2 rounded tablespoons sultanas (golden raisins)

4 pounds boneless pork loin (3½–4 inches in diameter)*
Salt and freshly ground black pepper to taste
1 carrot, coarsely chopped
1 onion, peeled and coarsely chopped
1 celery stalk, coarsely chopped

In a heavy saucepan, combine prunes, tomatoes and juice, sugars, vinegar, mustard seed, salt, cayenne, and onion. Bring just to a boil, then reduce heat to simmer.

*If roast is more than 4 inches in diameter, increase the roasting time by about 20 minutes.

Add garlic and ginger, stir well, and simmer, stirring often, for 1½ hours, until mixture is very thick. Remove from heat and stir in raisins. Adjust seasonings after mixture cools.

Preheat oven to 400°. Season roast with salt and pepper. Scatter carrot, onion, and celery in roasting pan and place pork loin on top, fat side up. Pour about a half cup of water in the pan. Insert a meat thermometer into the center of the roast. Put roast into the oven and reduce heat to 350°. Roast 1½ hours, adding more water as needed.

When thermometer reaches 155°, remove roast from the oven and cover with foil. Let rest 10 minutes, then cover with a large towel 5 minutes more.

Slice the roast and arrange on heated serving plates. Serve with a moderate amount of the cooked chutney mixture next to the meat.

Ginger-Poached Pears with Raspberry Mousse and Ginger Crème Anglaise

Serves 8

> 8 firm pears, preferably Bosc
> 5 cups water
> 1 cup sugar
> 3 slices fresh ginger

RASPBERRY MOUSSE
> 1 cup heavy cream
> 2 teaspoons unflavored gelatin
> ¾ cup plus 2 tablespoons confectioner's sugar
> 1 cup fresh raspberries, or 6 ounces frozen raspberries, partially thawed
> 1 egg white, beaten to stiff peaks
> 1 tablespoon Framboise liqueur

CRÈME ANGLAISE
> 6 large egg yolks
> ½ cup sugar
> 2 cups warm milk
> 3 slices fresh ginger

> Candied ginger for garnish
> Fresh raspberries for garnish

*P*eel the pears, then core them from the bottom. Bring the water and sugar to a boil in a small but deep saucepan. Scrape the ginger slices with a fork (to release flavor), add to the liquid, then drop the pears into the pot. Lower heat and poach over moderate heat 5 minutes. Turn heat off and let pears remain in the pot 5 minutes more. Remove the pears with a slotted spoon and cool to room temperature.

To make the raspberry mousse: Pour cream into a mixing bowl and sprinkle the gelatin over it. Add sugar and whip until soft peaks form. Fold in raspberries, egg white, and

The Best of the Midwest

Framboise. Carefully spoon this mixture into the cooled pears from the bottom. Fill the entire cavity made by removing the core. Chill thoroughly.

Next, make the crème anglaise: In the top of a double boiler over simmering water, whisk egg yolks and sugar until light in color. Temper by slowly whisking in the warm milk, a bit at a time, until all is added. Scrape the ginger slices with a fork and add to egg mixture. Cook until the mixture thickens, stirring constantly. Remove pan from heat and plunge into ice water to cool quickly, stirring often. Store in the refrigerator, well wrapped, until time to serve. Then remove and discard the ginger slices.

Spoon a generous amount of crème anglaise into each serving dish and place a pear in the middle. Garnish with candied ginger and a berry or two.

Stroud's

KANSAS CITY, MISSOURI

Mention Kansas City and you think barbecue. It is Calvin Trillin who is most responsible for that. He writes often about his hometown, but never more eloquently than when the subject is barbecue. So before our first visit we imagined the city to be covered with a special haze—smoke from its thousands of wood-fired pits. Much to our surprise, the air was clear. Moreover, we quickly learned that there were other very American foods that the city can claim as its specialties. Trillin has also written about our friend Larry "Fats" Goldberg, writer, pizza maker, consultant, and entrepreneur. Fats lost 250 pounds and has kept it off. He eats only on Wednesdays and Saturdays, and we were told to visit him only on an "eating day." This led to a remarkable food odyssey. We had the best doughnuts ever at Lamar's. The pies at Tippen's are better than most mothers will ever produce, and the burgers at Winstead's are superlative. And, of course, we had great barbecue. We don't know why all these wonderful American basics are better in Kansas City, but why think about it? Just eat!

And eat we did at Stroud's, where we had the best fried chicken we have ever had. Note that we did not say the best fried chicken in the world. A statement that definitive could lead to a fight or, at the very least, an argument. People all across this country are passionate about their fried chicken, so you have to be careful. No hyperbole allowed. Even the late Colonel Harlan Sanders, in an interview we did with him, stopped just short of saying that his chicken, Kentucky Fried, was the best in the world. We acknowledge that sometimes the Colonel's chicken can be awfully good; and even though grandmothers on both sides of our household had certain chicken "secrets" (Fred's father made great chicken for forty-nine years in his restaurant in Charleston, West Virginia), we must now repeat that Stroud's served us the chicken dinner of our lives.

While there are other things on the menu, this is really a place for chicken. The birds are delivered daily directly to the kitchen from the farm that has been raising Stroud's chickens for years. These may not be the "free-range" chickens of fancy restaurant fame, but they are birds raised with care, not filled with growth hormones and artificial feed. And, at Stroud's, each piece is fried to order in enormous cast-iron skillets. There are no real recipes here; everything is in the memories of the cooks. There is a century of experience represented by the six cooks at the stove and it shows: the chicken comes out cooked to perfection.

There are accompaniments, of course, and starters. The chicken soup, for example, is probably the richest we have ever had. Filled with chunks of chicken and homemade noodles that are rough-cut by hand, it is a soup that would bring tears of joy to the eyes of any Jewish grandmother. The huge bowl of mashed potatoes is not for the faint of heart. They are lumpy and loaded with butter, and the felony is compounded by the rich gravy made from the pan drippings of the fried chicken. Another bowl, filled with green beans that have been slowly simmered in a big pot with chunks of smoked ham, is also included. Home fries and cottage fries can be selected in place of the mashed ones—but as we looked around the room, almost every diner was spooning up the mashed. And as if all of this were not enough, there is a large basket filled with yeasty cinnamon buns, all sticky, buttery, and warm.

For those who frequent the place often enough to want an occasional change from the chicken, Stroud's offers a splendid example of chicken-fried steak. A dish that goes back to the chuckwagons of the Texas cattle range, chicken-fried steak is made with less expensive cuts of beef, soaked and breaded in the same fashion as their chicken, fried in cast-iron skillets, and served bathed in Stroud's famous chicken pan gravy. There are also fried shrimp and catfish on the menu, along with the ubiquitous Kansas City steak.

Dinner at Stroud's is an event; almost theater. The food comes from the kitchen piled on big trays and carried high overhead by

young men who rush it to the servers, and it is put before you while it is still almost too hot to touch. There is a cacophony of dishes clattering, servers rushing, a hundred different conversations, and piano music from Ray Searcy, who came to play the blues on the upright one night several years ago and never left. With an uncanny memory for the favorite songs of the regulars, he also charms the children in the room by responding with special warmth as they approach the piano.

Stroud's isn't much to look at. It's a big ramshackle building in an industrial district and parking can be a problem. Just inside the front door is a dark paneled bar where you stand and wait for your table. There is a certain camaraderie that develops among the waiting crowd as we sip our drinks, impatiently watching the diners who are too slowly gnawing their drumsticks or enjoying more potatoes. But most of all, there is the tantalizing fragrance of fried chicken.

The huge dining area seems to have evolved in stages over the years and spaces jut off at strange angles. The floors are of wood, heavily polished by time and use; the ceiling is almost claustrophobically low. Tablecloths are checkered in red and white, and the chairs are bentwood and cane, the kind that encourage you to eat quickly. This is a place for serious eating but not leisurely dining. It is a restaurant you come to with the family and with the kinds of friends who feel like family. You come here when you are ravenously hungry and want huge portions of simple food. We didn't leave a single spoonful of gravy, not one crumb of cinnamon bun. And when we looked at our bill we realized that we had just encountered one of the gastronomic bargains of the cosmos. The question we had for each other as we left was: How soon can we get back to Kansas City?

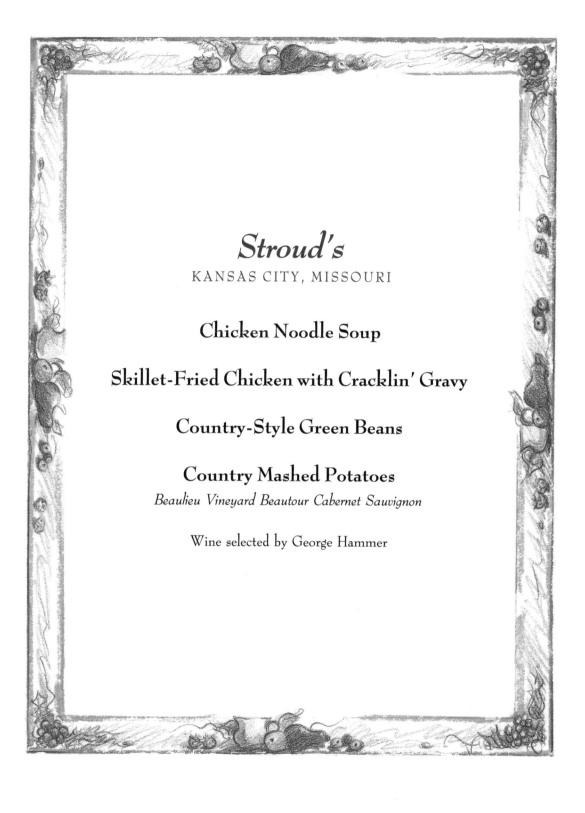

Stroud's
KANSAS CITY, MISSOURI

Chicken Noodle Soup

Skillet-Fried Chicken with Cracklin' Gravy

Country-Style Green Beans

Country Mashed Potatoes
Beaulieu Vineyard Beautour Cabernet Sauvignon

Wine selected by George Hammer

Chicken Noodle Soup

Serves 8

> 4 quarts Chicken Stock (see page 276)
> 12 chicken thighs
> 6 carrots, trimmed, scrubbed, and cut
>   in chunks
> ½ cup chopped fresh parsley
> 2 large eggs
> ½ teaspoon salt
>   Up to 3 cups flour
>   Salt and freshly ground black pepper
>   to taste
> 2 dashes Worcestershire sauce

Combine stock, thighs, carrots, and parsley in a large soup pot. Bring to a boil, lower heat, and simmer until the thighs are very tender, about 45 to 60 minutes.

Remove the chicken and cut the meat from the bones in chunks. Return chunks to the pot and remove from heat.

Beat the eggs and salt together in a large mixing bowl. Stir in 1 cup of flour. Then work in up to 2 cups additional flour, a bit at a time. The dough should be stiff but pliable and tender. Add 2 tablespoons water only if necessary. Knead briefly on a lightly floured board, then divide in half. Roll about 1/16 inch thick and cut with a knife into wide noodles. Roll and cut remaining dough.

Bring soup back to a simmer and add noodles, salt, pepper, and Worcestershire. Simmer about 10 minutes, or until noodles are done. Ladle into heated serving plates.

Skillet-Fried Chicken with Cracklin' Gravy

Serves 8

> 2 3–4-pound frying chickens
> 1 quart buttermilk
> 1¾ cups unbleached flour
> 1 cup whole-wheat flour
> 1 teaspoon salt, or more to taste
> 1 tablespoon coarsely ground black
>   pepper
> 1 pound lard
> 4 cups milk

Cut the chickens into at least 8 pieces each. Remove backbones and wing tips. Arrange chicken pieces in a large bowl and cover with buttermilk. Soak at least several hours. Drain.

Blend 1½ cups unbleached flour with the whole-wheat flour, salt, and pepper. Toss chicken in flour mixture to coat well; then let the pieces dry on a cake rack at least 10 minutes.

Heat the lard in a large cast-iron skillet until a bread cube put into the pan browns quickly. The lard should be at least ½ inch deep in the pan. Carefully add the chicken pieces without crowding. Cover the skillet and fry over medium heat 10 minutes. Turn the chicken and continue frying, covered, another 10 minutes. Check several times to make certain that the pieces do not burn. If the pieces are quite large, they may need a few more minutes. Remove the chicken, drain well, and keep warm.

Pour all the fat from the skillet through a large, coarse strainer into a bowl. Turn chicken bits that remain in the strainer into a small bowl and reserve. Spoon 4 tablespoons of fat back into

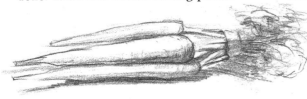

the skillet and return skillet to heat. Over very low heat, scrape the remaining browned chicken bits from the bottom of the pan. Pour contents of skillet and reserved bowl of bits into the strainer over another small bowl. Push the chicken bits and accompanying fat through a coarse strainer to further break up the pieces.

Return chicken bits and fat to the skillet and add ¼ cup unbleached flour. Stir over high heat so that the flour loses its whiteness and gets a bit tan. Gradually whisk in the milk and bring to a boil. Reduce heat and let simmer until the gravy has thickened. Add salt and pepper to taste.

Serve chicken Stroud's style—in a large bowl, with another bowl on the side for the gravy.

Country-Style Green Beans

Serves 8

2 sticks butter
1½ cups chopped onions
1 large (about 2 pounds) smoked ham
    hock
2½ pounds fresh green beans, trimmed
    and cut into 1-inch pieces
2 tablespoons freshly ground black
    pepper

6 cups water
   Salt to taste

*M*elt 1 stick butter in a heavy 3-quart saucepan. Add onions and cook over very low heat for a few minutes. *Do not brown.*

Add remaining ingredients except 1 stick butter and the salt, partially cover, and bring to a boil. Let boil 5 minutes. Lower the heat, cover completely, and simmer at least 15 minutes. Drain. Skin ham hock and cut meat off the bone. Return meat to the pan.

Add salt and remaining butter and toss until melted.

Country Mashed Potatoes

Serves 8

9 large Idaho potatoes, well scrubbed
1 stick margarine
   Up to 1½ cups milk
   Salt

*B*oil the potatoes until fork-tender, about 45 minutes. Drain and peel.

Put hot potatoes in the bowl of an electric mixer, cut in the margarine, and mash with a potato masher. Then, with mixer on low, slowly add enough milk to make the potatoes light and slightly creamy. Add salt to taste.

Jack Fiorella's Smokestack Bar-B-Que of Martin City

MARTIN CITY, MISSOURI

Selecting the best barbecue place in Kansas City is something akin to selecting a favorite among your children. You know you love them all, because they're all special for different reasons. But we decided that, at least as far as eating establishments were concerned, it would be an ugly job but somebody had to do it. We didn't manage to try every barbecue place in Kansas City but, again with help from Larry "Fats" Goldberg, the human food encyclopedia, we certainly managed to visit quite a few. We learned that fine art of short-ordering—standing in line; ordering for one, since that will usually provide more than enough food for two; sitting down at the ubiquitous Formica table; sharing the treasure. Linda learned to keep her glasses in her purse, lest she see how messy the floor was. We both learned also not to feel guilty about leaving some of the good stuff on our plates, since we had miles to go before we could stop eating. Until we saw for ourselves, we always thought Calvin Trillin, the incredibly chauvinistic Kansas Cityite, might be a bit nuts when he rhapsodized about the culinary delights of his native city. But now we under-

stand why people in K.C. are passionate about their barbecue. We agree with them that the best barbecue is, indeed, to be found in Kansas City. It's at Arthur Bryant's, it's at Gate's, it's at Richard's. Above all, it's at Jack Fiorella's Smokestack of Martin City. And Linda can even wear her glasses there.

Barbecue is much more than ribs, or brisket, or chicken; it's more than fire and smoke. One of the things we learned from our trip is that the secret might be more in the oven than in the sauce or the meat. At Smokestack the huge brick ovens are fired by hickory logs. All of this is watched over by a pit man, who keeps the fires burning properly. The huge racks hold massive amounts of ribs, turkeys, briskets, chicken, and pork loins. A talented pit man knows just where in the oven to put which cut of meat, so that the proper degree of doneness is achieved. Smoking is over low heat, so the cooking is very slow—it's "low and slow." Grilling is directly over the fire, so that the juices are seared into the meat.

While good barbecue places don't burn food, everyone has bits and pieces of ends that are very well done. We discovered the joys of eating "burnt ends" at Smokestack. Since nothing goes to waste here or at any other good barbecue place, the burned ends of roasts, ribs, and sausages all get cut off, drizzled with sauce, and sold as a lunch treat or an appetizer. Hard to believe that something burned could be so delicious! In addition, there are deep-fried mushrooms, chicken livers, and onion rings, all of which have a crispy coating that is perfectly drained of excess oil. But Smokestack is famous for its meats—the heavenly sausage with enough spice to stand up to the smokiness and sauce; the hams, pork roasts, briskets, and ribs of all kinds, all smoked to perfection and all flavorful enough to eat even without Smokestack's superlative sauces. Smokestack's barbecue sauces, by the way, come either hot and spicy or mild and smoky, with some good tang. Neither one is overly sweet, which pleased us.

Accompaniments at Smokestack are outstanding. The baked beans are better than the ones we make at home, which to us says a lot. On a busy Saturday, 350 pounds are served! Flavored with barbecue sauce, they are filled with tidbits of smoky pork and brisket, and are baked in the bottom of the pit to catch some of the juicy drippings from the meats above. Hard as it is, one must also save room for the cheesy corn, which is thick with Cheddar cheese and punctuated with bits of ham. This is our kind of soul food!

After all this, we must share with everyone one of the best parts about Smokestack—the fish menu. In response to customer demand for healthier food, Jack Fiorella developed a splendid menu of fresh hickory-grilled fish and skewered vegetables, grilled al dente on wooden skewers. Basted with an herb marinade, the vegetables make a satisfy-

ing accompaniment for those who opt to pass up the calorie-laden beans and corn. As for the fish, we cannot think of any place that does it better. The selection varies according to availability, but one can almost always find delicate Norwegian salmon, yellowfin tuna, and catfish with Cajun spices. While no sauce is needed for fish this moist and tasty, there are two served with each order. One sauce is delicious lemon butter with lots of pepper, and the other is a zippy creamy horseradish. Since barbecue food calls for lots of liquid refreshments as well, we enthusiastically recommend the vast selection of outstanding beers from around the world.

Jack Fiorella's Smokestack is a half-hour drive south from downtown Kansas City. While the family has other restaurants, Jack opened the Martin City place in 1974. It's a nifty old building that has grown in bits and spurts over the years. The kitchen is right in front as you enter, with aromas of hickory and barbecue sauce wafting into adjoining rooms. Most of the place is paneled; old beams support the ceilings. There is a great

The Best of the Midwest

stone fireplace to ward off the chill of winter. Old photographs and bric-a-brac adorn the walls, and marvelous antique light fixtures illuminate a delightful variety of collectible tables and chairs. Altogether, it is warm and welcoming. When filled, the restaurant seats 138 people inside, while the outside terrace accommodates some of those waiting for dinner. Although waiting is part of the game, the time passes quickly and tables turn over frequently, since the efficient serving staff keeps the food coming smoothly without seeming to rush those still dining.

The Fiorella family has been in the barbecue business since 1957. The family's first place is run by Jack's sister. Although his children are now coming into the business, Jack still works long hours. First he stays in the kitchen, tasting and touching; then he moves to the front, seating and greeting. It's hard to relax in this kind of business. Even when there might be a lull in the dining room, the telephone keeps ringing with orders "to go." In a city fabled for its barbecue, there seems to be no end to the demand. One of Jack's secrets is to buy the best meats he can; it is his method of quality assurance. He insists that there is no way to turn out a good product with inferior materials. Jack Fiorella knows that he cannot rest on his laurels, that demand continues only if the Smokestack of Martin City continues to be one of the best places in town. It is his mission to make certain that it does.

Jack Fiorella's Smokestack Bar-B-Que of Martin City

MARTIN CITY, MISSOURI

Fresh Vegetable Kabobs
McDowell Valley Vineyards White Zinfandel

Grilled Salmon with Drawn Butter and Horseradish Sauce

Cheesy Corn Bake
R. H. Phillips Vineyard Cabernet Sauvignon

Wines selected by John Giguirre

Fresh Vegetable Kabobs

The Horseradish Sauce (below) is a good accompaniment to this simple and delicious appetizer.

Serves 4

1 pound butter
½ teaspoon garlic powder
1 teaspoon minced fresh parsley
2 teaspoons lemon juice
2 small onions, peeled
4 ½–¾-inch carrot slices, cut
    diagonally, and blanched 3 minutes
4 ½–¾-inch zucchini slices, cut
    diagonally
4 2-inch slices corn on the cob
4 ½–¾-inch yellow squash slices, cut
    diagonally
4 mushroom caps
8 2-inch-square green bell pepper
    slices
4 12-inch wooden skewers, soaked in
    water
  Salt and freshly ground black pepper
    to taste
⅓ cup chopped fresh parsley

Melt the butter in a medium-sized saucepan over very low heat. Pour into a measuring cup and skim off the milky foam that forms on the top and discard. Chill remaining contents in the cup. Then transfer the solidified butter to a small saucepan and discard any sediment that remains in the bottom of the cup. Reheat the now clarified butter with garlic powder, parsley, and lemon juice. Set aside.

Carefully wash the vegetables and arrange on skewers, beginning and ending with the green pepper pieces. Brush with butter sauce and let rest while you prepare the grill (see instructions in the salmon recipe below).

When fire has reached its peak temperature, set kabobs on grill, baste with more butter, and grill, turning several times, until vegetables are tender but still firm. Sprinkle with salt, pepper, and parsley.

Grilled Salmon with Drawn Butter and Horseradish Sauce

Serves 4

HORSERADISH SAUCE
2 large egg yolks
1 tablespoon lemon juice
½ teaspoon dry mustard
½ teaspoon Dijon mustard
¼ teaspoon kosher salt
¼ teaspoon freshly ground white
    pepper
½ cup vegetable oil
½ cup light and fruity olive oil
⅓ cup prepared white horseradish
2 teaspoons dried parsley or 2
    tablespoons minced fresh parsley

1 pound butter
½ teaspoon garlic powder
2 teaspoons minced fresh parsley
2 teaspoons lemon juice
½ cup salt
2 teaspoons freshly ground white
   pepper
2 teaspoons freshly ground black
   pepper
Hickory logs or hickory chips
4 8-ounce fillets Norwegian salmon

Combine first 6 ingredients in bowl of a food processor or blender and blend. With the motor running, add vegetable oil and olive oil in a very slow but steady stream, so that the mixture will emulsify and thicken into mayonnaise. Add horseradish and parsley, and blend briefly. Transfer to a bowl, cover tightly, and refrigerate at least 2 hours.

Melt butter in a medium-sized saucepan over very low heat. Pour into a measuring cup and skim off the milky foam that forms on the top. Chill remaining contents in the cup. Then transfer solidified butter that remains to a small saucepan and discard any sediment in the bottom of the measuring cup. Reheat the now clarified butter with garlic powder, parsley, and lemon juice. Set aside.

Combine the next 3 ingredients in a small bowl and sprinkle some over the salmon fillets. Store the remainder for future use.

For best grilling results, stack grill with fresh-cut hickory logs. If unavailable, use hickory chips with charcoal. Wait until fire has reached its peak temperature and then set the grill 8 to 12 inches above the flame. Do not let the flame touch the grill.

Place the salmon fillets skin side up. Cook just until surface is seared (under 4 minutes). Turn carefully, baste with butter mixture, and continue to grill until done. Do not overcook. A fillet that is ¾ inch thick should need no more than 8 minutes of grilling. Baste with butter several times, but do not turn more than once.

Serve with Horseradish Sauce on the side.

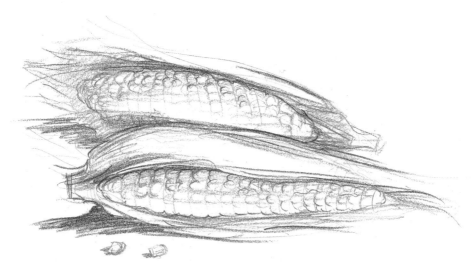

The Best of the Midwest

Cheesy Corn Bake

Serves 4

SAUCE

    2 tablespoons butter

    2 tablespoons flour

    ½ teaspoon dry mustard

        Up to 1½ cups hot milk

    ⅔ cup grated sharp Cheddar cheese

    7 ounces cream cheese, cut into pieces

    3 ounces smoked ham, diced

    2 teaspoons garlic salt

1¼ cups milk

    4 cups frozen corn kernels (don't defrost)

*I*n a small heavy saucepan melt the butter. Add flour and whisk well over low heat 2 minutes. Do not let flour mixture become brown. Blend in dry mustard. Whisking constantly, slowly add 1 cup hot milk and simmer sauce over low heat until thickened. Stir in grated cheese and stir until melted. Add remaining milk if sauce is too thick and will not pour easily.

Preheat oven to 325°. Combine cheese sauce, cream cheese, ham, garlic salt, and milk in a 2-quart casserole and bake in the preheated oven until cream cheese is melted, about 20 minutes. Remove from oven and stir. Add frozen corn, mix again, and bake another 30 minutes. Stir and scoop into individual casseroles. Place under a hot broiler to brown the top and serve.

Tony's

ST. LOUIS, MISSOURI

Until April 2, 1989, Tony's had to have been the last best restaurant in the world that did not take reservations. We only wish that we might have been the very first to have given our names on that day when the earth stood still and owner Vince Bommarito changed his policy. But then, there was something quite special about sipping wine at the bar, nibbling on deep-fried ravioli, and chatting with the bartender about the phenomenon of an elegant and pricy restaurant where everyone takes his or her turn to wait for a table. We had heard rumors that Vince's kitchen door had been known to swing open for a favored few. But that was just rumor. We also liked knowing that even the regulars—including the rich and famous—all had to submit to the ritual of pre-dinner drinks in the bar, and leisurely drinks at that. "The Wait," as it was called, was made even more amazing by the fact that it lasted the more than forty years that Tony's has been St. Louis's top restaurant. Linda remembers her twenty-first birthday dinner, given there by Uncle Dave and Aunt Roz Grosberg and cousins Don and Peggy Ross. And while it had

been at least ten years since she had last been there, the same warm greetings were being extended as guests came to the door. Some things never change. They just get better.

While there are always new and different dishes available at Tony's, the menu tries to feel the same as it always has. It is important that the restaurant offers new dishes to the regulars, but Tony's Italian roots are always evident, and the restaurant's history as the best place for steak continues, ensuring that the regulars will always feel comfortable. The problem comes in making selections from the menu. One of Vince's special openers is smoked salmon with mascarpone filling, rolled and sliced into beautiful spirals that are filled with flavor. Other cold antipasti include perfectly aged prosciutto wrapped around luscious melon and roasted red peppers in a heady, extra-virgin olive oil accompanied by fresh mozzarella and basil. On the hot side, there are luscious snail-filled ravioli rich with parsley butter, perfectly cooked sea scallops with truffles, and tender shrimp sautéed in garlic butter and finished with wine. After antipasti we move to a pasta course. From delicate cappellini with meat or mushrooms to the tiny ziti, we are tempted and teased. There are at least a dozen pasta sauces on any menu, including carbonara, with bacon and wine, a white clam sauce, and pesto, to mention just a few. And, to our delight, there is a nightly risotto, creamy and fragrant, always perfectly al dente.

Tony's offers a variety of salads. From a delicious house salad to thick slices of tomatoes, red onions, and anchovies, they are all dressed with flavorful extra-virgin olive oil and red wine vinegar. Now the stage is set for some outstanding entrees. The famous Lobster Albanello has been a specialty for years. Tender chunks of lobster meat and sautéed mushrooms are bathed in a rich cream sauce and served on a bed of fettuccine. For the health-conscious, there are impeccably fresh grilled salmon and trout. A tomato-rich zuppa di pesce is filled with chunks of fish and shellfish. And the fillet of fresh swordfish is tender and sweet, served with a heavenly sauce of tomatoes and capers punctuated with zesty olives. As we would expect, beef dishes are also extraordinary. We believe that Tony's manages to have the best beef in the world. But there is nothing wrong with their veal and lamb, either—or their stuffed breast of quail or lobster Fra Diavolo. And of course, all intentions to pass on dessert are thrown to the winds when one watches the clouds of egg yolks and Marsala rising in a nearby chafing dish, as a highly skilled captain whips up ethereal zabaglione. It looks so light, as do the torta di ricotta and the bananas flambé.

Located in downtown St. Louis, the several-story house has a long history in the neighborhood. After renovation, some of the brick walls are now exposed; other walls are richly paneled. The large cocktail lounge has a number of big sofas and many upholstered chairs.

No article has been written about this restaurant without making reference to the fact that the maître d' walks backward as he leads guests upstairs to the dining room, so that his back is never turned to a guest. It is a gesture that could easily become an affectation if it were not truly sincere. Tony's exudes warmth. Its Old World atmosphere, with fine touches of flowers, soft lights, and outstanding service, makes people welcome and comfortable. An outstanding wine list is presented and knowledgeable assistance is there for the asking. Wineglasses are kept replenished, courses perfectly orchestrated. A napkin dropped to the floor is retrieved and replaced in a quiet instant. Tableside preparation is not as prevalent as it has been in the past, but all food is transferred to hot plates right in the dining room.

Vince Bommarito has earned his place as a fabled restaurateur. What began as his father's spaghetti house for truckers, he built into today's legend. With the help of his brother Anthony and now with his sons, Anthony and Vincent, Jr., he has established a standard for the entire industry. Much has been written about the procedural handbooks at Tony's; they cover every aspect of restaurant operation, including the polishing of silver and the washing of floors. A microphone stands near the entrance to the kitchen. Orders are called out by the waiters, so that they control the flow of food to each table. It is a marvelous system indeed. All prep work is done away from the main kitchen, allowing for a chaos-free environment for the final cooking. Cleanliness has been a particular passion of Vince's. The kitchen is spotless, even during peak times. One really could "eat off the floors." Nevertheless, Vince Bommarito has time to greet every patron. Quietly walking among the guests, he knows exactly the right moment to chat at each table. For friends, it might be a long pause; for lovers, the visit will be briefer. And regardless of the hungry hordes waiting, not a single guest is rushed. It is the policy at Tony's to refrain from presenting a bill until it is requested. And so, even on a Saturday night, with its enormous crowds, dinner at Tony's is a wonderful experience, when we can savor every bite, relax between courses, and finally linger over an old brandy and celebrate the good fortune that has encouraged the Bommarito family to nurture the culinary soul of St. Louis. It was wonderful when Linda turned twenty-one; it was still wonderful when her son Andy turned twenty-one. We expect that we'll someday take our grandchildren there for their celebrations, too.

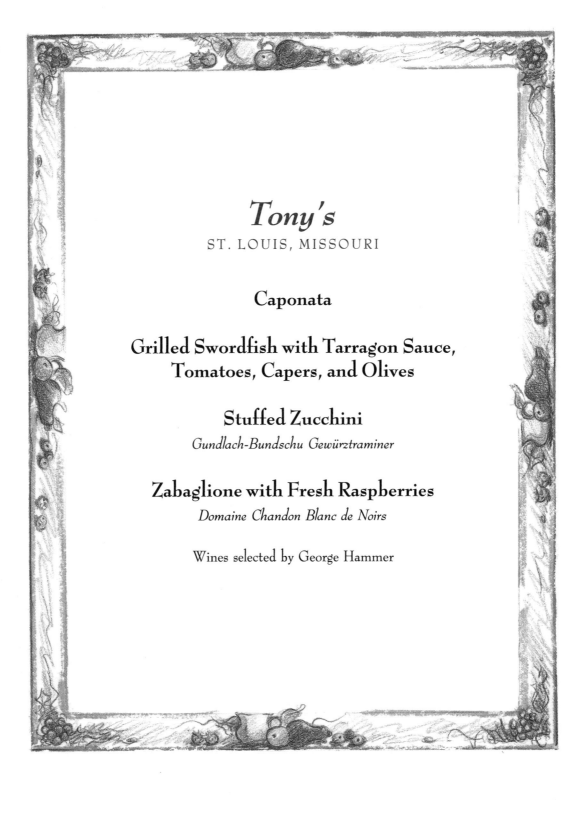

Tony's
ST. LOUIS, MISSOURI

Caponata

Grilled Swordfish with Tarragon Sauce, Tomatoes, Capers, and Olives

Stuffed Zucchini
Gundlach-Bundschu Gewürztraminer

Zabaglione with Fresh Raspberries
Domaine Chandon Blanc de Noirs

Wines selected by George Hammer

Caponata

Serves 4

    1 medium eggplant, peeled
    ¼ cup extra-virgin olive oil
    1 medium onion, chopped
14½ ounces canned Italian plum tomatoes
    ½ cup celery, cut into ¼-inch slices
    2 tablespoons capers, rinsed
    1 tablespoon sugar
    2 tablespoons wine vinegar
      Salt and freshly ground black pepper
        to taste

      Radicchio, curly endive, and fresh
        herbs for garnish

Cut eggplant into 1-inch cubes. Heat olive oil in a medium skillet and fry eggplant over high heat about 10 minutes, or until tender and lightly browned. Use a slotted spoon to remove eggplant from skillet to a medium saucepan.

Adding more olive oil if needed, sauté onion in skillet. When golden, add tomatoes and celery; simmer about 15 minutes, or until celery is tender. Add capers. Add this mixture to the eggplant.

Combine sugar and vinegar in a small saucepan. Add salt and pepper, and heat. Then add to the eggplant mixture. Cover and simmer about 20 minutes over very low heat. Stir occasionally to distribute the flavors evenly. Let cool and serve at room temperature, garnished with radicchio, curly endive, and herbs.

Grilled Swordfish with Tarragon Sauce, Tomatoes, Capers, and Olives

We find that this sauce is thick enough with ¼ pound less butter than Tony's uses.

Serves 4

TARRAGON SAUCE
  1½ cups white wine
    ½ cup tarragon vinegar
    2 tablespoons finely chopped shallots
    1 tablespoon finely chopped fresh
      tarragon
  1½ cups heavy cream
    1 pound butter, cut into pieces
      Salt and freshly ground white pepper
        to taste

    4 1-inch thick swordfish steaks
      Olive oil
      Salt and freshly ground white pepper
        to taste
    1 ripe tomato, peeled, seeded, and
      chopped
    2 tablespoons capers
  16 Niçoise olives, pitted

      Tarragon sprigs for garnish

In a large, heavy saucepan, combine wine, vinegar, shallots, and tarragon. Simmer briskly over medium heat until liquid is almost evaporated. Add heavy cream, bring to boil, and cook until slightly thickened—about 3 or 4 minutes. Turn heat to low and whisk in butter, a bit at a time. *Do not let this come to a boil.* When butter is completely incorporated, remove from heat and season with salt and pepper. Keep on a warm part of the stove or in a larger saucepan filled with hot water.

Rub fish with olive oil, sprinkle with more salt and pepper. Thoroughly clean grill top and spray with Pam. Heat until very hot and grill fish on both sides until done, about 4 minutes on one side and 3 on the other.

Center swordfish on warm serving plates. Spoon sauce around the fish. Sprinkle with tomato and capers; scatter olives. Add sprigs of tarragon and serve.

Stuffed Zucchini

Serves 4

4 small zucchini
2 tablespoons butter
2 tablespoons finely chopped shallots
1 tablespoon finely chopped prosciutto
½ cup finely chopped mushrooms
2 tablespoons dry sherry
1½ cups heavy cream
1 teaspoon minced fresh parsley
¾ cup grated Parmesan cheese
½ cup fresh white bread crumbs
Salt and freshly ground black pepper to taste

*P*reheat oven to 350°. Cut both ends off the zucchini so that each vegetable is about 4 inches long. Cut a flat strip off the bottom so that the zucchini will stand while baking. With a melon baller, scoop out the inside of the zucchini. Chop up the flesh and set aside.

In a skillet, melt the butter and add the shallots and prosciutto. Sauté over low heat until the shallots are glossy. Add the mushrooms and chopped zucchini. Cook until done, about 10 minutes. Add sherry and stir well. Then add cream. Cook about 4 minutes or until cream has thickened. Add parsley, Parmesan, and bread crumbs. Season with salt and pepper.

Stuff the zucchini with this mixture. Bake in preheated oven ½ hour, or until done.

Zabaglione with Fresh Raspberries

We think that there is nothing more wonderful than watching zabaglione swell and rise in the pot in response to the enthusiastic use of a balloon whisk! While a double boiler works almost as well, there is nothing prettier than a rounded copper zabaglione pot, which doesn't have cracks and corners to inhibit the whisk.

Serves 4

2 pints fresh raspberries
8 teaspoons sugar
Vanilla extract
8 ounces sweet Marsala wine
8 large egg yolks
Dash of salt

Ground cinnamon for garnish

Wash and drain the berries and distribute all but a few among four long-stemmed goblets. Reserve the remaining berries for the final garnish.

In a tall 3-quart saucepan that is narrow enough to support a zabaglione pot, or the bottom half of a double boiler, add water to a point *just below* the upper pot. Bring the water to a boil, then lower to a simmer. The top pot should not actually touch the water.

In the zabaglione pot itself, or the top half of a double boiler, combine sugar, a few drops of vanilla, and wine. Stir until sugar is dissolved. Add yolks and salt. Beat in a rapid folding motion with a balloon whisk over simmering water until the mixture swells in volume and becomes an airy and creamy custard. (It helps to be in good shape for this.) About the time your arm is ready to fall off, the zabaglione is ready. Pour over the berries. Garnish with the remaining berries and sprinkle with a dash of cinnamon.

Broadway Oyster Bar

ST. LOUIS, MISSOURI

The Broadway Oyster Bar is a place you hear about from someone who likes you. There is no sign in front—no identification at all, just a street number and an open door. We walked past it twice before we realized we were there. It is one of the few old houses still standing in an urban-renewal area a few blocks from Busch Stadium and downtown St. Louis. We were told to go there for wonderful and unpretentious seafood, and we were told to go there hungry.

The menu is written daily on chalkboards displayed both inside and in the courtyard. We went right for the oysters. Fresh and sweet, they are served a variety of ways, depending on the whim of the kitchen. If the grinder is offered, don't miss it. Imagine half a loaf of quality French bread, hollowed out in the middle and filled with a dozen succulent oysters sautéed in gobs of sweet butter, seasoned with a squeeze of fresh lemon, a sprinkling of parsley, and an eye-popping dose of cayenne. Raw oysters are always available, and are possibly the freshest in town. The sauces are marvelous but may be superfluous on oysters that good. Lucky patrons might also find

crayfish sautéed in a garlicky butter sauce or alligator tail in a spicy gumbo thickened by caramelized okra, an addition that contributes mightily to the gumbo's rich taste.

The kitchen staff is constantly planning new dishes that always reflect the best of the current season. The portions are huge, with a high ratio of shellfish to sauce. A scrumptious seafood salad is filled with tender scallops, plump mussels, and shrimp, then generously seasoned with fresh dill and rosemary. No phony fillers here. They concentrate on what goes into the bowl, not on the bowl itself, so food comes on plastic-coated plates and beer is served in the bottle. Presentation is not the priority here. Flavor and quality are.

The tiny kitchen, a simple lean-to of raw plywood sheeting, extends into the courtyard at the rear. Outside, barely screened from view by a large chalkboard, are the two items that are essential to producing the foods of the house: a half-barrel smoker, sooty from use, and a huge cauldron for steaming, precariously perched on a butane burner and blackened from its gases. There is a rough-built bandstand across the front of the courtyard that also blocks the sights and sounds of the heavy traffic rushing down Broadway. Another old house obviously was here long ago; its markings still show on the brick wall of the building itself, like a fossilized fern in a piece of prehistoric shale.

Devoted patrons possessing varying degrees of artistic talent have contributed murals and assemblages, along with a variety of sculptures, to the decor. At night, lanterns and candles soften the cracks in the furniture and add atmosphere to the clutter. Darkness is also an ally inside, adding an element of mystery to the oddball collection of art, bottles, clippings, posters, a baseball glove, and other contributions of customers past and present.

Dennis Connolly, a former Chicagoan, and Michael Thomas, a riverboat chef, started the place in October 1978 as a bar. At first they served only oysters, canned sardines, and hard-boiled eggs. Little by little, the menu grew. Some time later, Thomas left and Connolly ran the kitchen, while a new partner,

Donna Jeanne Hesseman, supervised the front.

Like most experienced cooks at home, successful professional chefs waste very little food in the kitchen. In fact, we have found that some of the best dishes we have created came about because we were trying to avoid wasting something in the kitchen. Dennis Connolly added some wonderful thoughts along these lines when he sent us his recipes. We couldn't resist sharing them with our readers:

All efforts at successful cooking are hopeless without a well-founded base. That is to say, most soups and sauces are made with herbs, spices, flavor builders, and some sort of a liquid. Water is the handiest, the cheapest, and also the least flavorful. When we cook commercially, we use some kind of stock for our liquid. Stocks are made in kettles with water, scraps of vegetables, and chunks of meat and bones—scraps of whatever flavor we wish to achieve. For instance, when shrimp is cooked, we use water flavored with herbs, spices, maybe a chopped onion, a touch of vinegar, and, finally, the shrimp itself. Save this liquid, strain it, and use it later for stock. Likewise, when a fish is filleted, don't discard the head and skeleton. Place them in a kettle with water, add some onion, celery, parsley, whatever vegetable bits are left from your meal prep, salt, pepper, and whatever herbs and spices you wish. Simmer this for about 30 minutes. What you will strain from this is a deep, rich fish stock to enhance whatever sauce or soup you are making. Do the same for chicken bones, fat, and leftover parts such as necks, backs, and gizzards.

Simmer the stock, never boil it. Allow it to cool, strain it through a sieve lined with cheesecloth, then refrigerate it. After it has cooled, you will notice that a layer of fat has risen to the top. This forms a natural sealant until you are ready to use the stock. This fat can also be worked in with flour to make a roux, a thickening agent for soups or sauces. When you make a roux, the object is to *slightly* burn the flour so it cooks and has a nutty flavor to it. Otherwise a dish will take on a pasty raw-flour taste and may even come up lumpy. In any case, a roux will take on the flavor of whatever it is made from and then can be used as a thickener instead of raw flour or cornstarch.

Here in a nutshell you have two secrets of budget management, because all this flavor comes from scrap, water, and a little flour. In other words, nothing goes to waste.

Other than saving time, there is really no reason to buy artificial flavor at an extra cost when there is such a bounty of natural flavor at your fingertips.

Recently a devoted patron made Connolly and Hesseman an offer they couldn't refuse; they sold the restaurant, but the new owner assures the patrons that they will still have an experience as comfortable and unpretentious as "going home," with a staff that treats everyone "like family." The food is creative and always delicious, the prices are low, and, most important, it is clear that everyone associated with the Broadway Oyster Bar is having fun.

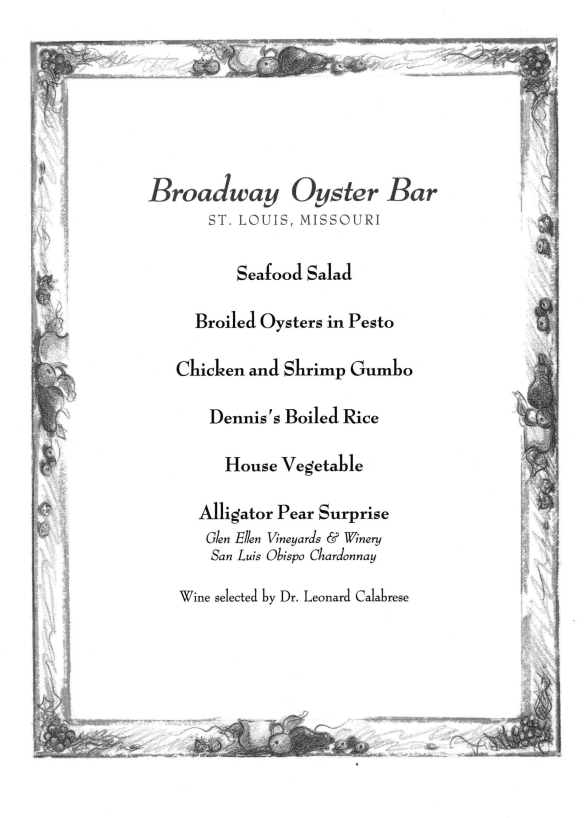

Broadway Oyster Bar
ST. LOUIS, MISSOURI

Seafood Salad

Broiled Oysters in Pesto

Chicken and Shrimp Gumbo

Dennis's Boiled Rice

House Vegetable

Alligator Pear Surprise

*Glen Ellen Vineyards & Winery
San Luis Obispo Chardonnay*

Wine selected by Dr. Leonard Calabrese

Seafood Salad

Serves 8 to 10

MARINADE

 ½ cup red wine vinegar
 ½ cup water
 2 teaspoons sugar
 1 teaspoon lemon juice
 1 teaspoon salt
 2 teaspoons black pepper
 1 teaspoon Worcestershire sauce
 4 tablespoons Dijon mustard
 4 teaspoons grated onion
 1 teaspoon minced garlic
 2 cups extra-virgin olive oil
 2 tablespoons poppy seeds

 2 tablespoons unsalted butter
 1 tablespoon minced garlic
24 mussels, scrubbed and debearded
 ¼ cup Sauvignon Blanc wine
 2 pounds bay scallops
 ½ pound (31 to 35) small shrimp
 1 tablespoon fresh rosemary
 1 tablespoon fresh dill weed
8 to 10 large leaves of red cabbage
8 to 10 large lettuce leaves
 4 to 5 cups shredded lettuce

  Celery stalks with leaves attached
   for garnish

*I*n a 2-quart bowl, combine all ingredients for the marinade except olive oil and poppy seeds. Whisk well, then slowly add olive oil, whisking continuously until all the oil is blended. Whisk in poppy seeds. Set marinade aside.

In a large skillet with a tight lid, melt butter, add garlic, and sizzle over medium heat. Add mussels. When sizzle begins again, pour wine over them, cover, and steam 6 to 8 minutes. Discard mussels that have not opened. Using a sharp knife, remove mussels from the open shells and put them into the bowl of marinade.

Reheat liquid in the skillet, add scallops, and simmer 5 minutes, turning several times. Use a slotted spoon to remove scallops from skillet, then add them to the marinade.

Reheat liquid again and add shrimp. Simmer until they turn pink and feel firm. Remove from liquid, peel and devein, cut in half lengthwise, and add to marinade.

Add rosemary and dill to marinade and let stand a minimum of 2 to a maximum of 48 hours, covered, in the refrigerator.

To serve, arrange cabbage and lettuce leaves in serving bowls so that they hang over the sides. Put ½ cup shredded lettuce on the bottom and distribute the shellfish among the bowls. Garnish with leafy stalks of celery.

Broiled Oysters in Pesto

You can increase or decrease the quantities in this recipe, depending on how many you want to serve. The pesto keeps very well in the refrigerator. You may also toss the oysters into your favorite pasta. If you do this, Dennis suggests that you garnish with chopped tomatoes and chopped black olives.

Serves 8 to 10

5 to 6 dozen oysters on the half shell, or 1
      quart shucked oysters, drained
  3 cloves garlic, peeled
  ½ cup fresh parsley
  1 cup fresh basil leaves
  ½ cup extra-virgin olive oil
  ⅛ teaspoon salt
  ¼ teaspoon freshly ground black
      pepper
  ⅓ cup grated Romano or Parmesan
      cheese, or combination thereof
  ⅓ cup pine nuts or walnuts

*A*rrange oysters on baking sheets if you are using them in the shell. If shucked, arrange them in a single layer in individual ovenproof gratin dishes or in a large ovenproof baking dish.

Put garlic, parsley, and basil in a food processor; pulse 3 times. With motor running, slowly add olive oil, salt, pepper, and cheese. Turn motor off, add nuts, then pulse enough to coarsely chop the nuts.

Spoon about 1 teaspoon pesto over each oyster. Broil 3 to 5 minutes, or until topping bubbles and the edges of the oysters begin to curl slightly. Serve immediately.

Chicken and Shrimp Gumbo

Since a gumbo is "built" from several different culinary building blocks, it is essential, for the success of the dish, to prepare all the ingredients in advance. Some items, such as the roux and the caramelized okra, may be prepared a day or two in advance. Then, on the day of the meal, prepare the chicken, peel and devein the shrimp, prepare the rice, and have the vegetables and spices all at the ready.

Makes 1 gallon, or 8 to 10 servings

SHRIMP STOCK
  4 quarts water
  2 tablespoons cider vinegar
  6 bay leaves
  1 small onion, chopped
  1 stalk celery, chopped
  1 tablespoon freshly ground black
      pepper
  1 tablespoon cayenne
  1 tablespoon dry mustard
  1 tablespoon minced garlic
  1 pound green (raw) shrimp

CARAMELIZED OKRA
  ¼ cup olive oil
  1 pound frozen okra (use fresh in
      season)

ROUX
  ¾ cup olive oil or chicken fat skimmed
      from the stock
  ¾ cup flour

  ½ stick margarine
  2 tablespoons olive oil
  1 large onion, chopped
  1 green bell pepper, seeded, deveined,
      and chopped

1 celery stalk, chopped
1 tablespoon minced garlic
1 large tomato, blanched, peeled, and
    chopped
1 bunch scallions, trimmed and
    chopped
  Pinch each of dried thyme, basil,
    oregano, marjoram, ground black
    pepper, cayenne, and ground white
    pepper
1 bay leaf, crushed
2 cups Chicken Stock (see page 276)
3 cups cooked chicken meat
1 recipe Dennis's Boiled Rice (see
    page 262)

*T*he day before serving, make the shrimp stock by bringing the water to a boil in a large pot. Stir in all the remaining ingredients except the shrimp. Continue to boil until the liquid is reduced almost by half.

Add the shrimp. Cook until the first shrimp floats to the surface. Remove the shrimp with a slotted spoon and place in a very large bowl. Add a tray of ice cubes and just enough of the stock to cover the shrimp. Let shrimp soak until completely cool. Transfer shrimp with a slotted spoon to a small bowl. Carefully cover shrimp with plastic and refrigerate until ready to finish gumbo. Strain stock and reserve.

In a large cast-iron skillet, bring to a simmer the ¼ cup olive oil and the okra. Stir frequently while simmering until seeds appear and the slices of okra attain a mushy consistency. This may take 30 to 40 minutes with frozen okra. If the okra is fresh, it will take 1 to 2 hours. This caramelized okra acts as a thickener and helps to build body and texture. Store in a tightly covered container in the refrigerator.

To make a roux, heat the olive oil or chicken fat in a cast-iron skillet. Add the flour and stir constantly all over the pan to make certain that nothing sticks. We use a long thin whisk as well as a wooden spatula, stirring constantly over medium heat so that the browning will happen slowly. If the flour browns too fast it will taste burned. When the roux becomes a rich brown, remove it from the heat. Keep stirring while it cools down. If you need to cool it in a hurry, add ½ cup of chopped onion. Store in a tightly covered container in the refrigerator.

The day of serving, heat the margarine and olive oil in a very heavy 8-quart pot. Sauté the onion, green pepper, celery, and garlic until tender but not limp.

Add the tomato, 2 quarts of hot shrimp stock, caramelized okra, and scallions. Simmer 10 minutes. Add ½ cup of the reserved roux, seasonings, and stock. Stir well and simmer, covered, 40 minutes. Add more stock if too thick. Be sure to stir very well each time you uncover the pot. (Store unused roux in refrigerator for other dishes.)

Peel and devein the shrimp that you used to make the stock, add them and the chicken to the pot, and stir until heated through. Taste and adjust seasonings.

Serve over mounds of rice in large flat soup bowls with plenty of crisp garlic bread.

Dennis's Boiled Rice

Makes 6 cups

6 cups water
½ stick butter
1 teaspoon salt
3 cups long-grain rice

*I*n a large heavy kettle or stockpot with a tightly fitting lid, bring water to a brisk boil. Add butter, salt, and rice. Stir once with a three-tined fork. Fit lid on tightly. Reduce heat to very low and simmer 25 minutes. *Do not even think about peeking or stirring.*

Remove from heat and allow to cool with the lid tightly in place 30 to 40 minutes. The pot should be cool to the touch, and all the water and steam should be absorbed.

House Vegetable

Serves 8 to 10

8 carrots, scrubbed
4 zucchini, scrubbed
32 mushrooms
8 to 10 spears broccoli
2 sticks butter
1 tablespoon plus 2 teaspoons minced garlic
¼ teaspoon dried basil
¼ teaspoon dried thyme
¼ teaspoon dried rosemary
⅛ teaspoon ground cinnamon
  Salt and freshly ground black pepper to taste
1 cup Sauvignon Blanc wine
1 tablespoon roux (see gumbo recipe, page 260)

*W*ash and cut all vegetables into bite-size pieces. Melt butter in a very large cast-iron skillet and add garlic and vegetables. Sauté over medium heat, stirring constantly for 5 minutes. Add the seasonings and continue to sauté and stir.

After a few minutes, add the wine and the roux. Stir and cook at least 2 minutes more. There should be a bit of crunch in the vegetables. Adjust seasonings and serve.

Alligator Pear Surprise

Serves 8 to 10

1½ cups Crème Fraîche (see page 275)
1 teaspoon honey
6 medium-sized ripe avocados

Juice of 6 lemons, strained
¾ cup sugar
1 tablespoon plus 2 teaspoons chopped
fresh mint

Sprigs of fresh mint and julienned
strips of lemon peel for garnish

*T*he day before serving, combine Crème Fraîche and honey in a small bowl and blend well. Cover tightly with plastic and refrigerate.

Halve the avocados and remove pits. Scoop fruit meat from avocado skin. Mash slightly in a large bowl. Add lemon juice and sugar. Transfer to the bowl of a food processor and purée until smooth. Add mint and pulse a few more times.

Transfer Crème Fraîche to the bowl of an electric mixer and whip into soft peaks. Divide avocado purée among 8 to 10 serving dishes. Top with whipped Crème Fraîche, a sprig of mint, and a bit of lemon peel. Chill until time to serve.

Richard Perry

ST. LOUIS, MISSOURI

Tiring of the publishing world, Richard Perry came to the restaurant business longing for some of the rich and comforting tastes he remembered from his childhood on an Illinois farm. His first restaurant, The Jefferson Street Boarding House, opened in St. Louis in January 1971. It wasn't long before it attracted the attention of dedicated local foodies. And it was inevitable that, with the burgeoning interest in American regional cuisine in the early eighties, a national following developed for this forward-thinking man. Richard Perry spent hours, from the very beginning, carefully researching the enormously varied traditional dishes of the St. Louis area—from boardinghouse to farm to riverboat to the early French settlers. While in the early days his food tended to be authentically tasty and stick-to-your-ribs, what has evolved is a cuisine deeply rooted in St. Louis traditions but interpreted with a contemporary touch. And while his food is elegantly presented, Richard Perry's dishes do not become precious and overly manipulated. Not only has the style of food changed over the years, but the restaurant itself has changed as well. After seven-teen years, Richard Perry finally moved from his unpretentious Jefferson Street location to the newly restored Hotel Majestic in downtown St. Louis in the summer of 1988. It is an elegant building and the move has been traumatic for some of the regulars, but whatever the location, the restaurant has lost none of the qualities for which it has been celebrated for so long. It is still a comfortable place that serves delicious and interesting food.

We like to order the tasting menu so that we can sample many different items in a single evening. Because of the owner's interest in wine, we can also have a different glass of wine to accompany each course. For starters, all pâtés are outstanding, as are the appetizers of soft-shell crab with Ozark honey-mustard sauce or grilled quail with lingonberry sauce. One might get lucky and find grilled sea scallops with their roe in a blood-orange sauce, a dish that is beautifully balanced with just the right amount of citrus. Strawberry shrimp, grilled over wood, accompanied by a hint of strawberry sauce and garnished with a red-onion chutney that is spiked with vinegar and capers is a splendid treat. All pastas are made on the premises and are both delicate and properly cooked. Linda's favorite is the spinach ravioli stuffed with duck and goat cheese, and delicately enhanced with a fresh tomato sauce. And the sweet-potato pasta with wild mushrooms is sublime, with its extraordinary blending of the woody shiitake, the tang of tomato, the silky texture of cream, and the crunch of scallions. This is also a place for soups. Our current favorite for cold weather is the hearty lamb shank and white-bean soup. You don't have to even like lamb to love this rich and flavorful soup. Summer soups are equally delicious.

We can tell that bread is important at Richard Perry because of the butter. Each table has a small bowl of creamy rich unsalted butter with a perfectly formed butter rosebud in the middle. There is also another bowl of fresh fruit butter, and always a variety of breads and muffins. We now bake the cracked wheat bread every week in our house. It is dense and chewy, with a bit of crackle from the wheat; thickly sliced and slathered with butter, it is perfect with coffee for breakfast or accompanying a hearty soup for dinner. Lemon bread and applesauce/strawberry bread are also rich and tasty. For the main course, Richard Perry prepares outstanding braised veal shanks with morels and cream, and lake perch delicately coated with pistachios and gently sautéed with Missouri bacon and grapes. The pork tenderloin with Nauvóo blue cheese accompanied by a spicy golden pear sauce is especially delicious. There are always grilled chops and fish accompanied by some seasonal fruits and vegetables. Marinated and grilled lamb chops, almost caramelized on the outside, might be accompanied by red currants in the summer; a veal porterhouse served on onion marma-

lade is a splendid winter combination. Vegetables, including the fabled Bellville white asparagus, are from the region. The area around the city has long been a lush garden center, providing fruits and vegetables for a large portion of the Midwest. Richard Perry makes certain that his restaurant capitalizes upon that fact, and his menu always includes some creative and delicious vegetable dishes. Fragrant corn, freshly picked just hours before dinner, makes a marvelous addition to the menu during its season. From the asparagus in the spring to tomatoes in late summer, from cultivated strawberries to extraordinary melons, the best of the crops will be presented to diners at their peak of freshness.

It is the desserts, however, that have made Richard Perry famous. In addition to seasonal fruit buckles and ice creams, there are light-as-a-feather chiffon pies. Chocolate lovers will always find a variety of their favorites on the menu. We still can taste the crème anglaise generously flavored with Grand Marnier and coconut that accompanied a velvet-rich slice of chocolate cake. And lovers of white chocolate will delight in the sinful richness of the creamy mousse.

While the name of the restaurant changed in 1981 to that of its proprietor, Richard Perry is very much the work of two men today. St. Louis–born Gregg Mosberger began working for Richard Perry in 1975 as a busboy at the restaurant while still in high school. Over a seven-year period he learned every facet of restaurant work—by doing it—and in 1981 he became chef. Today he is also responsible for all training in the restaurant, and finds some time to teach cooking outside the city as well. But it is still the imposing, jovial face of the peripatetic Richard Perry that greets every diner each night. And it is he who still guides the overall details of the restaurant. A serious student of the history of the region, Perry has finally seen food trends around the country catch up with what he has been doing for almost twenty years. And now he is regarded by many as a real pioneer—a guru in St. Louis!

The restaurant is lush and welcoming. The dark paneling is relieved by light from the large windows that line two exterior walls. Dark green velvet upholstery covers the plush banquettes and chairs. Shining brass sconces grace the walls and brass billiard-table lights with green glass shades hang from the ceiling. It is a comfortable elegance. Because of its location in a hotel, the restaurant is open for breakfast, lunch, and dinner seven days a week. This is a tall order for any restaurant, and the energies of the two men are sorely tested. But with the help of their large, dedicated staff, we know that Richard Perry will continue to be one of the finest and most creative restaurants in the Midwest.

Richard Perry
ST. LOUIS, MISSOURI

Country Pork Loaf with Marinated Cucumbers
Girard Winery Blue Jay Zinfandel

Lamb Shank and White-Bean Soup

Sweet-Potato Fettuccine with Shiitake Mushroom Sauce
Winterbrook Vineyards Zinfandel Reserve

Grilled Veal Porterhouse Steak with Onion Marmalade
Robert Stemmler Winery Pinot Noir

Celery Root and Apple Purée

Cracked Wheat Bread

Strawberry-Applesauce Bread

Bourbon Chiffon Pie
Hidden Cellars Chanson D'Or

Wines selected by Sandra Jordan Earl

Country Pork Loaf with Marinated Cucumbers

Serves 8 to 10

½ pound chicken livers
2 pounds pork shoulder

MARINADE

2 teaspoons salt
2 teaspoons dried thyme
1 teaspoon cracked black peppercorns
¼ teaspoon freshly grated nutmeg
¼ teaspoon dried sage
8 garlic cloves, minced
½ cup Sauvignon Blanc or Chardonnay
    wine

CUCUMBERS

¼ cup plus 2 tablespoons red wine
    vinegar
½ cup sugar
2 tablespoons olive oil
1 cup paper-thin sliced cucumber
1½ cups paper-thin sliced onions

3 tablespoons lard
1½ cups minced onion
1 bay leaf
¼ cup Sauvignon Blanc wine
2 large eggs, beaten
¼ cup flour
½ cup shelled and peeled unsalted
    pistachios
¾ pound sliced bacon

Cut livers and pork into 1-inch pieces. Put each into a separate glass or ceramic container. Combine salt, thyme, pepper, nutmeg, sage, garlic, and ¼ cup of white wine. Divide mixture between the two meats and toss well. Cover tightly and marinate overnight in the refrigerator.

In a large mixing bowl, combine vinegar and sugar; let stand 1 hour. Add olive oil; combine with cucumbers and onions. Cover and marinate at least 12 hours in refrigerator.

Melt lard in a large skillet and sauté onions and bay leaf until onions are golden. Add ¼ cup white wine and cook until most of the wine has evaporated. Add the marinated pork to the skillet and sauté 5 minutes; then add the liver and sauté until the surface has lost its red color. Cool meats in the skillet 30 minutes. Then put meats, eggs, flour, and nuts into the bowl of a food processor and process thoroughly.

Preheat the oven to 350°. Line a 6-cup loaf pan with slightly more than half the bacon, pack pork mixture into the loaf pan, and cover with the remaining bacon. Bake in preheated oven 1½ hours, or until the loaf reaches an internal temperature of 140°. Put a large plate under a cooling rack, then turn loaf out on the rack and cool completely. Transfer loaf to a serving dish, cover, and refrigerate. Slice and garnish with marinated cucumbers.

Lamb Shank and White-Bean Soup

In the cold winter, this flavorful soup makes a perfect meal when accompanied by a warm fragrant loaf of Cracked Wheat Bread (see page 272) and unsalted butter.

Serves 6 to 8

1 pound dried Great Northern beans
2 tablespoons butter
1 cup chopped onions
1 clove garlic, minced
2 1-pound lamb shanks

1½ cups peeled and diced tomatoes
1 bay leaf
6 sprigs parsley, tied in 2 bundles
½ teaspoon dried thyme
2 whole cloves
20 black peppercorns
1 tablespoon kosher salt
10 cups water

Chopped fresh parsley for garnish

Place beans in a large bowl and cover with cold water. Soak overnight. The next day, drain the beans and set aside.

Melt butter in a 5-quart pot; sauté the onions, garlic, and lamb shanks 5 minutes. Add remaining ingredients to the pot, bring to a boil, and simmer 2½ hours.

Remove the shanks from the soup, trim the meat from the bones, and return the meat to the pot. Adjust seasonings and heat thoroughly. Ladle into heated soup plates and garnish with chopped parsley.

Sweet-Potato Fettuccine with Shiitake Mushroom Sauce

Serves 6 to 8

FETTUCCINE DOUGH
1 medium sweet potato
2 large eggs
3 cups semolina flour

2 tablespoons butter
1 tablespoon minced shallots
10 cloves garlic, minced
½ cup port wine
½ cup Beef Stock (see page 276)
2 cups fresh tomatoes, peeled, seeded, and diced

½ teaspoon salt
¼ teaspoon freshly ground black pepper
1 tablespoon cornstarch dissolved in 3 teaspoons water
1 tablespoon fresh thyme, or 2 teaspoons dried thyme
1 cup sliced shiitake mushroom caps
½ cup sliced scallions, cut diagonally into ½-inch pieces
1 cup heavy cream

Preheat oven to 350°. Puncture the sweet potato with a fork and bake it in the preheated oven until tender, about 1 hour. Scrape the inside of the potato into the bowl of a food processor, add the eggs, and process while adding the flour through the feed tube, little by little, until the mixture rolls easily into a soft ball. Transfer dough to a mixing bowl, cover with a towel, and let rest 10 minutes. Follow instructions on page 274 to knead and roll dough in the pastry machine. Then cut into fettuccine. After the pasta is cut, let it dry on a pasta rack or spread on a floured tray.

While pasta is drying, melt butter in a large sauté pan and sauté shallots and garlic just until golden. Add port and scrape bottom of pan to loosen any browned particles that are adhering to it. Add stock and cook over high heat until liquid is reduced by one-third. Add tomatoes, salt, pepper, and cornstarch mixture. Cook over medium heat, stirring often, until sauce has thickened. Remove from heat and stir in thyme.

Combine mushrooms, green onions, and cream in a small saucepan and cook over high heat until cream is slightly thickened. Add mushroom mixture to tomato mixture. Heat thoroughly before serving.

Just before serving, bring a large pot of salted water to a boil and add pasta. Cook until al dente, about 3 minutes. Drain, return fettuccine to pot, add heated sauce and toss well together. Divide among warm serving plates and serve.

Grilled Veal Porterhouse Steak with Onion Marmalade

Serves 6 to 8

MARMALADE
4 tablespoons clarified butter
4 cups thinly sliced onions
2 teaspoons salt
½ teaspoon freshly ground black
    pepper
2 cups Chicken Stock (see page 276)
1 tablespoon red wine vinegar
½ cup port wine
2 tablespoons butter

6 tablespoons butter, softened
3 tablespoons port wine
2 cloves garlic, finely minced
3 tablespoons finely minced fresh
    parsley
6 1-inch-thick veal porterhouse steaks
    Salt and freshly ground black pepper
1 cup heavy cream

Melt clarified butter in a skillet and sauté onions until transparent. Add salt, pepper, 1½ cups stock, and vinegar. Cook over high heat until liquid has evaporated. Add the remaining stock, port, and butter. Simmer briskly until liquid is reduced by two-thirds. Cover and refrigerate until you are ready to prepare the meat.

Combine softened butter, port, garlic, and parsley in a small mixing bowl and blend very well. Using a sheet of wax paper, roll butter mixture into a log and chill.

At dinnertime, thoroughly clean grill and spray with Pam. Heat grill to hot. While grill is heating, rub steaks with salt and pepper. Cook to desired doneness over the hot grill.

Just before serving, combine onion mixture with heavy cream in a heavy medium-sized saucepan. Cook over high heat until thickened.

Place a grilled steak on each heated serving plate, top with a slice of the butter log, and garnish with onion marmalade.

Celery Root and Apple Purée

Serves 8

2½ cups peeled celery root, cut into 1-
    inch dice
2¼ cups peeled and cored Granny Smith
    apples, cut into 1-inch dice
½ cup heavy cream
2 teaspoons salt, or more to taste
¼ teaspoon freshly ground white
    pepper

Put the celery root in a heavy 3-quart saucepan and cover with hot water. Bring to a boil and continue to boil 10 minutes. Add the apples and boil until the celery root and the apples are both quite tender, perhaps 20 minutes.

Drain very well and transfer to a food processor. Purée while adding the heavy cream, making certain that the mixture is very, very smooth. Add the salt and pepper and combine well. Taste and adjust seasonings. Transfer to a medium-sized bowl and keep warm. This can be reheated by placing bowl in a saucepan of hot water and simmering slowly over low heat until purée is thoroughly warmed.

Cracked Wheat Bread

Sliced thin, this bread is delicious for sandwiches; sliced thick, it makes luscious toast.

Makes 2 9 × 5-inch loaves

1½ cups cracked wheat
¾ cup dark brown sugar, firmly packed
¾ tablespoon salt
1½ tablespoons butter
1⅔ cups boiling water
2 tablespoons active dry yeast
1 cup warm (about 90 to 110°) water
6 cups bread flour, plus more if necessary

Combine cracked wheat, brown sugar, salt, and butter in a large mixing bowl. Pour in boiling water and stir until the butter has melted. Let cool.

Meanwhile, combine yeast and warm water in the bowl of an electric mixer. Set aside in a warm place and allow to bubble.

After about 15 minutes, check the cracked-wheat mixture to make certain it has cooled to at least 110°. Then add it to the yeast.

Using the mixer paddle, slowly stir flour into the combined yeast and cracked-wheat mixture. Then replace the paddle with a dough hook. Knead on lowest setting 20 minutes. Add up to 1 cup additional flour, just enough to make a light, but not sticky, dough. We find that a total of 7 cups of flour will be enough. Knead by hand for a few minutes to finish.

Preheat oven to 350°. Transfer dough to an oiled bowl, cover with plastic wrap, and let rise in a warm place until doubled in volume, about 1 to 2 hours.

Punch dough down, divide in half, and form into 2 loaves by patting each half into a flat oval. Then fold each oval in half and flatten down on the seam, tucking the ends under. Divide dough between two greased 9 × 5-inch loaf pans. Cover with plastic wrap and let rise until dough almost reaches the top of the pans. Bake in preheated oven 1 hour, or until done. Brush with melted butter. Remove from pans after a few minutes and let cool on racks.

Strawberry Applesauce Bread

Makes 3 9 × 5-inch loaves

3 cups applesauce
1 cup coarsely puréed strawberries
5 jumbo eggs
5½ cups cake flour
1¾ cups raisins
¼ cup melted butter
3 cups granulated sugar
1 tablespoon salt
1 tablespoon plus 1½ teaspoons baking soda
1 tablespoon ground cinnamon
1½ teaspoons ground cloves
¾ cup chopped pecans
1 tablespoon plus 1 teaspoon baking powder

Preheat oven to 350°. Combine all ingredients in the bowl of an electric mixer and stir with paddle—or by hand—just until all ingredients are combined thoroughly. *Do not overmix.*

Fill three buttered and floured 9 × 5-inch

loaf pans a little over half full. Bake in preheated oven about 20 minutes, then quickly rotate pans in the oven to ensure even cooking. Bake another 20 minutes, or until a toothpick inserted in the middle comes out clean.

Remove pans from the oven and transfer to a baking rack to cool. Turn loaves out of pans after 5 minutes, and continue cooling right side up. These freeze very well if wrapped tightly as soon as they are cold.

Bourbon Chiffon Pie

Makes 1 10-inch pie

CRUST
    1¼ cups graham cracker crumbs
    ¼ cup sugar
    ½ teaspoon freshly grated nutmeg
    ¼ cup melted butter

FILLING
    1 envelope unflavored gelatin
    ½ cup black coffee
      Pinch of salt
    ⅓ cup sugar
    3 large egg yolks, beaten
    5 tablespoons bourbon
    ¼ cup Kahlua
    1¼ cups heavy cream
    ¼ cup egg whites
    ⅓ cup sugar

TOPPING
    ¾ cup Crème Fraîche (see page 275)
    ¼ cup confectioner's sugar

    Bittersweet chocolate for garnish

*P*reheat oven to 350°. To make crust: Combine crumbs, sugar, and nutmeg in a medium-sized bowl and mix well. Then add melted butter. Blend carefully, then press evenly into an ungreased 10-inch pie plate. Bake in preheated oven 12 minutes; remove and cool.

For filling: Combine gelatin, coffee, salt, and sugar in a small saucepan with a heavy bottom. Bring to a simmer, stirring until gelatin dissolves. Gradually add this to the egg yolks, whisking carefully. Then pour the mixture back into the saucepan and whisk over low heat until it is thickened and coats the back of a spoon. Remove from heat and let cool, whisking occasionally. Whisk in bourbon and Kahlua.

Whip cream until stiff and fold it into the cooled custard mixture.

In a medium-sized mixing bowl, whip egg whites until soft peaks form. Slowly add sugar, beating constantly, until shiny and firm. Fold into the custard mixture, spoon into the pie shell, and chill 24 hours.

Whip Crème Fraîche, gradually adding sugar, until stiff peaks form. Spoon the mixture into a pastry bag fitted with a decorative tip, and decorate the top of the chilled pie. Garnish with grated chocolate.

Appendix

How to Bone Fowl

*I*f you ever have an opportunity to watch Jacques Pepin bone a fowl, you will be watching the absolute master. One day he did it in less than two minutes on Linda's radio show, talking his way through step by step. Fred loves having him as a guest on *The Morning Exchange* so that Jacques can give him a refresher course. There is always some kind of fowl for Jacques to bone—even if he is there to cook fish!

It is absolutely essential to use a very sharp knife for this. Place fowl on a carving board that will not slip. First, remove the wishbone. Use your finger to lift skin back under the neck and insert the knife up along the wishbone. Cut completely around the bone from shoulder to shoulder. Pull bone out with your fingers.

Turn fowl on its side. Hold leg and thigh up, and slice right along the skin around the thigh area. Hold leg out and cut through the sinews of the thigh, parallel to the backbone, to separate it from the carcass.

To remove the breasts, place the fowl on its back and, using a very sharp knife, cut along each side of the breastbone to separate the two halves of the breast. Turn bird on its side and work your finger under the skin and flesh along the ribs. Then slide your knife along the rib cage into the shoulder joint and cut it loose. Hold the wing in one hand and the carcass in the other to pull the breast half off in one piece. Repeat the process on the other side. Remove the remaining fillets that are on the sternum with your fingers. Each fillet has a long sinew that can be removed by holding it at one end and scraping the meat away with the knife. Pat fillet into place on the bottom of each breast half. Then carefully remove wings and drumettes from breasts.

Using a Pasta Machine

*O*ur wonderful friend Marcella Hazan encourages people to roll pasta by hand because it will be more tender than pasta rolled in a machine. She is right! However, because of her arthritis, Linda could never manage to roll it thin enough; consequently, we never had fresh pasta. Then we bought an Atlas pasta machine (under $30) and discovered how easy it is to handle. So, Marcella, we hope you forgive us for encouraging people to use a machine instead of a rolling pin—but it does work.

Begin by dividing dough into balls of about ⅓ to ½ cup each. While working on one portion, keep remaining portions covered with a towel. Set pasta machine rollers to their widest setting. Flatten first portion with your hands on a lightly floured surface and feed it through the rollers. Fold it in thirds, as you would a letter. Feed it through the rollers again. Flouring as needed, folding as described, and turning in 45-degree rotations, repeat this rolling (kneading) process a total of 10 times.

Then reduce setting one number at a time and roll strip of pasta thinner and thinner, dusting lightly with flour as needed. You do not fold the pasta strip during this process. For ravioli, roll to within one setting of the thinnest and proceed to fill pasta immediately. For all other pastas, roll as thin as possible and allow the pasta to dry on towels 15 minutes before you proceed to cut.

After the pasta is cut, let it dry on a pasta rack or dust it very well with cornmeal, coil it in bunches, and freeze until needed.

Crème Fraîche

Crème fraîche is a somewhat tart heavy cream that is commonly used in France in the preparation of desserts and sauces. While it can now be purchased in most markets in this country, it is far less expensive to make it at home. Linda's recipe works very well, and keeps more than a week if properly sealed.

Makes 1–2 cups

> 1 cup heavy cream
> 2 tablespoons buttermilk, or 1 cup
>   sour cream

Combine heavy cream with buttermilk or sour cream. If using sour cream, whisk very well to make a smooth mixture. Pour blended creams into a container that has a close-fitting lid. Cover loosely and let stand 8 hours at room temperature. Then seal tightly and refrigerate.

This mixture will whip quite nicely. To make a delicious whipped cream, add 1 tablespoon confectioner's sugar and whip in the bowl of an electric mixer.

Fish Fumet

Let your fish merchant know a few days ahead of time that you want to make a fish fumet, so that he has time to gather some good bones for you. Do not use bones from strong fish like tuna or oily fish like mackerel. Linda likes halibut, salmon, and bass. Please note that when we sweat the vegetables we do not use butter, because fat will make the stock rather cloudy.

Makes 3–4 cups

> 2 cups chopped onions
> 1 cup carrots, peeled and chopped
> 1 cup chopped celery
> 2½ quarts water
> 3 pounds fish heads, bones, and
>   trimmings
> 1 bunch celery
> 1 bay leaf
> 2 sprigs fresh thyme
> 10 white peppercorns, bruised
> 2 cups Sauvignon Blanc wine

In a large stockpot, place onions, carrots, celery, and 1 quart water. Cover with wax paper directly on the vegetables and bring to a boil. Reduce heat immediately and simmer 15 minutes. Discard wax paper, then add the rest of the water and the remaining ingredients. Bring to a boil, reduce heat to a brisk simmer, and cook 1 hour. Remove scum as it accumulates on the surface of the liquid.

After 1 hour, remove from heat. Use a large, flat Chinese strainer to remove as much of the fish and vegetables as you easily can. Then pour stock through a colander that has been lined with two layers of cheesecloth. Chill.

Chicken Stock

Makes 1 quart

> 5 pounds chicken bones
> 5 quarts water
> 8 carrots, scrubbed
> 2 large onions, unpeeled, each studded
>   with a clove
> 1 leek, trimmed, split, and washed
> 1 bunch parsley
> 2 stalks celery
> 1 parsnip
> 1 turnip
> 1 bay leaf
> 2 sprigs thyme
> 10 black peppercorns, bruised
> 5 white peppercorns, bruised

*P*lace chicken bones and water in a large stockpot and bring to a boil. Reduce heat slightly, still allowing to boil slowly, and re-

move scum as it forms on top of the liquid. Continue to do this until scum ceases to form. Replace discarded liquid by adding an equal amount of warm water to the pot.

Add remaining ingredients. Reduce heat, partially cover, and simmer 8 hours.

Strain stock through a double layer of cheesecloth into a large saucepan. Bring to a boil and reduce heat. Simmer, uncovered, until stock is reduced to 1 quart.

Beef or Veal Stock

We must thank our good friend Lydie Marshall for suggesting the addition of a knuckle bone to the stockpot. We are certain that it adds more flavor and body. Please note that we do not add any salt to our stocks. We feel that it is better to do that when whatever dish you are making from the stock is finished.

Makes 2 quarts

> 5 pounds beef or veal marrow bones
> 1 pound beef or veal flanken
> 1 large veal knuckle bone for beef
>   stock, or beef knuckle bone for
>   veal stock
> 5 quarts water
> 6 carrots, washed
> 2 parsnips, washed
> 1 turnip, washed
> 4 stalks celery
> 2 large onions, unpeeled, each studded
>   with a clove
> 1 bunch fresh parsley
> 10 black peppercorns, bruised
> 1 bay leaf
> 2 sprigs fresh thyme

276　　　　　　　　　*Appendix*

Combine meat and bones in a large stockpot. Add water and bring to a boil. Reduce heat to a slow boil and remove scum that forms at the top. Each time you do that, replace the discarded liquid with an equal amount of warm water.

Coarsely chop carrots, parsnips, turnip, and celery. When scum ceases forming on the top of the liquid, lower heat to a simmer and add remaining ingredients. Add more water if needed. Simmer, partially covered, for 8 hours. Strain through a double layer of cheesecloth. There should be about 2 quarts of stock; if there is more, return liquid to a large saucepan, bring to a boil, reduce heat, and simmer briskly until stock is reduced to 2 quarts. Chill. Remove fat from top before using. This stock freezes very well.

Dark Brown Beef or Veal Stock

Makes 2 quarts

> 5 pounds beef/veal soup meat, marrow, and knuckle bones
> 2 large onions, unpeeled
> 6 carrots, washed
> 2 parsnips, washed
> 1 turnip, washed
> 5 quarts water
> 4 stalks celery
> 1 bunch fresh parsley
> 10 black peppercorns, bruised
> 1 clove
> 1 bay leaf
> 2 sprigs fresh thyme
> 6 garlic cloves, unpeeled
> 3 large ripe tomatoes, coarsely chopped

Preheat the oven to 425°. Place meat and bones in a large roasting pan and roast in the preheated oven, turning frequently, for 45 minutes.

Meanwhile, cut onions in chunks: chop carrots, parsnips, and turnip roughly. After meat begins to brown, add vegetables to roasting pan. Keep turning meat, bones, and vegetables until very brown all over. This will take up to 2 hours.

With a slotted spoon or large, flat Chinese strainer, transfer meat, bones, and vegetables from roasting pan to a very large stockpot. Add the water and bring to a boil.

Meanwhile, if the bottom of the roasting pan has not been burned during the browning process, deglaze by carefully pouring off fat, adding 1 to 2 cups water, and placing roasting pan over heat on the stove top. Slowly stir and scrape browned bits from the bottom of the pan. When this process is complete, add the mixture to the stockpot.

After liquid in stockpot comes to a boil, reduce heat slightly and boil slowly, removing any scum that comes to the top of the pot. Replace discarded liquid with an equal amount of warm water. When there is no more scum forming, lower heat to a simmer and add remaining ingredients. Simmer 8 to 10 hours.

Strain stock through a double layer of cheesecloth and measure; if more than 2 quarts, return to a large saucepan, bring to a boil, reduce heat, and simmer briskly until stock is reduced to 2 quarts. Chill. Remove fat from top before using. This stock freezes very well.

Demi-glace

Yields 1 quart

Prepare 1 recipe Dark Brown Beef or Veal Stock (page 277) and chill overnight. Then skim off fat and discard. Return skimmed stock to a large saucepan and bring to a boil. Reduce heat and simmer briskly until stock is reduced by half. This ultra-rich stock is highly gelatinous and superlative for sauces.

Dark Brown Duck Stock

If you make this stock for the Tapawingo duck dish (page 74), rub these vegetables and giblets with some of the duck fat and roast them until brown. Then combine them with the already roasted carcasses.

Makes 3 to 4 cups

    2 duck carcasses, broken into pieces, including giblets
    1 large onion, quartered
    3 carrots, scrubbed and cut into chunks
    1 parsnip, scrubbed and cut into chunks
    1 turnip, scrubbed and cut into chunks
    2 stalks celery
    1 bay leaf
    2 sprigs thyme
    1 clove
  10 black peppercorns, bruised

Preheat oven to 450°. Place duck carcasses and giblets in the bottom of a large roasting pan. Roast in the preheated oven 30 minutes, turning frequently. Add onion, carrots, parsnip, and turnip, and continue roasting until everything is dark brown. This may take up to 1 hour.

Transfer browned duck pieces and vegetables from the roasting pan to a large stockpot. Cover with cold water and bring to a boil over high heat. Remove scum as it forms, replacing discarded liquid with an equal amount of warm water. When scum no longer forms, add remaining ingredients and simmer, partially covered, for 3 hours.

Strain liquid through a double layer of cheesecloth into a large saucepan. Briskly simmer stock until liquid is reduced to 3 to 4 cups. Chill. Remove fat before using. This stock freezes very well.

Addresses
and Phone Numbers

Ristorante Giovanni
25550 Chagrin Boulevard
Beachwood, Ohio 44122
216-831-8625

Z Contemporary Cuisine
20600 Chagrin Boulevard
Shaker Heights, Ohio 44122
216-991-1580

The Baricelli Inn
2203 Cornell Road
Cleveland, Ohio 44106
216-791-6500

Johnny's Bar
3164 Fulton Road
Cleveland, Ohio 44109
216-281-0055

The Palace
The Cincinnatian Hotel
601 Vine Street
Cincinnati, Ohio 45202
513-381-3000

The Restaurant at The Phoenix
812 Race Street
Cincinnati, Ohio 45202
513-721-8909

Peter's Restaurant
936 Virginia Avenue
Indianapolis, Indiana 46203
317-637-9333

The Carriage House
24460 Adams Road
South Bend, Indiana 46628
219-272-9220

Tapawingo
9502 Lake Street
Ellsworth, Michigan 49729
616-588-7971

Chez Raphael
27000 Sheraton Drive
Novi, Michigan 48050
313-348-5555

Cousins Heritage Inn
79954 Ann Arbor Road
Dexter, Michigan 48130
313-426-3020

Yoshi's Café
3257 North Halsted Street
Chicago, Illinois 60657
312-248-6160

Charlie Trotter's
816 West Armitage
Chicago, Illinois 60614
312-248-6228

Frontera Grill
445 North Clark
Chicago, Illinois 60657
312-661-1434

The Everest Room
4410 South Lasalle Street, 40th Floor
Chicago, Illinois 60605
312-663-8900

Jackie's
2478 North Lincoln Avenue
Chicago, Illinois 60614
312-880-0003

Printer's Row
550 South Dearborn Street
Chicago, Illinois 60611
312-461-0780

Café Provençal
1625 Hinman Avenue
Evanston, Illinois 60201
312-475-2233

Old Rittenhouse Inn
301 Rittenhouse Avenue
Bayfield, Wisconsin 54814
715-779-5765

L'Étoile
25 North Pinckney Street
Madison, Wisconsin 53703
608-251-0500

River Wildlife
Kohler, Wisconsin 53044
414-457-0134

D'Amico Cucina
100 North 6th Street
Minneapolis, Minnesota 55405
612-338-2401

Tejas
The Conservatory on Nicollet
800 Nicollet Mall
Minneapolis, Minnesota 55402
612-375-0800

Goodfellow's
The Conservatory on Nicollet
800 Nicollet Mall
Minneapolis, Minnesota 55402
612-332-4800

Schumacher's New Prague Hotel
212 West Main Street
New Prague, Minnesota 56071
612-758-2133

Strawtown Inn
1111 Washington Street
Pella, Iowa 50219
515-628-4043

Lacorsette
629 First Avenue East
Newton, Iowa 50208
515-792-6833

Stroud's
1015 East 85th Street
Kansas City, Missouri 64131
816-333-2132

Jack Fiorella's Smokestack Bar-B-Que of Martin City
Holmes at 135th Street
Martin City, Missouri 64145
816-942-9141

Tony's
826 North Broadway
St. Louis, Missouri 63102
314-231-7707

Broadway Oyster Bar
736 South Broadway
St. Louis, Missouri 63102
314-621-9606

Richard Perry
1019 Pine Street
St. Louis, Missouri 63101
314-771-4100

Index

apple: and celery root purée, 271–272; consommé, 160; honey-nut muffins, 179; pecan relish, baked pumpkin soup with honeyed crème fraîche and, 200; walnut pie with streusel topping, 65–66

applesauce strawberry bread, 272–273

artichoke: fritters with fresh tomato sauce, 8–9; hearts, carpaccio with parmigiano, truffles, balsamic vinaigrette and, 6

asparagus: cassoulet of morels, fiddleheads and, 73–74; chilled with creamy lemon vinaigrette, 104–105; warm crayfish, sun-dried tomatoes and, with avocado, lemon butter sauce, and salmon caviar, 136

avocado: alligator pear surprise, 262–63; basil sorbet, chilled tomato soup with, 114; warm asparagus, crayfish, and sun-dried tomatoes with lemon butter sauce, salmon caviar and, 136

bananas foster, 33

bananas foster cheesecake with caramel sauce, 50–51

bass: black, broiled with natural juice of seasonal mushrooms, 144; black, tartare with buckwheat blini and Asian vegetables, 113; striped, with white peppercorn sauce, 151–52

bean(s): black, and goat cheese relish, 193; country-style green, 237; crisped green, mallard duck with beet mousse, roasted pearl onions and, 86–87; fava, filling, oval masa cakes with green tomatillo sauce and, 121–22; white, and lamb shank soup, 269–70

beef: carpaccio with artichoke hearts, parmigiano, truffles, and balsamic vinaigrette, 6; collared, 220; poached Coleman's natural, over baby lettuces with herb vinaigrette, 84–85; smoked tenderloin with damson plum and ginger glaze, 49–50; stock, 276–277

bitterballen, 218

blackberry-raspberry buckle, 204

blini, buckwheat: black bass tartare with Asian vegetables and, 113; with eggplant caviar and smoked salmon, 22

blueberry: and cream pie in hazelnut meringue, 145; tart, Michigan, 99

bread pudding: basil and pine-nut, 186–87; chocolate, with red wine sauce, 187

breads: buttermilk potato doughnuts, 179; cracked wheat, 272; crispy Czech, 212–13; honey-nut apple muffins, 179; serrano chile blue cornbread, 194; strawberry applesauce, 272–73; sweet-potato rolls, 201–202; walnut, 170–71; white chocolate muffins, 161

cabbage: red, fillet of John Dory with Michigan Chardonnay sauce and, 129–30; tomato soup, 95

calamari: salad, 22–23; stuffed, 30–31

capon, roasted stuffed, with red bell pepper coulis, 105–106

caponata, 251

carrots, herbed, 212

cassoulet of morels, fiddleheads, and asparagus, 73–74

caviar: Osetra, mosaic of wild Maine salmon and, en gelée, 128; salmon, warm asparagus, crayfish, and sun-dried tomatoes

with avocado, lemon butter sauce and, 136

celery root and apple purée, 271–272

cheese(s): baked chèvre, with marinated mushrooms and olive paste, 168–69; balls, 218; Cheddar-and-beer soup, Capitol, 169; cheesy corn bake, 245; chèvre coeur à la crème with raspberry sauce, 171; chèvre terrine with black olive quenelles, 87; four, soup of roasted garlic, herbs and, 38; goat, and black bean relish, 193; herbed feta, in phyllo pastry with shrimp and tomato butter, 227

cheesecake, salsa, 159

cheesecakes, dessert: bananas foster, with caramel sauce, 50–51; candied ginger, 106–107; chocolate mint, 40–41

cherry, tart red, granita, 74

chicken: free-range, with Door County cherries, 169–70; noodle soup, 236; Schumacher Hotel pâté, 210; and shrimp gumbo, 260–61; skillet-fried, with cracklin' gravy, 236–37; stock, 276

chile: ancho, flourless chocolate cake, 194–95; serrano, blue cornbread, 194

chocolate: ancho chile cake, flourless, 194–95; bread pudding with red wine sauce, 187; cream sauce, 107; marquise with Sauternes-infused sultanas, 115; mint cheesecake, 40–41; pecan truffle torte, 66–67; terrine with mocha sauce, 131; three-berry fudge tart, 138–39; white, muffins, 161

coconut: flan, fresh, 123; and sweet potato pie, 59

cookies: pecan lace with raspberry cream, 76–77; rolled sugar, 89·

corn: bake, cheesy, 245; grilled, grilled pike with chanterelle mushrooms, Cabernet butter sauce and, 15–16

cornmeal: blue-corn griddlecakes, 192; oval masa cakes with fava bean filling and green tomatillo sauce, 121–22; serrano chile blue cornbread, 194

crab(s), soft-shell: grilled, with cucumber-and-bell-pepper salad and tarragon butter, 38–39; warm, salad, 14–15

crabapple jelly, 162

crayfish, warm asparagus, sun-dried tomatoes and, with avocado, lemon butter sauce, and salmon caviar, 136

crème anglaise, 107; ginger, ginger-poached pears with raspberry mousse and, 230–31

crème fraîche, 275; honeyed, baked pumpkin soup with apple-pecan relish and, 200

demi-glace, 278

desserts: alligator pear surprise, 262–63; apple walnut pie with streusel topping, 65–66; bananas foster, 33; bananas foster cheesecake with caramel sauce, 50–51; blueberry and cream pie in hazelnut meringue, 145; bourbon chiffon pie, 273; chèvre coeur à la crème with raspberry sauce, 171; chocolate bread pudding with red wine sauce, 187; chocolate marquise with Sauternes-infused sultanas, 115; chocolate mint cheesecake, 40–41; chocolate-pecan truffle torte, 66–67; chocolate terrine with mocha sauce, 131; Dutch letters, 220–21; flan de coco, 123; flourless chocolate ancho chile cake, 194–95; ginger ice cream, 88; ginger-poached pears with raspberry mousse and ginger crème anglaise, 230–31; gratin of summer fruit, 16–17; Michigan blueberry tart, 99; pecan lace with raspberry cream, 76–77; poached plums with port wine cinnamon sauce, 88; raspberry-blackberry buckle, 204; rhubarb cobbler, 77; rolled sugar cookies, 89; sabayon of red raspberries with dark rum, 25; snow eggs in red raspberry sauce, 163; strawber-

ries brandi, 213; sweet cream tart with red-fruit compote, 152–153; sweet potato and coconut pie, 59; three-berry fudge tart, 138–39; tiramisù, 9; vanilla ice cream, 204–205; zabaglione with fresh raspberries, 252–53

doughnuts, buttermilk potato, 179

duck: appetizer, beer-battered, 210; breast of, grilled with sesame oil, 144; grilled ducklings with wild-rice burrito and onion confit, 74–76; hash with fried eggs, 177; mallard, with beet mousse, crisped green beans, and roasted pearl onions, 86–87; roast, with sweet kraut dressing, 211–12; salad of arugula, radicchio and, with raspberry vinaigrette, 56; Schumacher Hotel pâté, 210; smoked, quail with walnut dressing, Cabernet-elderberry sauce and, 47–48; smoked Barbary, roasted red pepper ravioli with New York State goat cheese, 23–24; stock, dark brown, 278

Dutch letters, 220–21

eggplant: caponata, 251; caviar, buckwheat blini with smoked salmon and, 22; red snapper wrapped in, with tomato-orange sauce, 184–85

eggs, fried, duck hash with, 177

escargot-stuffed plum tomatoes in poultry broth, 83–84

fiddlehead ferns: cassoulet of morels, asparagus and, 73–74; sautéed walleye with lobster and smoked-trout sauce and, 95–96

fish, see seafood

fowl: chicken and shrimp gumbo, 260–61; chicken noodle soup, 236; chicken stock, 276; free-range chicken with Door County cherries, 169–70; how to bone, 274; roasted stuffed capon with red bell pepper coulis, 105–106; Schumacher Hotel pâté, 210; skillet-fried chicken with cracklin' gravy, 236–37; see also game fowl

fritters: artichoke, with fresh tomato sauce, 8–9; wild-rice, 203–204

fruit: red, compote, sweet cream tart with, 152–53; salad, late-summer, with ginger dressing,

65; summer, gratin of, 16–17; see also specific fruits

game fowl: lasagne of quail, foie gras, and wild mushrooms, 114–115; pheasant pot pie, 176–77; quail with smoked duck, walnut dressing, and Cabernet-elderberry sauce, 47–48; roast pheasant with prune sauce, 96–97; Schumacher Hotel pâté, 210; smoked breast of pheasant with wild-rice compote and cracked-pepper pear sauce, 202–203; see also duck

ginger: candied, cheesecake, 106–107; and damson plum glaze, smoked tenderloin with, 49–50; dressing, late-summer fruit salad with, 65; ice cream, 88; lemon jus-lié, steamed lake perch fillets in, 83; poached pears with raspberry mousse and ginger crème anglaise, 230–31

grapefruit-tequila ice, 192

griddlecakes, blue-corn, 192

ham, pan-roasted Northern pike fillet with leeks, orange sauce and, 200–201

ice cream: ginger, 88; vanilla, 204–205

jelly, crabapple, 162

John Dory, fillet of, with Michigan Chardonnay sauce and red cabbage, 129–30

kaasbolletjes, 218

kapusta, 95

lamb: chops, grilled baby, with Roma tomatoes and rosemary-garlic beurre blanc, 48–49; loin in potato crust, 130–31; rack of, with Madeira, 65; salad, grilled, with warm goat cheese, 150–51; shank and white-bean soup, 269–70

lingonberry citrus sauce, 76

lobster: with sea scallops, fettuccine, and lemon butter sauce, 137–38; and smoked-trout sauce, sautéed walleye with fiddlehead ferns and, 95–96

marinara sauce, 31–32

masa cakes, oval, with fava bean filling and green tomatillo sauce, 121–22 meats: pan-roasted Northern pike fillet with ham, leeks, and orange sauce, 200–201; roast venison, 98; venison sausage, 192–93; *see also specific meats*

mushroom(s): chanterelle, grilled pike with grilled corn, Cabernet butter sauce and, 15–16; marinated, baked chèvre with olive paste and, 168–69; morels, cassoulet of fiddleheads, asparagus and, 73–74; porcini, veal chop Sergio with, 7–8; porcini sauce, risotto cakes with, 185; seasonal, natural juice of, black bass broiled with, 144; shiitake, giant ravioli with brandy cream sauce and, 64; shiitake, sauce, sweet-potato fettuccine with, 270–71; wild, lasagne of quail, foie gras and, 114–15; wild, medallions of veal tenderloin Madeira with, 24–25; wild, whole roasted veal strip with leeks, tomatoes and, in brandy demi-glace, 39–40

noodle(s): Japanese buckwheat, bay scallops on, with pesto sauce, 104; soup, chicken, 236; *see also* pasta

olive(s): black, quenelles, chèvre terrine with, 87; grilled swordfish with tarragon sauce, tomatoes, capers and, 251–52; paste, baked chèvre with marinated mushrooms and, 168–69

onion(s): confit, grilled ducklings with wild-rice burrito and, 74–76; marmalade, grilled veal porterhouse steak with, 271; roasted pearl, mallard duck with beet mousse, crisped green beans and, 86–87

orange(s): navel, romaine lettuce, and cashews with balsamic vinaigrette, 48; sauce, pan-roasted Northern pike fillet with ham, leeks and, 200–201; tomato sauce, red snapper wrapped in eggplant with, 184–85

oysters, broiled, in pesto, 260

pancakes, veal sweetbread, with hazelnut yogurt, 58

pasta: giant ravioli with shiitake mushrooms and brandy cream sauce, 64; lasagne of quail, foie gras, and wild mushrooms, 114–115; lobster with sea scallops, fettuccine, and lemon butter sauce, 137–38; puttanesca, 30; roasted red pepper ravioli with smoked Barbary duck and New York State goat cheese, 23–24; sweet-potato fettuccine with shiitake mushroom sauce, 270–71; trenette with rock shrimp and crushed red pepper, 6

pasta machine, using, 274–75

pâté, Schumacher Hotel, 210

pea soup, Dutch, 219

pear(s): butter, 229; ginger-poached, with raspberry mousse and ginger crème anglaise, 230–231; sauce, cracked-pepper, smoked breast of pheasant with wild-rice compote and, 202–203

pepper(s), bell: and cucumber salad, grilled soft-shell crabs with tarragon butter and, 38–39; red, coulis, roasted stuffed capon with, 105–106; roasted red, ravioli with smoked Barbary duck and New York State goat cheese, 23–24; soup, chilled red, 14

perch, steamed lake, fillets in ginger-lemon jus-lié, 83

pheasant: pot pie, 176–77; roast, with prune sauce, 96–97; smoked breast of, with wild-rice compote and cracked-pepper pear sauce, 202–203

phyllo pastry, herbed feta cheese in, with shrimp and tomato butter, 227

pies: apple walnut, with streusel topping, 65–66; blueberry and cream, in hazelnut meringue, 145; bourbon chiffon, 273; sweet potato and coconut, 59

pike: fillet, pan-roasted Northern, with ham, leeks, and orange sauce, 200–201; grilled, with chanterelle mushrooms, grilled corn, and Cabernet butter sauce, 115–16

plums, poached, with port wine cinnamon sauce, 88

pork: chops in cream, 160–61; loaf, country, with marinated cucumbers, 269; loin, roasted, with persimmon-bread stuffing and applejack and port wine sauce, 56–58; medallions, sautéed, with Marsala cream sauce, 186; roast loin of, with tomato-prune chutney, 229–30

potato(es): buttermilk doughnuts, 179; chips, olive-oil roasted, 16;

country mashed, 237; crust, lamb loin in, 130–31

poultry, *see* fowl

pumpkin soup, baked, with honeyed crème fraîche and apple-pecan relish, 200

quail: lasagne of foie gras, wild mushrooms and, 114–15; with smoked duck, walnut dressing, and Cabernet-elderberry sauce, 47–48

radicchio cream soup with semolina quenelles, 129

raspberry(ies): blackberry buckle, 204; cream, pecan lace with, 76–77; fresh, zabaglione with, 252–253; mousse, ginger-poached pears with ginger crème anglaise and, 230–31; sabayon of red, with dark rum, 25; sauce, chèvre coeur à la crème with, 171; sauce, red, snow eggs in, 163

rhubarb cobbler, 77

rice: Dennis's boiled, 262; risotto cakes with porcini sauce, 185; wild, burrito, grilled ducklings with onion confit and, 74–76; wild, compote, smoked breast of pheasant with cracked-pepper pear sauce and, 202–203; wild, fritters, 203–204

rollade, 220

sabayon of red raspberries with dark rum, 25

salads: of arugula, radicchio, and duck with raspberry vinaigrette, 56; arugula, radicchio, and watercress, alla Trevisiana, 7; of Belgian endive, radicchio, and sun-dried tomatoes, 228; calamari, 22–23; cucumber-and-bell-pepper, grilled soft-shell crabs with tarragon butter and, 38–39; grilled lamb, with warm goat cheese, 150–51; late-summer fruit, with ginger dressing, 65; seafood, 259; spring, 170; summer, with lemon vinegar and walnut oil, 137; warm soft-shell crab, 14–15; watercress, 162

salmon: grilled, with drawn butter and horseradish sauce, 243–44; smoked, buckwheat blini with eggplant caviar and, 22; smoked and tartare, roulade of, 150; wild Maine, mosaic of Osetra caviar and, en gelée, 128 salmon caviar, warm asparagus, crayfish, and sun-dried tomatoes with avocado, lemon butter sauce and, 136

salsa cheesecake, 159

sauces: chocolate cream, 107; crème anglaise, 107; lingonberry citrus, 76; marinara, 31–32

scallops: bay, on Japanese buckwheat noodles with pesto sauce, 104; sea, lobster with fettuccine, lemon butter sauce and, 137–38

seafood: bay scallops on Japanese buckwheat noodles with pesto sauce, 104; broiled oysters in pesto, 260; calamari salad, 22–23; fillet of John Dory with Michigan Chardonnay sauce and red cabbage, 129–30; fish fillets with cheese sauce, 219; fish fumet, 275–76; grilled pike with chanterelle mushrooms, grilled corn, and Cabernet butter sauce, 15–16; grilled soft-shell crabs with cucumber-and-bell-pepper salad and tarragon butter, 38–39; grilled swordfish with tarragon sauce, tomatoes, capers and olives, 251–52; lobster with sea scallops, fettuccine, and lemon butter sauce, 137–38; millet-and-almond-coated walleye with Brie sauce, 178; pan-roasted Northern pike fillet with ham, leeks, and orange sauce, 200–201; red snapper wrapped in eggplant with tomato-orange sauce, 184–185; salad, 259; sautéed walleye with lobster and smoked-trout sauce and fiddlehead ferns, 95–96; steamed lake perch fillets in ginger-lemon jus-lié, 83; stuffed calamari, 30–31; swordfish baked in spicy peanut mole, 122–23; warm asparagus, crayfish, and sun-dried tomatoes with avocado, lemon butter sauce, and salmon caviar, 136; warm soft-shell crab salad, 14–15; see also bass; salmon; shrimp

shrimp: and chicken gumbo, 260–261; rock, trenette with crushed red peppers and, 6; and tomato

butter, herbed feta cheese in phyllo pastry with, 227

snapper, red, wrapped in eggplant with tomato-orange sauce, 184–185

snow eggs in red raspberry sauce, 163

soups: apple consommé, 160; baked pumpkin, with honeyed crème fraîche and apple-pecan relish, 200; cabbage tomato, 95; Capitol beer-and-Cheddar, 169; chicken noodle, 236; chilled red pepper, 14; chilled tomato, with basil-avocado sorbet, 114; cream of spring greens, 73; Dutch pea, 219; of four cheeses, roasted garlic, and herbs, 38; lamb shank and white-bean, 269–70; old-fashioned Bohemian goulash, 211; radicchio cream, with semolina quenelles, 129; winter squash bisque, 228

squash bisque, winter, 228

stock: beef, 276–77; chicken, 276; dark brown duck, 278; demi-glace, 278; fish fumet, 275–76; veal, 276–77

strawberries brandi, 213

strawberry applesauce bread, 272–273

sweet potato: and coconut pie, 59; fettuccine with shiitake mushroom sauce, 270–71; frites, 145; rolls, 201–202

swordfish: baked in spicy peanut mole, 122–23; grilled, with tarragon sauce, tomatoes, capers, and olives, 251–52

tarts: Michigan blueberry, 99; sweet cream, with red-fruit compote, 152–53; three-berry fudge, 138–39

tiramisù, 9

tomato(es): cabbage soup, 95; escargot-stuffed plum, in poultry broth, 83–84; grilled swordfish with tarragon sauce, capers, olives and, 251–52; marinara sauce, 31–32; orange sauce, red snapper wrapped in eggplant with, 184–85; prune chutney,

roast loin of pork with, 229–230; Roma, grilled baby lamb chops with rosemary-garlic beurre blanc and 48–49; sauce, fresh, artichoke fritters with, 8–9; and shrimp butter, herbed feta cheese in phyllo pastry with, 227; soup, chilled, with basil-avocado sorbet, 114; sun-dried, salad of Belgian endive, radicchio and, 228; sun-dried, warm asparagus, crayfish and, with avocado, lemon butter sauce, and salmon caviar, 136; whole roasted veal strip with leeks, wild mushrooms and, in brandy demi-glace, 39–40

trout, smoked, and lobster sauce, sautéed walleye with fiddlehead ferns and, 95–96

vanilla ice cream, 204–205

veal: chop Sergio with porcini mushrooms, 7–8; demi-glace, 278; grilled, porterhouse steak with onion marmalade, 271; medallions over braised romaine with thyme beurre blanc, 32; savory balls, 218; stock, 276–77; strip, whole roasted, with leeks, wild mushrooms, and tomatoes in brandy demi-glace, 39–40; sweetbread pancakes with hazelnut yogurt, 58; tenderloin Madeira, medallions of, with wild mushrooms, 24–25

vegetable(s): Asian, black bass tartare with buckwheat blini and, 113; fresh, kabobs, 243; house, 262; see also specific vegetables

venison: roast, 98; sausage, 192–193

walleye: millet-and-almond-coated, with Brie sauce, 178; sautéed, with lobster and smoked-trout sauce and fiddlehead ferns, 95–96

zabaglione with fresh raspberries, 252–53

zelniky, 212

zucchini, stuffed, 252